the new garden designer's handbook

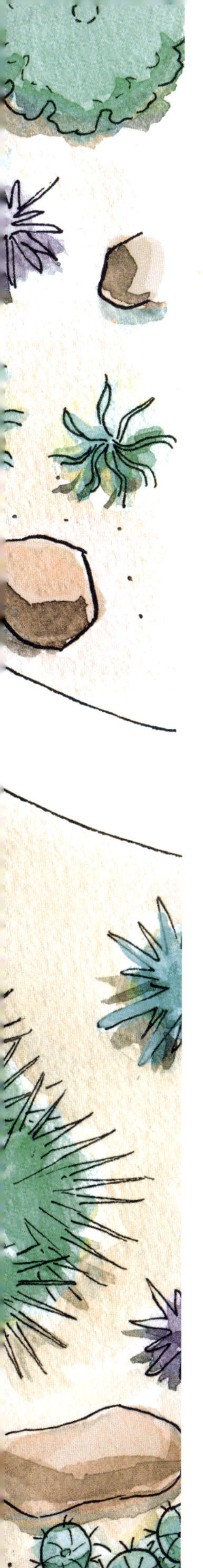

the new garden designer's handbook

How to Design Useful, Beautiful Gardens from Start to Finish

DARYL BEYERS

Illustrations by Elara Tanguy

TIMBER PRESS
Portland, Oregon

To Carrie,

for her constant kindness, patience, love, and understanding

Photo and illustration credits appear on page 275.

Timber Press
Workman Publishing
Hachette Book Group, Inc.
1290 Avenue of the Americas
New York, New York 10104
timberpress.com

Timber Press is an imprint of Workman Publishing, a division of Hachette Book Group, Inc.
The Timber Press name and logo are registered trademarks of Hachette Book Group, Inc.

Printed in Dongguan, China (TLF), on responsibly sourced paper

Text design by Adrianna Sutton and Sarah Crumb
Jacket design by Adrianna Sutton and Sarah Crumb
Illustrations by Elara Tanguy

The publisher is not responsible for websites (or their content) that are not owned by the publisher.

ISBN 978-1-64326-469-1

A catalog record for this book is available from the Library of Congress.

CONTENTS

Preface

A Life with Gardeners

Traditionally, a preface is where the author shares their background with the reader to make the case for why they are qualified to write the book in hand. So, this is where I should tell you about my degree in environmental design, my time as an estate gardener, my experiences as a garden magazine writer and editor, and of course mention the many client gardens I have designed and created over a span of three decades of professional work. That said, I want to share what I have learned from a few of the many gardeners I've met along the way, and how the design philosophy I developed through these interactions has shaped my approach to garden design.

The first person who made a difference was my first landscape foreman, Steve. I met Steve one summer break when I was hired to work on a landscape crew, not because I had any experience working on a landscape crew, but because I told the job interviewer I was studying landscape architecture at the University of Minnesota and wanted to "learn landscaping from the ground up." They put me on a three-man crew tasked with small jobs. Each day we went to several modest homes throughout the city suburbs to correct drainage problems around foundation walls before laying sod and planting daylilies or juniper shrubs to dress things up. Besides learning how to hold my own during bouts of blue-collar work-truck banter, Steve taught me how to read a grade elevation by eye. Much of our work involved building up the soil against foundations and shaping swales (more about swales in chapter 4) in the lawn around the house to direct surface water away and out toward the street. As Steve explained it, water always flows downhill no matter how small the grade. Even a 1 percent slope will move water, but an untrained eye can't see a 1 percent grade. It looks flat. By the end of summer, I was starting to see it, and I have been able to read grades by eye ever since.

My next watershed experience was working with a design team on an estate. Joe and Wayne were the garden designers, and I was the head gardener, which meant I installed the garden they designed. I don't really like to say "install" to refer to making a garden, but it felt that way then. The property was a ten-acre English country-style estate, all of it fully gardened, with many mature specimen trees and shrubs in place. The gardens were old and outdated and were being renovated along with the house. I was hired as head gardener because someone with a design degree and experience with landscape crews was needed on-site to facilitate the work. My responsibilities included making the gardens as explained to me by Joe and Wayne, however, they did not provide drawings. Instead, on visits they would describe the gardens they had conjured in their heads, all with a flurry of words and waves of their arms. A week or so later a truckload of trees, shrubs, and perennials would arrive, which were then planted, and it became my responsibility to keep them alive.

To their credit, Joe and Wayne were consummate plantspeople, and though they were talented at the art of combining plants, it became clear to me they were less practiced in laying out multiple garden spaces on a large property. As head gardener, it was my job to give garden tours, and I soon realized the different garden "rooms" didn't hold together. There was no drama; no story being told. These guys treated garden rooms (more about garden rooms in chapter 8) like separate entities. They were interesting when you were in them, but as parts they did not add up to something greater. Worst of all, when touring the gardens we hit dead ends without destinations, and all too often crossed through spaces already visited. What I learned from Joe and Wayne was how not to lay out gardens and that some of the best design lessons are seeing how things shouldn't be done.

Next, I received a comprehensive course in how great gardens are made when I became an editor for *Fine Gardening* magazine. I was hired to write two special issues on garden design called Great Gardens. Each issue featured ten private gardens from across the United States and my assignment was to study each garden, interview the designer, who in most cases was also the owner and head gardener, and write a design lesson based on the unique features of each garden. It was two years of in-depth exposure to an amazing collection of garden designs and designers. From Dennis Schrader, on Long Island, New York, I learned about zone-busting; from James David in Austin, Texas, I learned how to design circulation through a garden that works; from Marcia Donahue in Berkeley, California, I learned how to add art objects to a garden; from Little and Lewis, on Bainbridge Island, Washington, I learned how to make a small garden feel big; and from Craig Bergmann in Chicago, Illinois, I learned how to create true garden rooms.

My time as a magazine editor brought other lessons, through Q and A interviews with other great garden designers, such as Lynden Miller, Brandon Tyson, Raymond Jungles, and Sydney Eddison. What I've learned from these interactions was unique to the time I met each person, matching my growth as a garden designer with their life in gardens. In the years that followed, I found a new generation of designers who were thinking beyond traditional gardening ideas and were now designing meadows, creating habitat gardens, and working with indigenous plants and a sustainable approach. All these aspects of garden design continue to inform my work as a designer, teacher, and writer.

Garden designers grow. We start by learning the fundamentals, such as those found in this book, then we emulate others we admire, develop our own signature style, and ultimately evaluate the work of the next wave of designers and adapt what we like into our work. The timeline of my education and career puts me in a unique position. I transitioned through the days of ornamental gardening, inspired by the English school of controlling nature to create beauty, to sustainable gardening practices that treat nature as a partner in design. That journey has brought me to writing this book, in which each chapter provides lessons on the fundamentals of garden design, all informed by my personal and professional experience, ideas, ethics, and attitudes toward designing great gardens.

Introduction

Dynamic Nature and the Art and Craft of Creating Gardens

Designing gardens is fun, but it's also kind of tricky. The fun part is that you get to work outside, play with plants, dig in the dirt, and discover new things about nature. The tricky part is you have to work outside, keep plants alive, respect your soil, and learn daily lessons from nature. The point is that what makes designing gardens interesting and rewarding are the same things that often make it difficult and frustrating. It's good to understand this from the start and manage your expectations. Anyone can design and implement a garden, but it takes time, patience, practice, and experience to make memorable gardens. I still shudder to think of the mistakes I made in my first gardens, and I am sometimes disappointed with more recent work, yet I remind myself that my design skills and preferences continue to grow and evolve, just like the gardens.

Garden design, like any other type of design work, follows rules of form and function, texture and color, symmetry and scale, contrast and harmony, and balance and mass. The big difference is that most other design work employs nonliving, mostly static materials, whereas the medium of gardens is alive. Nature is alive and therefore dynamic, and dynamic nature is what makes designing gardens so rewarding when you get it right.

One of my favorite slogans, whether I am teaching a design masterclass or a basic gardening course, is, "A tree is not a chair." What do I mean? Well, an interior designer can pick the right chair and set it in the right place in the right room, and the chair will stay the same. It won't grow too big for the space, change shape over time, or ultimately die and rot. The chair is static. Conversely, trees are dynamic. Trees grow and change with the seasons, they respond to weather and climate as well as what the gardener does when caring for them, like fertilizing or pruning. The dynamic nature of garden design makes it challenging and fun, but it also makes it difficult to do it well unless you understand

Walking path through Sagano Bamboo Forest in the Arashiyama district of Kyoto

how it's done. Once you grasp the nature of the medium—of plants, wind, rain, soil, and wildlife—and learn the rules, designing a garden gets easier. It becomes a lifelong pursuit, filled with ideas, experiments, and adventures.

Embracing the themes of ideas, experiments, and adventures, the chapters that follow include a behind-the-scenes glimpse at how I have worked through the design process for my own home property, newly purchased in a part of the country where I have never gardened before: Northern California at the top of the Sacramento Valley. You'll also find designs from previous client work across several states and regions, including the East Coast, the Midwest, and the Southeast, though I have slightly redesigned the designs for this book—like I said, all garden designers evolve and change, just like were now designing meadows, creating habitat gardens, and working with indigenous plants and a sustainable approach. All these aspects of garden design continue to inform my work as a designer, teacher, and writer.

Garden designers grow. We start by learning the fundamentals, such as those found in this book, then we emulate others we admire, develop our own signature style, and ultimately evaluate the work of the next wave of designers and adapt what we like into our work. The timeline of my education and career puts me in a unique position. I transitioned through the days of ornamental gardening, inspired by the English school of controlling nature to create beauty, to sustainable gardening practices that treat nature as a partner in design. That journey has brought me to writing this book, in which each chapter provides lessons on the fundamentals of garden design, all informed by my personal and professional experience, ideas, ethics, and attitudes toward designing great gardens.

our gardens. There are also design plans I have simply dreamed up but hope to turn into reality somewhere, someday.

Dreaming up and making gardens is an art and a craft. As a familiar trope for many creative pursuits, the distinction between art and craft is informed by the goals of each. It is said that artists are committed to their self-expression, not the medium, while great craftspeople create exactly what is wanted, and needed. My assertion is that garden design touches on both. It is a form of self-expression through the arrangement of plants and other features like paths and patios, but the design is just the first step in a process that fulfills the desired usefulness and beauty of our outdoor spaces. Because a garden designer's work is never done—because a garden is never done—the art of design joins the craft of gardening to produce something better than both.

Perhaps this sounds grandiose for someone simply planning to position a few plants outside their house, but that's the promise of garden design. You can choose the heights to which it strives, from a bit of suburban curb appeal to the expression of a personal land ethic or philosophy. It's up to you. Keep that in mind as I lay out the fundamentals of garden design, and treat this book as a friendly, talkative guide, not a strict taskmaster. Promise me that, and I promise you will enjoy the lessons that follow and find good uses for them in your gardens for years to come.

CHAPTER 1

The Elements of Garden Design

The importance and implications of *landforms*, *structures*, and *plants* as the three major elements of any garden design.

Throughout this book, especially in the next few chapters, I repeat the terms *landforms*, *structures*, and *plants*. These three elements work like overlays in a garden. In fact, thinking and working in layers is the best way to describe how we make gardens. There is a landform layer, referring to geological features like hills and plains; there is a structure layer, which includes every human-made object on the property; and there is a plant layer, itself comprising additional layers like canopy and understory. Learning to work with these three elemental layers is how I learned landscape design in school, is how I practice design professionally, and is how I've taught garden design to hundreds of students.

Landforms, structures, and plants are also the layers that make the landscape and garden as we find it before the design begins. They are what we examine and map during our site survey stage, which I describe in detail in chapter 2. Garden designers must learn to recognize and evaluate pre-existing landforms, structures, and plants to determine how each can either be part of the design or added or subtracted to shape the new garden as envisioned.

Landform

Landform is, quite literally, the lay of the land. It is how the ground undulates, sinks, rises, falls, and generally flows, or doesn't do any of those things but simply lies flat. The extent of the rise and fall of the ground plane, or topography, plays a key role in the design potential of any outdoor space. A simple flat patch behind the house makes things easy, but also relatively dull. In such case, we may want to create landform. A super-steep slope, however, poses many challenges but, as you will learn, challenges are the best engines for interesting designs. I believe it's more difficult to design an interesting garden on a flat, empty patch compared to what may appear possible on a crowded mountainside. There are three types of landforms commonly found in gardens: slopes, bedrock or boulders, and natural water features. Each poses problems or potential for a garden design in different ways.

◀ Maya Lin's *Storm King Wavefield* at Storm King Art Center in New Windsor, New York, is a large-scale example of landform treated as intentional design.

Dig a Lake. Make a Mountain.

I am reminded of a Chinese proverb on garden making: "Dig a lake. Make a mountain." To me, that is the epitome of landforming. I earned my first A+ in design school when we were assigned to make models of a landscape featuring landform. While my classmates focused on stacking layers of cardboard and clay to represent mounds and hillocks, I started with a foot-thick piece of Styrofoam and started digging down. In the end, I created a cave-like tunnel connecting a flat section to a terraced space above. It was a simple concept, I must admit, I lucked into. I was just trying to find an easy way to complete the assignment, and the simplest way turned out to be a great way (more on the importance of simplicity in chapter 8).

SLOPES

The most important type of landform to recognize and understand is the slope. Slopes are the ups and downs of the ground. They can be steep or subtle, wavy or planar. The key thing to remember about a slope is that it affects how surface water moves through a garden. Water runs downhill so if the ground slopes toward the house, rainwater will flow that way, which could lead to a wet basement. If the ground has low spots, rainwater will fill them and, perhaps, take a long time to percolate into the soil. Most plant roots don't like to sit in saturated soil for long periods of time, but some do, and low spots like these could become a rain garden filled with plants that like wet feet.

Existing landforms can present problems or potential, but we don't know which until we recognize it. By understanding the slopes in our gardens, we understand how the surface water moves and how people may move through those spaces. Flat ground is easy to traverse, steep slopes take effort, while gentle undulations are interesting. Hilltops provide moments of prospect once we climb to the top, and valleys make us feel at home, sheltered and safe. Garden designers work with the ups and downs of slopes, taking advantage of what is there or making changes as needed.

BEDROCK AND BOULDERS

Some regions have a lot of ledge or bedrock, either protruding from or located just a few inches beneath the soil, making it difficult to grow grass and planting large trees or shrubs impossible. Luckily there are many shallow-rooted plants that will grow over buried bedrock, though one useful move is to expose the bedrock ledges and make them a design highlight. Stone is beautiful so take advantage of what nature provides. Beyond bedrock, there may be large boulders on-site, deposited by glaciers and randomly scattered or stacked. Or they may have been dug up and left during construction of the house. Harvest them and use them in the design as a boulder wall, though this will require large machinery, skill, and some courage. Watching an excavator lift a 6-ton (5.4 metric tons) boulder with straps and set it in place is harrowing, but with the right crew and equipment it can be done.

NATURAL WATER FEATURES

Rivers, streams, creeks, ponds, lakes, and oceans are all natural landforms. A pond is just a low spot filled with water. A stream is a channel with water running through it. If any of these features are on a property, they may require design solutions to work around them, but in most cases bodies of water should be seen as something special. The music of a trickling stream or the peaceful scene of a misty-morning pond can inspire a design. If a river runs through it, even just a short stretch through a small property, that's special. Intermittent streams are suggestions of the season. When dry, they are a pattern of rocks and plants, but when the rain arrives, they come to life. The best is a shoreline. There is no simpler way to create a beautiful view than to open it up to a lake or ocean. There's a reason people gather and build along the shore, and it's not just for the fishing or surfing. Proximity to large bodies of water that stretch to the horizon instills a sense of sublimity into a design that is difficult to duplicate. Only distant mountain tops and desert expanses do the same.

Natural vs. Human-Made Landforms

While there is little land left on earth completely untouched by humans, there is a distinction to be made between landforms created by nature and those shaped by human activity. Rolling farm fields and suburban foothills may possess the human touch, but their size and scale set them apart from the endeavors of residential garden designers. Gardens are located within a larger natural topography, just a small patch of a larger pattern. It's where a garden sits within the landscape at large that makes a difference. If it's up on a ridge, it will be windswept with wide views. Deep in the valley, it will feel safe and secure, though night will arrive earlier. Either instance will influence the garden's character in terms of growing conditions as well as its sense of place.

There are, however, large-scale human-made landforms that influence garden making. These are more akin to land art, or earthworks, where the size, shape, and character of the landforms are the design. The wave fields of Maya Lin, designer of the Vietnam Veterans Memorial in Washington, DC, are an exercise in landform and slope—a perfect example of reshaping landform for aesthetic purposes and a testament to what can be accomplished by simply moving around some soil, albeit a lot of soil! Maya Lin turned a gravel pit into a work of art, and any garden designer presented with a flat, uninteresting plot can do the same just by reshaping the ground.

LANDFORM WITH STRUCTURE

Some landform changes require the use of structures to make them work, like retaining walls that hold back the soil to create a flat terrace on a slope, or switchback steps installed on a hillside to help people walk up the easy way. Once we start shaping the land to make it either more useful or interesting, we often need to include structures to make it work—a natural transition from thinking about landform to considering structure in a garden.

A garden glasshouse is the epitome of structure that is both useful and beautiful.

Structure

Structure in garden design is anything human made on the property. This includes the house and other buildings, walls, walks, paths, and steps, patios and decks, fences, gates and arbors, pergolas, swimming pools, firepits, furniture and more. Outdoor grills, and utilities like air-conditioning units, garbage cans, composters, and irrigation systems, are also structures. That's a lot to think about and, in many ways, except for the plant layer, which is complex by nature, structures are the most complicated element to deal with when designing gardens. Because gardeners are so interested and excited about plants, we often forget about the structural elements in the garden; however, when we define structures as "anything human made" the vast numbers of structures intrinsic in gardens becomes clear.

The purpose of any structure in a garden design is a factor of function. Paths make it easy to walk from place to place, fences provide privacy, and retaining walls turn steep slopes into level fields.

How we work with structures determines the usefulness of our gardens, and the levels of function within them. A walkway can be designed as ADA (Americans with Disabilities Act) compliant, with ramps and an adequate width for wheelchair access, or it can consist of a sequence of steps and landings made of roughhewn stone set in a hillside.

The easiest way to start a garden design is with a structure element, for example, a seating area. Imagine a backyard that no one uses. We step out the back door from the kitchen and all we find is a patch of grass, some weeds, maybe a tree or two and some shrubs, and a fence along the property line. There's not much to do out there; nothing to engage us. It's not comfortable or inviting because we have to stand so the visit is quick. In a few minutes' time we'll go back inside. It's not a garden. The easiest way to start that garden is to add a structure, a patch of patio or stone where we can place a chair or two, and perhaps a small table where we can sit and enjoy our morning coffee or an adult beverage in the evening. It's a place to sit a spell. A spell in a magical sense as well, because as we sit outside, pausing to look up at the sky, listen to the birds, or feel the breezes as they blow through the trees, that backyard is now a garden, albeit in the most minimal way. Maybe it's not a beautiful or especially interesting garden, but it's now a useful space where we can spend time thinking of how to make it better.

The structure of that first viewing ground can be made from whatever is at hand, even just

An Origin Point

Every garden I design has an origin point. It doesn't have to be permanent, just some cleared ground for a camp chair. However, a vestige of this special spot where I first envision a garden is often included in the final plan as an acknowledgment of the origins of my process and those early days spent observing, meditating, and finding the ideas that guided the design.

a canvas camp chair. While the materials our garden structures are made of are less important than the structure's function, the materials we choose determine their quality and appearance. Stone, wood, glass, metal, ceramics, and more contribute to the look and feel of a thing as much as its shape or style. Compare a privacy fence made of redwood to one made of PVC plastic. Each achieves the usefulness of a fence, but with a different aesthetic. Redwood will rot in time, though some say elegantly, whereas PVC won't, though it could lose its luster, if it ever had any. Fortunately, we have composite materials that are both beautiful and durable. The trick is to introduce the structures we need to make the garden work, then select their fit and finish for the appearance we want.

OUTBUILDINGS

All the building structures other than the house are outbuildings. The list is long: ADUs (accessory dwelling units), art studios, barns, berry houses, cabanas, detached garages, doghouses, gazebos, greenhouses, potting sheds, she-sheds, solar saunas, toolsheds, tree houses, woodsheds, and more. Basically, they're any built structure with walls and a roof. Outbuildings add usefulness in obvious ways, but they also provide settings for our gardens. Treat them like mini houses that need landscaping and design a garden around them. There's nothing sadder and lonelier than a shed sitting in the middle of an empty lawn, disconnected from the rest of the garden. Take time to think it through and make every outbuilding a key feature of the design.

WALLS

There are two types of garden walls: retaining walls and freestanding walls. Either can be made from a variety of materials, such as natural stone, engineered block, or large timbers. The type of stone and the size, shape, and patterns employed are as diverse as the imagination of the stonemason. Engineered blocks can be almost as diverse in color and character as natural stone, but they tend toward an engineered look not everyone likes. Timbers work well but, in time, will rot and fail, unless they are used in an exceptionally arid climate. All things considered, the aesthetics of form, texture, and color are at the designer's discretion.

Retaining Walls

The most important attribute of a retaining wall is its ability to withstand the lateral forces of the soil on the upslope, to hold back the soil to accomplish a change in ground elevation from the back side of the wall (uphill) to the front side (downhill). Most often used for terracing, retaining walls allow us to carve out a flat area on a slope to make it more useful. Speaking of slopes, let's take this opportunity to talk about something called angle of repose, which, by definition, is "the steepest angle at which a sloping surface formed of a particular loose material is stable." The angle of repose is different for different soils, but you can assume that the slope of an existing hill is at or below that angle. What a retaining wall allows is the ability to cut into that hillside to change the angle of the slope—in most cases to flatten it out. Beyond

Thoughtfully designed retaining walls allow you to shape landforms, providing opportunities for beauty and usefulness.

Unlike a retaining wall that holds back soil, freestanding walls let you "hold back" space, delineating garden areas.

pure function, retaining walls also add interest and style to a design by shaping the spaces above and below the wall's location. The wall can be straight or curved, even zigzag. Its face can be textured or smooth, with a regular or irregular pattern. Depending on the forces being applied to the retaining wall, it can be monumental or slight, blocky, or sleek. Clearly, there's more to a retaining wall than its function, and the same holds true about every structure in a garden.

Freestanding Walls

The purpose of a freestanding wall is different from a retaining wall. Freestanding walls are space definers. Their function is to separate one part of the garden from another, and they can range in height from just a foot to 6 feet (1.8 m) or more–though once a wall gets that tall, we need an engineer to provide construction drawings for permits. The same is true for retaining walls: For anything over 6 feet (1.8 m) tall, call an architect or engineer.

The beauty of a freestanding wall is that it helps us create outdoor rooms, which is a key to garden design. If we're making a room, what better way to do it than to include some walls?

However, these walls don't have to be solid or tall. A pony wall, so called because it was first introduced in English gardens to keep pet ponies away from the roses, is just 18 to 24 inches (45.7 to 61 cm) tall. They effectively segregate spaces, but without blocking views. They also provide places to sit around a firepit or near a swimming pool. Many amazing garden designs employ freestanding walls, even if only as sculptural features or interesting backdrops for plantings.

WALKS AND STEPS

Walks and steps make it easier to move through and get from place to place in the garden. This could be from the sidewalk to the front door, the back door to the composting pile, or a ramble through the woods. Steps, quite simply, are a walk that goes up or down, and walks and steps should always be conceived as spaces in themselves, not just a conveyance from one spot to another. A key characteristic of walks or steps is their width, and there is a good general rule to go by: Four feet (1.2 m) is the minimum width for a walk if we want two people to comfortably walk side by side, for example, when approaching the front door of a house. Too many front walks are 3 feet (91.4 cm) wide or narrower, and they need to be widened (more about doing that in chapter 8). Three feet (91.4 cm) works for someone delivering a package, but single file isn't how we want guests to arrive, and 4 feet (1.2 m) is good, but 5 feet (1.5 m) is better. The reason so many new construction homes have 3-foot (0.9 m) instead of 4-foot (1.2 m)-wide walkways is cost. The builder saves 25 percent on the materials and labor by knocking off that foot (30.5 cm) of width. There is, however, a limit to how wide a walkway should be. An 8-foot (2.4 m)-wide walk is getting grandiose, and anything wider is almost imperial. Conversely, a 2-foot (61 cm)-wide path is best suited for a lane between vegetable beds, and something a foot (30.5 cm) wide should be intended as a secret trail.

Five-foot (1.5 m)-wide walkway; design your entry walkways wide enough to accommodate two people comfortably side by side.

Walkways, Paths, and Trails

The width of a walk is its first defining feature, but there is a lot more to it than that. The next important consideration are the materials to be used, which, in turn, directly corresponds to the type of walk desired.

Walkways have a solid, level, stable surface, suitable for wheels or high heels. Walkways are typically wide enough for two and tend to be rectilinear, though not necessarily. Usually made of brick, concrete, manufactured pavers, or stone, walkways come in many shapes and sizes.

- Brick walkways in herringbone, running bond, or basket weave patterns are popular in gardens for their formal look.
- Concrete can be formed and stamped in a variety of ways that improve upon the familiar sidewalk.
- Pavers come in many shapes, sizes, and colors that fit together in multiple motifs of circles, arcs, and chevrons.
- Stone can be irregular pieces of flagstone, arranged in a pattern, or different-size squares and/or rectangles, or even laser-cut slabs.

Paths are, by nature, winding. Though this is not a hard-and-fast rule, when we think of a path, the immediate image for most is a ribbon winding up a hill or wending around a corner. Paths are also often narrow, less than the 4-foot (1.2 m) rule, though they can be wider when space allows. What really makes a path is the material it is made of. Peastone or gravel are familiar choices, available in a multitude of colors and textures. They work well in informal gardens but must be kept in check with an edging, like metal or bricks.

Continued ›

Two- to 3-foot (61 cm to 0.9 m)-wide path; use narrow paths where you want just one person at a time to pass through.

One-foot (30.5 cm)-wide trail; establish an intuitive trail where you want a casual yet efficient passage through the landscape.

Grass paths are a favorite, especially when cutting through a swath of meadow or wildflowers. Some vegetable gardeners sow grass paths between their beds for a rustic look. However, a 4-inch (10 cm) layer of bark mulch on top of landscape fabric to suppress weeds will keep feet in bounds and prevent soil compaction in the adjacent beds.

Trails are a special type of path. Whereas paths are contained and often defined by distinct edges, a trail is wild, less predictable, and not wheel or high-heel friendly. Trails, more than any other form of walk, are intuitive. They follow the land and the instincts of the people, or wildlife, who blazed them, like following a deer run to lay out a trail through the woods. Every landscape design student has been taught that a great way to locate a walk that people will use is to fashion it according to how people have instinctively moved through that space on their daily rounds. This may lead to trails being upgraded into paths, and paths promoted to walkways as the garden design develops on paper or in real life.

Stairways and Ramps

Stairways are walkways with steps that help us climb or descend a slope. It's helpful to think of a garden area that needs steps as a stairway, a space in and of itself, or a room connecting two gardens, one up and one down. Long stairways need landings, and landings reinforce this sense of space, making stairways interesting, and easier to climb. There may also be room on a landing for a bench or container plantings to dress it up. Long, steep stairways, without landings to provide places to pause, rest, and look around, are intimidating.

Another important consideration regarding stairways is the measure of each step. Where width is the watchword for walks, the character of steps is determined by the depth of the treads and the height of the risers. The ideal ratio for interior steps is a 7-inch (17.8 cm) rise with a 10-inch (25.4 cm) tread, but designing gardens allows a little leeway. In most cases, the goal is to create a comfortable climb, and the deeper the tread the shorter the riser. An important safety rule is to keep all risers in a length of steps the same height so people don't stumble!

Ramps are, by definition, inclined planes that join two different levels of ground. While ramps serve an important role in making gardens safe and comfortable for folks who use wheelchairs or walkers, they also provide people with baby strollers easier access and may attract skateboarders, rollerbladers, and bicyclists, though it's unlikely the latter will find our gardens the best place to practice or play. However, ramps also make it easy for gardeners to gain access with wheelbarrows and carts. They also allow us to make our way up and down throughout the garden in interesting ways without steps. There is a formula for ADA compliance of ramps: 1:12, which means 1 inch (2.5 cm) of rise for every 12 inches (30.5 cm) of ramp length. It also must be a hard surface. If ADA compliance is not part of the program, however, ramps can be grass or gravel, maybe even moss, and as steep as desired.

PATIOS AND DECKS

Patios and decks are the primary gathering places in gardens, so much so that they are almost ubiquitous. Most, if not all, good residential gardens have a patio or deck. As part of a garden room, they function as a floor, but the chief reason to include a patio or deck is as a location for tables and chairs or other outdoor accoutrements, like plants in pots or barbecue grills. Conceiving of a patio or deck as an outdoor room is exactly how we should approach the design because they provide a direct connection between the house's indoor rooms to the garden. As transition spaces, they play an important role in how we begin to shape the garden. Transitions from indoors to outdoors, from garden room to garden room, from formal spaces to wild ones, from sun to shade are big-picture examples, but transitions also occur when we step from a wooden deck to a stone patio, then from that stone patio to the lawn, and finally from the lawn to a mulched trail.

When designing structures on the ground plane, how they connect to other spaces matters, as does how the material they are made of holds together. Consider the gaps between patio stones. How wide are they? Are they filled with cement, stone dust, or moss? Garden designers pay attention to the material connections and transitions between important structures like patios and decks because how we handle them contributes directly to the success or failure of our designs.

What About Terraces and Porches?

Patios and terraces are both paved outdoor areas adjacent to a house and, for this reason, the terms are often used interchangeably without much confusion. However, to be precise, *patios* are constructed on flat, level ground whereas *terraces* are typically built at a ground level elevated above the surroundings, such as at the brow of a hill. Patios are also considered less formal than terraces.

Is there a difference between a deck and a porch?

Decks are private livable outdoor spaces built at the back or side of a house that tie the house to the garden. A porch is most often part of a home's entrance, functioning as a semipublic space connecting the house to the sidewalk or driveway. Typically, porches are covered by a roof or overhang whereas decks are commonly open to the sky, or partially shaded with pergolas or umbrellas.

FENCES AND GATES

If patios and decks are the structured floors of a garden room, then fences and gates are the walls and doors. When it comes to designing gardens, these two types of structures go a long way toward defining our outdoor spaces. They can be used simply, such as a privacy fence installed along a property line, or subtly, like a gate signaling the transition from one garden to another. A gate at the end of a path is an excellent example of a focal point designed to guide us through a garden, and focal points are one of the most useful components of any garden design (more about focal points in chapter 5).

Typically, material choices for fences and gates are limited to wood, metal, or composite, but all can make a statement and lend style to a structure.

- Wood is traditional but often used in modern designs with simple geometry and clean lines.
- Metal is perfect for contemporary structures, adding a light yet resilient air, unless we're working with cast iron for an antique touch.
- Composites usually mimic wood but possess a durability unattainable with natural materials.

Whatever the material used, the need for and use of fences and gates is always under the purview of the garden designer.

ARBORS AND PERGOLAS

Arbors are doorways without a door that lead to and from one space to another. They should never stand alone as a decorative object on the lawn. When set along a path, they are the perfect visual cue to tell us we are passing from one garden room to another. They also work as focal points that help lead us through a garden. Deep arbors create hallways, and the space under the arbor can become a garden in its own right.

Pergolas do the same thing, but without walls. In terms of a garden room, pergolas function as incomplete ceilings. They create partial shade while also maintaining views of the sky, unless they are covered with vines growing up them.

Material choices for arbors and pergolas are the same as for fences and gates: wood, metal, or composite. The trick to using either structure is to focus on how they change the character of the space beneath them and how they can be used to signal a transition from one part of the garden to another.

SWIMMING POOLS AND SPAS

A swimming pool may be a luxury for many, but as popular additions to many suburban backyards, their impact on a garden means they should be thoughtfully planned and considered during the garden design phase. One big mistake homeowners make is having a pool installed without thinking about how it will affect the garden.

The pool's shape and scale are important considerations, as is its location in relation to other garden areas, the house, and adjoining features like decks or outbuildings. The goal is to make the pool more useful and comfortable by introducing a place for furnishings and including complementary plantings. There's no rule that a swimming pool should be a stand-alone affair with nothing of interest around it. The best

Think of an arbor as a formal passageway between garden rooms.

Use a pergola if you want an outdoor ceiling open to the sky.

examples are part of an overall outdoor plan that works with the landform and plant layers to soften the effect of such a significant structure.

The same is true for spas or hot tubs. Often added in conjunction with a swimming pool, they are excellent destinations. Ultimately, pools and spas define the function of the outdoor area they are in so it's best that the designer finds solutions to help them fit in.

FIREPITS, KITCHENS, AND BARS

Nothing says "outdoor entertainment" like a firepit or outdoor kitchen and bar. Often reminiscent of campfires, a firepit can be as simple as a circle of stones in an open space, but more often is a refined piece of masonry work. Actual outdoor fireplaces with a chimney are excellent focal points on a terrace, but so is a basic clay chiminea on a patio.

Many firepits use gas for fuel and can be turned on and off with a switch, adding a level of convenience to decorative tabletop fires and heating towers. Outdoor kitchens can range from a simple charcoal grill and tabletop to a full-on kitchen with cooktops, granite counters, refrigerators, and beer taps. Seating areas, especially at bars and high-top tables, are common in and around an outdoor kitchen and create that resort-style vibe.

FURNISHINGS

Items like tables and chairs, benches, umbrellas, or anything that makes a garden space an outdoor room, are considered furnishings. They play an important role in making our gardens comfortable places to spend time and relax. Dining areas require ample table space and chairs, while poolside we may want chaise longues or a bistro table with simple stools. Comfy couches and recliners with weather-resistant upholstery make great gathering places to enjoy the outdoors with family and friends, while a simple wooden bench set amid some plantings is the perfect spot for a meditative pause. My favorite is a pair of Adirondack chairs arranged to watch the sun set or rise with a loved one or best friend.

ART OBJECTS AND ACCESSORIES

Pots and planters, birdbaths, sundials, gazing balls, sculptures, urns, and almost any other object you can think of can be included in a garden's design. They make great focal points and help establish a theme within a garden room. Mirrors can be used to create the illusion of a larger space, and wall hangings enliven an unremarkable shed wall. We're limited only by our imagination when it comes to these structures, but the key is to treat them as contributors to the outdoor décor, introducing style as well as substance.

UTILITIES

Utilities are also structures, but in most cases our designs try to mitigate their visual and auditory presence in the garden. The list is long and includes air-conditioning units, gas and electric meters, power and cable lines, downspouts from rain gutters, rain barrels, water spigots, wellheads, irrigation boxes and controllers, mailboxes, flagpoles, security lights and cameras, landscape lighting, pool equipment, French drains, leach fields, septic tanks, garbage cans, and composters. Utility structures are often preexisting and unchangeable, but good garden design can rearrange things so they are less intrusive. Skilled designers find ways to include utilities in the design. For example, composters arranged as part of a demonstration garden turn what was once an eyesore into a main attraction.

Plants

If "water is life" (an adage I use to open my chapter on watering the garden in *The New Gardener's Handbook*), then "plants are life" for garden design. Without plants a garden would be just a collection of inanimate objects (structures) positioned on the ground (landform). Plants make gardens, and they are why I transitioned from being a landscape architecture student, to a landscape designer, to a garden designer and creator. In recent years as I began to see gardens as ecosystems and habitats, the role of plants in my professional work finally caught up with what I learned years ago in my ecology design studios.

Having come full circle, I see garden design as a way to work hand-in-hand with these living creatures called plants. Most landscape architects don't use plants as plants, they see them as architectural elements, and while this concept can be useful, it's missing something. It's missing life. Landscape architects may see plants as communities, and systems, but rarely do they consider each plant an individual. Landscape designers get a little closer, but tend to see plants as objects, not lifeforms. They are interested in how plants affect space, but not necessarily how each plant affects the people in that space. Garden designers think differently. We see plants as partners. They provide beauty and color, scent, touch, and taste. In turn, we provide them with sun and soil, nutrients and water, and the appropriate care such as pruning, and protection.

So, the most important layer in any garden design is the plant layer, and the plant layer is comprised of three distinct layers: canopy, understory, and ground plants. Those three layers have layers too, making the plant layer more elaborate and complex than the landform or structure layers by far. More than any other design element, plants make gardens, and plants are special because they are the true dynamic feature of any garden design. While wind, rain, sky, sun, and time contribute to a garden's dynamic nature, plants are the living things garden designers choose and use. Designing with plants is unique because they respond to stimuli, making them simultaneously predictable and unpredictable. Garden designers learn how two genetically identical plants can be grown in the same conditions but one may die while the other may thrive. This is because plants are individuals, just like people. They live and work together; some even help each other by sharing nutrients through their roots or sheltering their companions from the sun or storms.

Because the plant layer makes a garden, it also makes a good garden designer. By embracing a love of plants and our relationships with them, our garden designs can transcend the simple pursuits of beauty and comfort and attain a higher station, as unique places for psychic and spiritual health. Some of the best designed gardens I have visited were designed by botanists, true plant people who just happen to be good at design. My best advice is to strengthen your relationship with plants and come to understand all that the plant layer can provide.

CANOPY

Garden designers are visionaries. We envision how the plants we choose will grow and mature, and there is no better example of this than when working within the canopy layer of plants. The canopy plants are, by definition, the tallest plants on the property, usually mature trees, like maples and oaks, but not necessarily. It's a matter of scale. If the tallest tree in a garden is a 15-foot (4.5 m) Japanese maple, then that's the canopy. However, in many cases the canopy consists of pre-existing older specimens, trees that have been growing on that patch of land for many years, because trees take time. Trees don't necessarily grow slowly, but to reach 40, 50, 60 feet (12, 15, or 18 m) or more takes at least as many years to achieve.

While most garden designers inherit a canopy, we can also start one. That's where our visionary skills kick in. When we plant a long-lived oak tree, which grows slowly, just a few inches a year, we're not planting that tree for us, we're planting it for our grandchildren's children. No one we know is going to swing on the tire hung by a rope tied to one of its limbs. But we plant it anyway because planting a tree is an exercise in our faith in the future—a legacy for those who come next.

This vision of the future also works when we plant smaller, faster-growing trees, but within a shorter time frame. Instead of fifty or sixty years hence we're looking at fifteen or twenty, and if there is already a mature canopy in place, this new layer of trees is called a subcanopy. In this instance, the canopy consists of mature upper canopy trees and a newly planted subcanopy of trees. The subcanopy can be younger versions of the same trees in the canopy, planted as a sort of insurance policy for the day the elder trees weaken and begin to die. Or they can be companion trees, like dogwood, hornbeam, and redbud, that thrive in the shade of their larger cousins.

Although the canopy is typically less diverse than the understory and much less diverse than the ground layer, it's rarely monolithic. In fact, botanically speaking, it's best if it isn't monolithic because a balanced diversity of species is how plants coexist in the wild. Plants like to live with each other, and there are many known, and perhaps some unknowable, beneficial relationships that occur between the plants we use in our designs and the plants we inherit on the site. It's one of many complexities of designing with plants that keep us honest and engaged (more about playing with plant partners in chapter 7).

UNDERSTORY

At the understory layer, we again encounter the dynamic nature of designing with plants. The understory grows under the canopy, consisting of mostly shrubs, woody plants with multiple stems instead of a singular trunk. Understory plants don't grow as tall as the canopy or subcanopy but thrive in their shade. However, some members of the understory may be species of trees waiting for an elder tree to die and make an opening to the sun and sky so they can join the canopy or start a new one. This process, called succession, is how forests evolve. Succession can also be initiated when a forest fire removes the canopy after which ground-layer plants take over, followed by an understory of shrubs and

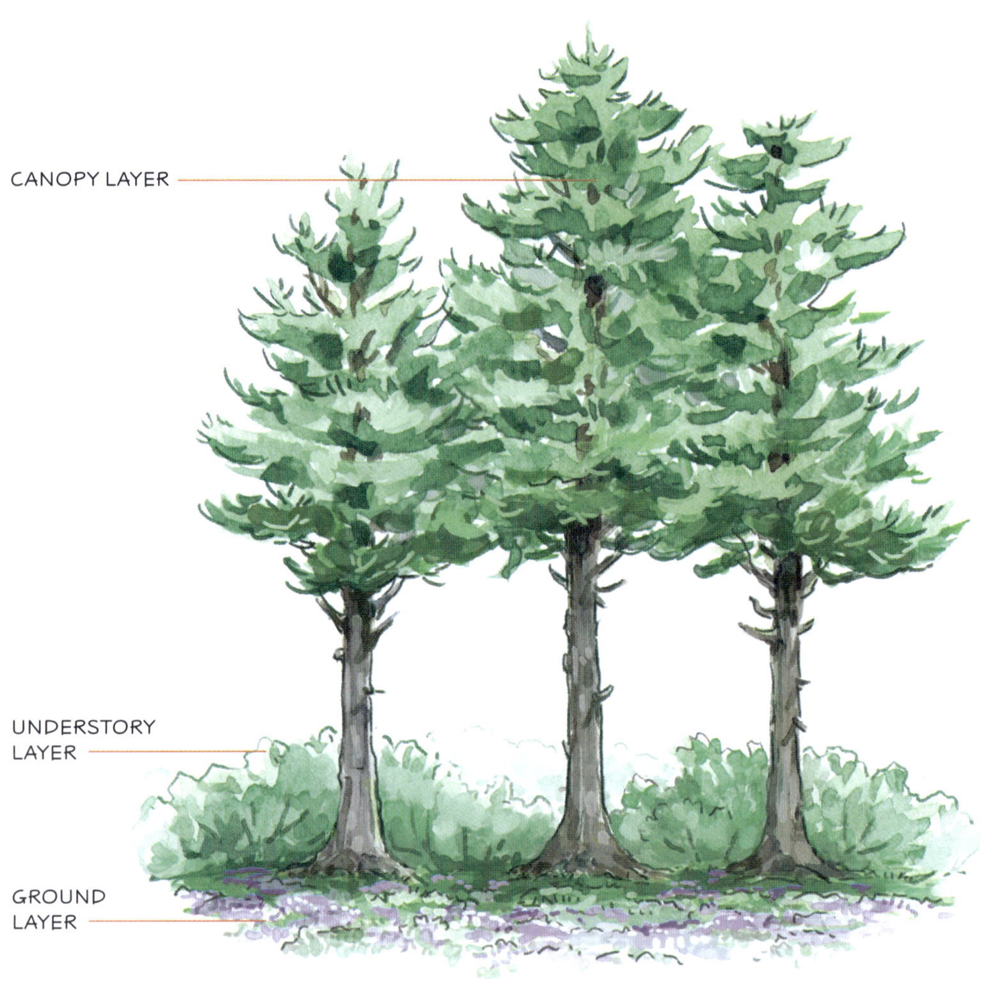

Each layer of plant life, from the treetops down to the ground, provides complexity and interest to your design.

small trees. Plant succession is something garden designers should be familiar with. Many new homesites are cleared of the original vegetation, in which case we can design a succession planting that will develop over time. Succession helps us understand the future effects of our plant choices on the garden, and the landscape at large. The forests we walk in today weren't always there. They were preceded by a succession of plant communities and habitats, perhaps a completely different forest populated with different kinds of trees.

Because understory plants need less sunlight to thrive, understory species, in general, are useful for our designs, especially when we've inherited a dense canopy. It would be foolish to knock down a woodland of old oak trees to make a garden. Instead, a good designer sees the potential for a woodland garden. All woodlands, designed or wild, have understory plants, plants we interact with intimately when we visit a garden. The canopy is above our heads, supported on an arrangement of tree trunks, and while we can weave in and out of the tree trunks,

Trees Don't Live Forever

Trees have a life span. No individual plant lives forever, though our affection for trees may make us hope so. Some trees, like the giant California redwood (*Sequoiadendron giganteum*), can live for thousands of years. That's why they're so tall. Multiply 1,000 years by several inches of new growth each year and you're getting up there. But a Lombardy poplar (*Populus nigra*) is much shorter lived, just ten to fifteen years, yet they still grow tall before they die because they grow fast. For a college landscape design assignment, I selected a Lombardy poplar because its growth habit perfectly fit a tight spot near the house, but my instructor, a horticulture professor, chastised me for using it because of its short life span and the need to replace it one day. This was a common rookie mistake, and a good example of a young landscape architecture student seeing a tree as a pillar, not the living organism it is.

the understory shrubs, often functioning as obstacles or walls, will directly affect our experience in the garden.

However, not all understory plants reside directly beneath the canopy. There are edge species that need more sun and live half under half out from under the shade of the trees. Plants like hydrangea, elder, and holly. In fact, an understory does not require a canopy. Though that sounds strange, an understory can grow as an independent shrub layer, in full sun, on its own. Think of a hedge between two properties, or a group of shrubs in the middle of a meadow.

With or without a canopy, the understory will also have layers due to the different species of shrubs growing together. Some smaller shrubs will live in the shade of larger ones, which creates layering through cooperation, a little like the succession scheme exhibited between canopy and subcanopy trees.

Understory plants also provide excellent habitat for birds and other wildlife, including butterflies and bees. Not all trees bear sufficient fruits or nuts best suited for the animals that live around us, but many shrubs do, and typically in a seasonal sequence that provides what the animals need when they need it, like nuts and seeds in fall to help them fatten up for winter, and summer berries when they're thirsty (more about planting for habitat in chapter 6). The understory also provides nesting spots for species like cardinals and mockingbirds that prefer shrubs over trees.

GROUND LAYER

The ground-layer plants, sometimes called groundcovers, are mostly herbaceous plants, like grasses, herbs, forbs, and flowers. These are the low growers that cover the ground beneath the canopy trees as well as in and around the understory shrubs. "Groundcover" is not the best term because it often refers to and suggests only plants that spread low across the ground, like lawn, myrtle, or pachysandra. Although these plants are part of the ground layer, they are just one example of ground-layer plants. The ground layer consists of **all** the plants that are not the canopy and understory. Though there are woody ground-layer plants, such as spreading junipers or creeping vines, the most prevalent ground-layer plants are nonwoody, herbaceous plants that have soft stems and die down to the ground in cold winter climates. If they are perennials, they will re-emerge the following spring when the air and soil temperatures initiate growth. If they are annuals, they won't return, but they will have most likely dispersed their seeds the previous season that may germinate and grow.

The ground layer is, by all accounts, the most complex layer of the three main plant layers. It includes species that hug the ground and never grow more than an inch high, those that can grow 6, 7, even 8 feet (1.8, 2.1, even 2.4 m) tall, and everything in between. They may grow in shade, in sun, or a combination but, most important, ground-layer plants populate areas not already occupied by the trunks of the canopy trees or the stems of the understory shrubs. Nature abhors a vacuum and sooner or later any bare ground, fertile or not, will sprout plants—fast-growing species first, followed by colonizing native plant communities. As garden designers, we get to choose which plants establish first and which will follow.

Ground-layer plants are good at coexisting with others. In fact, plant diversity is a hallmark of a healthy ecosystem, something we try to duplicate in sustainable garden design. While nature knows what it's doing and just does it if left undisturbed, humans must think it out first, then follow nature's lead to reproduce a planned version of what works.

The ground layer has many layers, and not just because of the different plant heights. They also emerge, grow, flower, and fruit in unique sequences. Plants called spring ephemerals, like trillium and toad lily, emerge in spring, then fade back into the ground after they flower, fruit, and set seed. Other plants start slowly, allowing their neighbors to grow first, but then suddenly shoot up to make a show in summer or fall. All perennial flowers have a specific bloom time—spring, summer, or fall—that typically lasts just two or three weeks, maybe a month. Spring bulbs, like crocus and daffodils, emerge and bloom before the trees even have leaves. They finish and then lie dormant underground for the rest of the year but return the next spring.

A list of ground-layer plants is long and could potentially include almost every herbaceous plant in the world, except for epiphytes, air plants like orchids that grow in trees with their roots as anchors on the upper branches. There are, however, distinct plant categories to choose from when working within the ground layer: mosses; ferns; grasses, forbs; perennial, annual, and biennial flowers; vines; and ground-hugging shrubs.

All garden designers work with landforms, structures, and plants as interrelated layers to shape and define outdoor spaces. The interactions between these elements determine how we experience, use, and enjoy the landscapes we live in, especially our gardens. If we approach each element in a comprehensive and complementary way, we can create cohesive designs with the look and feel of a true house and garden. We don't want a house plopped inside a garden, or a collection of gardens located outside of a house; we want the house and garden unified. However, before we can begin to make this happen and initiate any changes to the landforms, structures, and plants of a property, we must first record what's already there to help us choose what to keep and what to remove or replace. As a result, the first step of any new design is to inventory and evaluate the existing landforms, structures, and plants by performing a site survey and analysis, the topic of our next chapter.

CHAPTER 2

Analyzing the Garden

A lesson on how to conduct a *site survey and analysis* of what exists on the property, use the results to determine the *scope of the design*, and then create a *base map* to begin the design process.

The Site Survey and Analysis

In chapter 1, I discuss the three main elements of garden design: landforms, structures, and plants, and the ways garden designers see them as layers that make up a greater whole. I describe examples of each and discuss what makes each layer unique and important within a design. Now we are ready to take the first actionable step of starting a garden design: the site survey and analysis.

A site survey and analysis is an exercise in objective observation coupled with subjective evaluation that leads to design. The survey consists of accurately mapping what is already on the property by taking an inventory of the landforms, structures, and plants currently in place. The analysis portion is an assessment and/or description of those elements, for example describing a slope as steep or gentle, a fence as well built or in need of repair, a tree as beloved or a nuisance. The analysis determines whether each inventoried and mapped element is a potential pro or con within the design site. The completed survey and analysis aids the designer's thought process leading to the actual design sequence.

The fact that the site survey and analysis is conducted outside, on-site, is what makes it the crucial first step of every garden design process, during which we become intimately familiar with the garden as is, and whether the existing elements on-site add or detract from the purpose and appearance of the property. This is especially important for unfamiliar gardens as the process helps the designer see what is there and understand how different garden areas and elements relate to each other. The more time spent on the ground the better. It leads to more familiarity and a better understanding of the site details, hence an increased potential for better design ideas. For instance, the property used as the case study for the site survey and analysis in this chapter is my new home property in Northern California. We lived there for a little over a year before I started to truly understand how I wanted to redesign the outdoor spaces. This luxury of time is rarely, if ever, available to me when I design for clients, but anyone looking to design their own home property should have a certain amount of familiarity with the site so they feel ready to map it, assess what's there, and start considering design ideas. It's important to remember that design is a process and that

◀ As a new garden designer, you will graduate from *looking* at the elements of a garden to *seeing* how landforms, structures, and plants shape a garden.

Garden Designer Talk

SITE An area of ground on a property where the proposed design work will take place.

PLAT MAP A map of a land parcel that provides property line measurements and location, locations of streets and public utility easements, as well as ingress and egress easements and sometimes hazard zones. Typically, the map attaches to the property deed at the local county assessor's and recorder's office.

SCALE The ratio of the drawing's size compared to the actual area of the design: for example, 1" = 10' means a measurement of 1 inch (2.5 cm) on the drawing corresponds to 10 feet (3 m) on the site.

CONTOUR MAP A topographic map on which the landform is shown by contour lines indicating the relative slope of the surface.

ORIENTATION The relative physical position of the site in relation to the direction of north on a map.

SCOPE OF DESIGN The purpose and physical parameters of a proposed design plan.

BASE MAP A site survey of the proposed design redrawn without the elements deemed unwanted during the analysis phase.

good design ideas take shape over time. Outside inspirations make a difference and are often the origin of great gardens, but the site itself should be the primary source for our ideas (more about this in chapter 8).

SITE SURVEY

In the first session of the garden design workshop I teach, I ask students to perform a site survey in class, mapping it by memory, and then completing and correcting it at home. Almost invariably, when they compare their in-class survey map to reality at home they discover discrepancies. There could be trees they never knew existed, or the size and shape of the house may be different from what they thought it was. The point of the exercise is to use the process of the site survey to recognize what is there and evaluate it. Although it is not actual design work, we can't help but begin to formulate some design concepts while we perform the site survey and analysis. However, these early ideas will not be included on this site survey, though we can take note of any inspirations as they arise. In fact, experienced garden designers develop some of their best design ideas during this phase.

Color Coding

It helps to color code the elements on a site survey and analysis: **black** for constants; **blue** for structure; **brown** for landform; **green** for plants; and **red** for the analysis. Though not required, it makes it a little easier to read. It is, however, important to remember that the site survey drawing is meant only for the designer and is not typically shared with anyone else. Think of it as notes. All that matters is that the designer can read and understand it. Surveys become quite messy and scrawled with edits and erasures out in the field, but that can be cleaned up later.

Constants

Start with a black pencil. Locate and draw all the constants, the unchangeable property attributes—the first of which are the property lines, unless there are plans to buy the neighboring lots. A good shortcut is to find a property plan or plat map, often available in the real estate documentation from purchase, or from town records. A plat map will clearly indicate the property lines. If a plat map isn't available, it could be worthwhile to hire a professional land surveyor to establish the location of the property lines and map other key elements, like buildings and utilities. A professional survey map may also include elevation contours indicating landform and even mark the location of large specimen trees. Starting with any type of pre-existing map or plan makes the site survey and analysis process much simpler because a lot of time-consuming measurements will be provided. Another way to start is using a digital map application to get a bird's-eye view of the site to locate the property lines and major structure elements, like driveways and roads.

The property map or aerial photo is then reduced to fit on an 8.5 × 11-inch or 11 × 17-inch (21.5 × 28 or 28 × 43.1 cm) piece of graph paper and affixed to a clipboard, making it easier to work with outside in the elements. Use the entire sheet of paper so the property outline is as large as possible. It's best if the property's entry point, such as the driveway or walkway entry, is located at the bottom of the page to make it easier to visualize how the property is approached and for others to understand the plan once it reaches the design phase. The site survey and analysis should always include the entire property, even if just a portion of the property is planned. This helps ensure that a sense of unified thought is being applied to the whole property from the start.

The next constant that needs to be included on the map is orientation. Determining orientation means finding "north." Obviously, that's never going to change. Garden designers care which direction is north because they need to know which direction is south as that will affect the sun and shade patterns on the ground. Find north and draw an arrow on the sheet that points in that direction. The arrow may or may not point to the top of the page, but it must point north.

The final category of constants comprises adjacent public features, like roads, sidewalks, utility poles, and, in cases where they infringe

Determining the Drawing's Scale

Find the drawing's scale by measuring a known length in the real world, such as a property line, and dividing it by the length of the line on the drawing. For example, if a property line is 100 feet (30.5 m) and the corresponding line on the drawing is 10 inches (25.4 cm), the scale is 1" = 10' (2.5 cm = 3 m). This ratio can be used for all additional measurements taken outside and translated onto the survey map. (Note: The scale will likely change when the site survey is converted into a base map.)

on or loom over the property, neighboring buildings. If the wall of a neighboring building is right near the property line, it should be considered unchangeable and indicated on the survey. Roads and sidewalks define the geography surrounding the site, suggesting whether it is in a city, the suburbs, or out in the country. All this matters and must be recorded. Nearby public infrastructure should also be mapped on the survey since things like street poles will remain unchanged.

Structures

Structures are all the human-made features on the site, the most important of which in residential garden design is the house. In chapter 1, I discuss the elements of landforms, structures, and plants, in that order, and that is how we will approach them during the actual design phase, but for the site survey it is easier to draw the structures first, then the landforms and plants. The first structure we draw should be the house, accurately placed within the property lines. The house may already be on a plat map or aerial map, but if it isn't, the best way to locate it is to triangulate the distance from a corner of the house to a known location, such as the closest property corner. Measure in right angles, up (or down) and over (left or right), from the property corner to the corner of the house and then translate those measurements onto the survey map to locate the corner of the house on the plan.

From that corner point, walk around the house, measuring the length as best as possible and noting the direction of each wall, window, or doorway, and indicate if it is a wall, window, or doorway. Work around counterclockwise and the footprint of the house will form. Use a measuring tape or wheel, or pace it off. Don't worry if it's not precise, or if the exact line measurements on the survey sheet aren't absolutely accurate to scale. They can be cleaned up later. The most important thing is that the shape of the house and the location of the walls, windows, and doors are correct. Also on the drawing, include the location of rain gutter downspouts, water spigots, light fixtures, electrical receptacles, drains, and other utilities adjacent to or attached to the house.

Use a triangle graphic to indicate a doorway by placing it inside the building pointing to the exit. Once the footprint of the house is mapped, it helps to label the interior spaces, like kitchens, bedrooms, and bathrooms. This will be useful because what we decide to design in the garden

Your site survey constants are those things that cannot be changed, like adjacent roads, fixed property lines, and which way is north.

outside the kitchen will be different from what we include outside the bathroom window. Label front and back porches or balconies. Upper-story balconies should be included because they tie interior rooms to the outdoor spaces below.

Next, add all the other structures on the site, locating them in relation to the house, starting with any other buildings including garages and sheds, even doghouses. Use the same method of triangulation used to locate the house to locate each additional building.

Draw the driveway, walkways, and paths, including casual paths like stepping-stones. Indicate their dimensions, especially width, and what they are made of, such as asphalt, concrete, cut stone, pebbles, boards, or woodchips.

Draw any existing patios and decks, indicating their material, such as "bluestone patio" or "treated lumber deck," as well as any helpful dimensions, like the thickness of the patio stone or the height of the deck. Some properties have odd patches of concrete or asphalt left over from an old shed or an abandoned driveway. Be sure to include these in the survey because they may need to be removed or somehow incorporated into the design.

Next, draw the garden walls, including retaining walls and decorative freestanding walls within the garden as well as any significant neighboring walls not previously indicated as a constant feature. Note the material and height of each wall, for example, "3-feet-tall, 2-feet-wide (91.4 cm tall, 61 cm wide) fieldstone wall."

Locate any fences and add those using a hatched line. Indicate the height and material of the fence as well as the type of fence, such as chain-link, deer, picket, privacy, security, or stockade fence. Indicate the location of any gates attached to the fences, walls, or buildings.

Include pergolas, arbors, gazebos, trellises, and canopies, either stand-alone or attached to other structures.

Locate and draw the swimming pool or hot tub and indicate whether it is above- or below-ground. If there is a designed water feature with pumps, such as a koi pond or artificial waterfall, include it here. Built water features are considered structures, not landforms.

Draw any permanent planters. This includes raised beds made from brick, stones, or timbers as well as large, heavy pots and planters that stay in place year-round. Don't include small pots, unless it's a large collection always kept in the same location, for example a group of terra-cotta pots for an herb collection on a platform. If there are any window boxes attached to the house, draw those too.

Add any permanent art objects or furnishings. These can include birdbaths, feeders and houses, sundials, fountains, gazing balls, statues, totem poles, and anything like that. Furnishings run the gamut and include patio tables and chairs, outdoor couches, chaise longues, garden benches, potting benches, and more.

Add any recreational structures like playsets, horseshoe rings, bocce courts, tennis courts, volleyball nets, firepits, and more.

▶ As you add each structure to your survey, always include an accurate and descriptive label. For example, "5-foot (1.5 m) green chain-link fence" or "concrete walk."

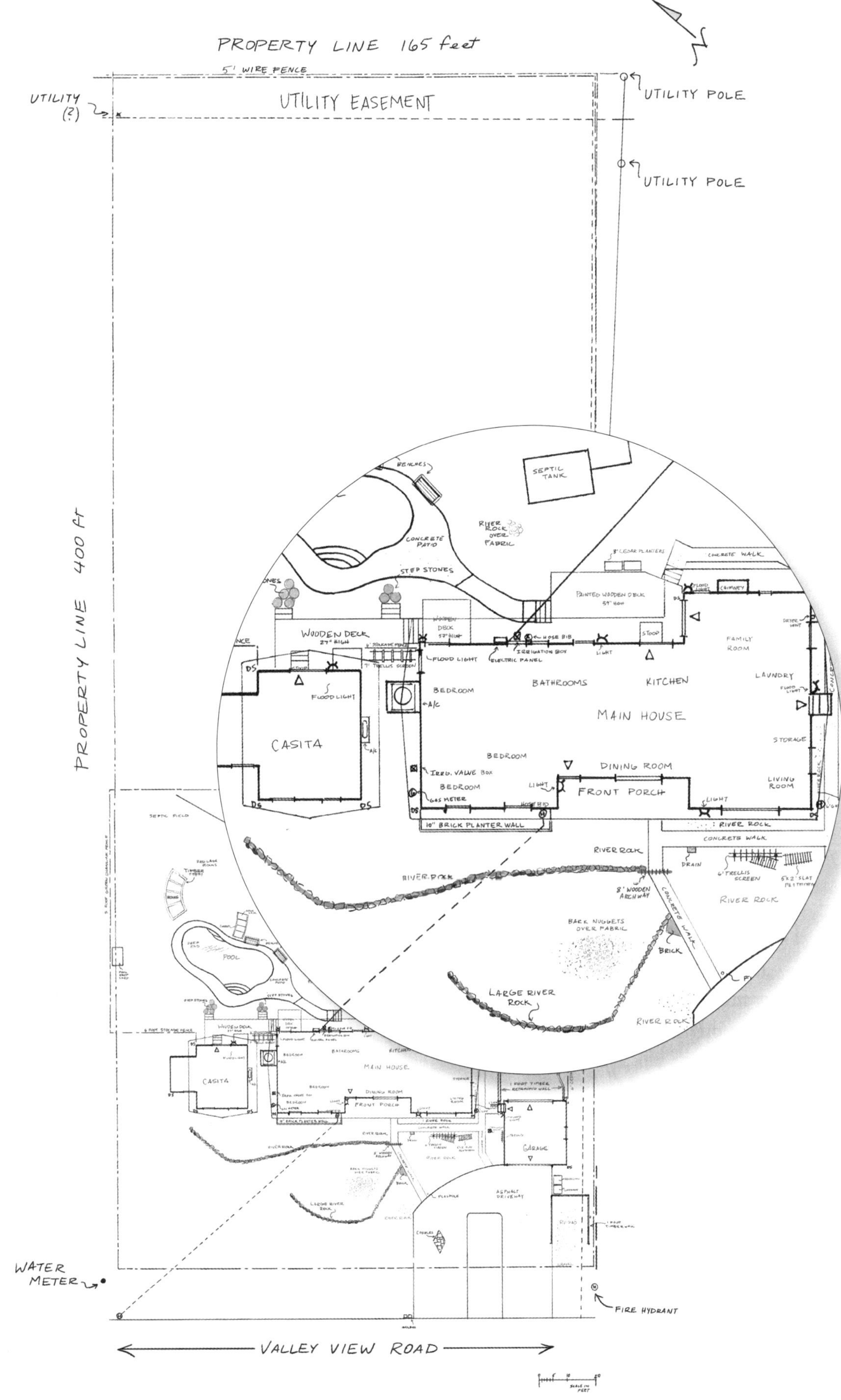

PROPERTY LINE 165 feet
5' WIRE FENCE
UTILITY (?)
UTILITY EASEMENT
UTILITY POLE
UTILITY POLE
PROPERTY LINE 400 ft
SEPTIC TANK
BENCHES
CONCRETE PATIO
RIVER ROCK OVER FABRIC
STEP STONES
CEDAR PLANTERS
CONCRETE WALK
PAINTED WOODEN DECK
WOODEN DECK 27" HIGH
HOSE BIB
IRRIGATION BOX
ELECTRIC PANEL
FLOOD LIGHT
LIGHT
STOOP
CHIMNEY
FAMILY ROOM
LAUNDRY
BEDROOM
BATHROOMS
KITCHEN
MAIN HOUSE
CASITA
A/C
STORAGE
BEDROOM
IRRG. VALVE BOX
BEDROOM
GAS METER
DINING ROOM
FRONT PORCH
LIVING ROOM
10" BRICK PLANTER WALL
RIVER ROCK
CONCRETE WALK
DRAIN
6' TRELLIS SCREEN
8' WOODEN ARCHWAY
CONCRETE WALK
BARK NUGGETS OVER FABRIC
BRICK
LARGE RIVER ROCK
POOL
GARAGE
ASPHALT DRIVEWAY
WATER METER
FIRE HYDRANT
VALLEY VIEW ROAD

The list of utility structures is long, but all these objects should be included on a site survey:

- Air conditioner
- Barbecue grills
- Cable box
- Composters
- Electric and gas meters
- Firewood racks
- Garbage cans
- Generator
- Irrigation boxes
- Lampposts
- Landscape lighting
- Mailbox
- Outdoor kitchens; pizza ovens; refrigerators
- Pool equipment
- Power lines that cross the property
- Propane tank
- Septic tank and leach field
- Solar panels
- Stereo speakers
- Utility boxes
- Well heads
- Windmills

Landform

The landform layer is more than just the site topography, though that is an important aspect of it. Landform also consists of exposed bedrock and natural water features. Although most city and suburban sites tend to have relatively simple landforms, sometimes even completely flat with no grade changes at all, other properties can exhibit multiple topographic features and elevation changes. The key for the garden designer during a site survey and analysis is to identify and describe significant landform features that will affect how the garden can be used and should be designed. It is an exercise in recognizing the limitations of a property, but also identifying unique characteristics that make the site special. The landform layer is often where the "genius of the site" resides, meaning whatever is wholly unique and memorable on a property, what sets it apart from any place else. The landform element is too often overlooked by garden designers who, understandably, focus more attention on the plant layer. However, landforms, whether pre-existing or developed during the design, are perfect for creating exciting and interesting outdoor spaces.

Slopes, Low Spots, and High Spots

The easiest way to record slopes is with a topographic contour map produced by a land surveyor. Contour maps are valuable resources

▶ Your primary focus when surveying the landform layer is to record the lay of the land and the location of any significant geologic features.

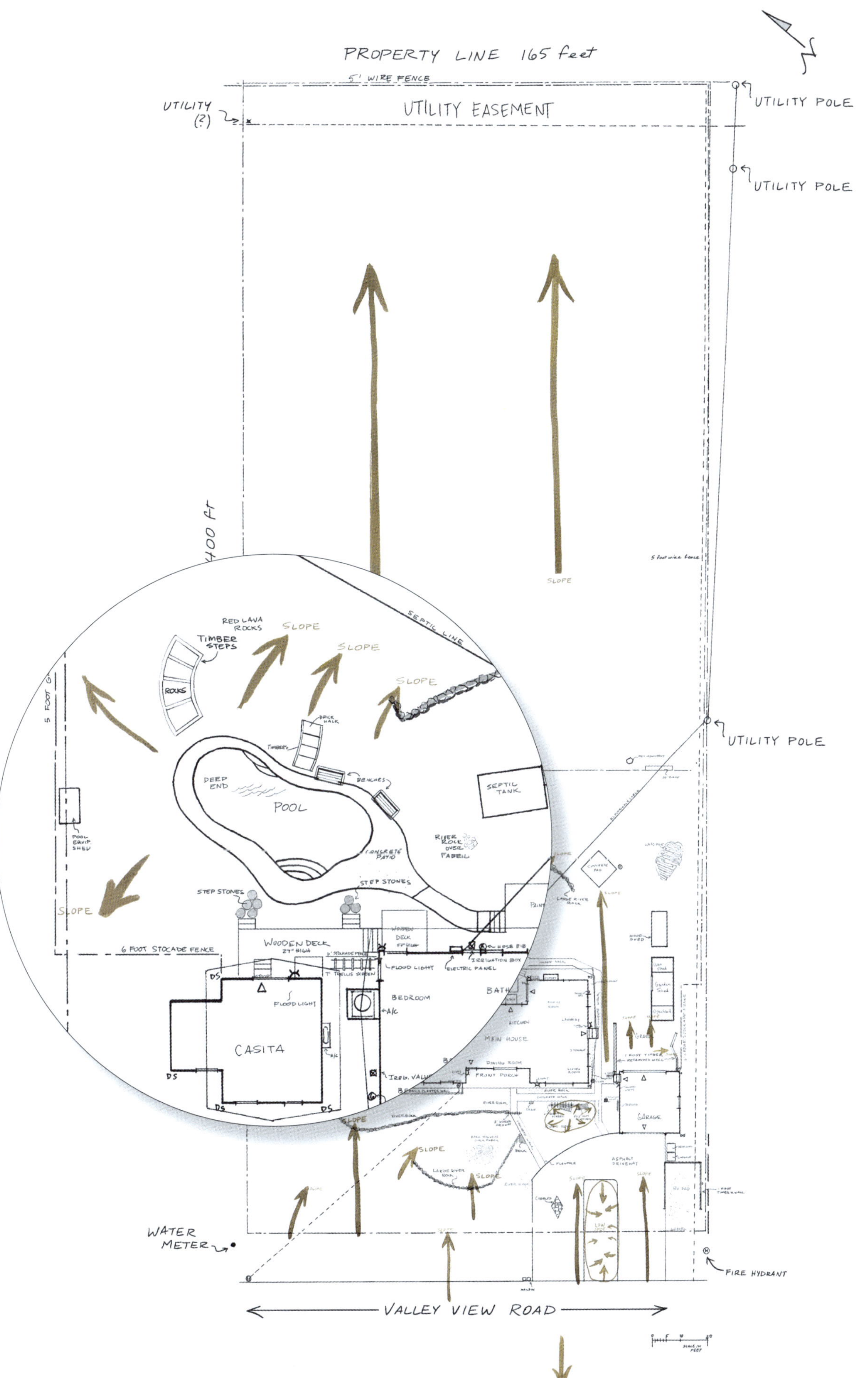

PROPERTY LINE 165 feet
5' WIRE FENCE
UTILITY (?)
UTILITY EASEMENT
UTILITY POLE
UTILITY POLE
400 ft
5 foot wire fence
SLOPE
UTILITY POLE
SEPTIC LINE
RED LAVA ROCKS
SLOPE
TIMBER STEPS
SLOPE
ROCKS
SLOPE
BRICK WALK
TIMBERS
BENCHES
DEEP END
POOL
SEPTIC TANK
5 FOOT G
POOL EQUIP. SHED
RIVER ROCK OVER FABRIC
CONCRETE PATIO
STEP STONES
STEP STONES
SLOPE
6 FOOT STOCADE FENCE
WOODEN DECK 27" HIGH
HOSE BIB
IRRIGATION BOX
FLOOD LIGHT
ELECTRIC PANEL
DS
FLOOD LIGHT
BEDROOM
A/C
BATH
CASITA
A/C
KITCHEN
MAIN HOUSE
DINING ROOM
FRONT PORCH
DS
DS
DS
GARAGE
SLOPE
SLOPE
SLOPE
ASPHALT DRIVEWAY
WATER METER
FIRE HYDRANT
VALLEY VIEW ROAD

for any garden design project; however, few homeowners have such maps, and not everyone can afford to pay for one. Fortunately, what we really need is a recognition of the lay of the land and how the ground is affected by hills, swales, humps, and dips. For our purposes at this stage, any topographical feature that is recognizable to the eye should be indicated on the site survey. Slopes are indicated by arrows. The arrows always point downhill. The fatter the arrow the steeper the slope, and the length of the arrow indicates the extent, or run, of the slope. We draw low spots by outlining their shape and location, then use slope arrows, pointing in toward the center of the shape, to indicate steepness and depth. Draw high spots the same way but aim the arrows from the center of the shape to the outer perimeter to indicate the basic character of the hillock.

Ponds, Lakes, Seas, and Oceans

These are low spots in the topography filled with water. Ponds can be small enough to fit on a property, and their water level may change during the year, filling in spring or rainy seasons and diminishing during times of drought. A healthy pond is an excellent habitat for turtles, frogs, and birds as well as many water-loving plants, like sweet flag or water lilies. Ponds and lakes also breed mosquitos and may become choked with weeds and algae, making them smell bad when stagnant so it's good to know one is nearby. Lakes are larger than ponds and most often a site lies adjacent to a lake, forming a wetland zone that must also be indicated on the site survey. Seas and oceans are always edge elements that mostly influence the site as a view, or weather maker. The location and character of a shoreline near the site must be indicated, such as sand with dunes, rocky, or cliffside. Indicate the view to the water on the survey because an ocean view is definitely something special.

Rivers, Streams, Creeks, and Drainage Ditches

These landforms are channels with volumes of water that flow permanently, seasonally, or intermittently. Rivers are the widest and typically flow continually. They are often adjacent to the site rather than located directly on it, unless it is a very large property. Adjacent rivers should be included in the survey because they are significant features that can affect the site even from a distance, either as views or flood threats. Streams and creeks are smaller and may transect the site. They are often tributaries that feed a larger river system and are unique features that can either add to or detract from the goals of a design. Drainage ditches may occur naturally or be built. They differ from rivers, streams, and creeks in that they are usually dry but fill with running water during and after a rainstorm. Sketch the location of these natural water features with parallel lines that indicate their length, width, and overall character, then label accordingly, for example "seasonal creek" or "dry riverbed."

Boulders, Outcroppings, and Ledge

Rock formations can be excellent features of a garden design, but they can also pose problems. Boulders, whether partially buried or laying on the surface, are often remnants from when the land was originally cleared for construction, or the foundation of the house was excavated.

What About Wetlands?

Wetlands are a unique example of a landform where the water might appear to be standing still but is, in fact, moving, though slowly. Wetlands are the sponges of our ecosystems. When it rains, wetlands slow surface drainage, allowing water to either percolate into the soil or direct it to a stream or river where it can pass through the local watershed and discharge into a lake, sea, or ocean. Due to their role within the surface water system and because they serve as excellent habitats for native plants and wildlife, wetlands are ecologically critical and must be mapped during a site survey to prevent any interference in how they function, or perhaps suggest a way to highlight them within a design. States and municipalities designate wetlands and legislate their protection, issuing guidelines as to what can be done on or near them in terms of landform changes and adding structures or plants. So, if there is a wetland, or a portion of one on a site, it absolutely must be indicated.

Even though they may have been moved or purposely placed, we always include boulders as a landform feature. Any stones too large and heavy to be moved without machinery should be drawn where they lay. Map any exposed stone outcroppings that emerge from the ground and use them to locate shallow bedrock just below the surface. It's important to find out if there is bedrock near the surface since it will affect what can be planted there. If it's just a foot below, there is no way trees will grow, though smaller, shallow-rooted plants could work. We can spot bedrock beneath a lawn where the grass turns brown first during a hot, dry spell in summer. Plant roots can't grow deeply over bedrock so that grass will turn brown first. Another trick is to use a length of rebar hammered into the ground to find out exactly how deep the bedrock lies.

Plants

Finally, we reach the plant layer. When drawing the site survey, envision the plant layer from the top down and draw the canopy first, then draw the understory, and finally, the ground-layer plants. Of course, all three plant layers also have layers within them, and there are also plant categories, like hedges and edible plants, within layers. While the primary purpose of a site survey is to inventory and locate all the plants, this can be difficult to accomplish when working on properties over an acre (0.4 ha) in size. To fit on an 8.5 × 11-inch or even an 11 × 17-inch (21.5 × 28 or 28 × 43.1 cm) sheet, the drawing's scale could be 1 inch = 20 feet (2.5 cm = 6 m) or more, making it impossible to draw individual small shrubs and ground-layer plants. A scale of 1 inch = 10 feet (2.5 cm = 3 m) allows us to locate and label all the trees and shrubs within the canopy and understory along with most herbaceous ground-layer plants, and at a scale of 1 inch = 5 feet (2.5 cm = 1.5 m), every plant can be easily located and labeled, assuming they are all found and identified. However, at this point it is best to stick with the scale that allows the entire property to fit on a sheet that fits on the clipboard and simply represent the plant layer on the site as accurately as possible, no matter the scale. Remember, a site survey is like taking notes. It's not a finished product for presentation.

Canopy

These are the tallest woody plants on the property and can be broken down into several categories, including large shade trees, medium-size ornamental trees, small patio trees, and evergreen screening trees. Draw a canopy tree by locating its trunk and marking it with a dot or X. If it's a very large tree, with a big trunk 2 feet (61 cm) or more in diameter, measure it and draw the dot as a filled-in circle. If there is more than one main trunk add more dots to show that.

Next, draw a circle the size and shape of the tree canopy. This is important because it indicates how much shade the tree casts on the ground beneath the canopy (something good to know). Measure from the tree trunk to the drip line, the edge of the farthest reach of branches and leaves, and draw the canopy as a circle, oval, or ellipse. Label each tree as accurately as possible, such as "oak," or more specifically "valley oak." If unsure of the name, simply describe it. For example, a "beautiful, old tree with lobed leaves." That's good enough for now.

Draw smaller trees as smaller circles, and if they are growing close enough to each other to intersect, draw them as intersecting circles. This is often the case with screening trees, a common category of tree in the canopy layer. Screening trees tend to be planted close together to block views, create privacy, or mitigate nearby noise. In time they will grow into each other to form a connected canopy, like a hedge. Since the trees function more like a single plant it's okay to locate each trunk with a small dot or X and then draw a sequence of connected circles to show the extent of the screening, or just draw an encompassing rectangle shape showing the entire grouping as one and label it as a screen or hedge, like "arborvitae hedge" or "spruce screening grove."

Woodlots are also part of the canopy, but there is no need to draw each tree. Simply draw a "blob" outlining the size and shape of the woods and label it "woods." Most trees in woodlots aren't special, but if there is a nice specimen, locate, draw, and label it. It might become a feature tree in the design later, such as a destination for a walk in the woods or a place to make a small clearing.

Understory

The understory is next and consists of woody plants, mainly shrubs, that grow beneath the canopy if there is one. Understory plants often grow in groups, such as foundation plantings alongside the house, as individual specimens in lawn areas, or within a mixed planting bed. Use the same graphics convention as for the canopy. Mark the location of each plant with a dot or an X, then indicate the size and shape of

▶ By adding the plant layer, you bring the site survey to life, manifesting it as a recognizable landscape garden.

PROPERTY LINE 165 feet

5' WIRE FENCE

UTILITY (?)

UTILITY EASEMENT

UTILITY POLE

UTILITY POLE

LIVE OAK SHRUBS

MIXED GRASSES & FORBS

LIVE OAK

VALLEY OAK

GRAY PINE

SLOPE

MIXED GRASSES & FORBS

PROPERTY LINE 400 ft

WEEDS

SEPTIC FIELD

WILD LAWN

POOL

CASITA

SLOPE

WATER METER

VALLEY VIEW ROAD

FIRE HYDRANT

LIVE OAK

5' GREEN CHAINLINK FENCE

CHERRY TREE (WEAK)

APPLE TREE

CROWN VETCH

PEACH TREE

PRUNUS

VALLEY OAK

STUMP

SLOPE

ROSES (PINK)

SEPTIC LINE

SLOPE

SLOPE

VALLEY OAKS

CONCRETE PAD

SPREADING MYSTERY SHRUB

BOTTLE BRUSH

FAN PALM SHRUB

BRICK WALK

FAN PALM TREE

LARGE RIVER ROCK

SLOPE

PYRACANTHA

BENCHES

BRIDAL'S WREATH

SEPTIC TANK

SPREADING JUNIPER

GRASSES

STUMP

NANDINA

RIVER ROCK OVER FABRIC

CONCRETE PATIO

CYCAD STAR PLANT

STONES

CONCRETE WALK

CAMELLIA

PAINTED WOODEN DECK

CHIMNEY

its branching as a circle or blob. For multistem shrubs, use three or more dots to show it's not a single trunk (find more tips on how to draw plants in chapter 3). Some understory plants may be located under the canopy of larger trees; draw them inside the circle of that canopy and label them accordingly. If it's an unknown quantity of shrubs filling a large area, draw them like we draw woods, as a blob, but labeled with the plant name, such as "juniper" or "oleander." Shrub hedges are a category of understory plants and can be drawn as a single shape or with individual connected circles or squares for each plant.

Ground Layer

As the most complex part of the plant layer, ground-layer plants may be woven together out in the open or beneath the canopy or understory. They may grow as individual groups of the same species, or as individual plants of many different species in the same planting bed. The trick to recording ground-layer plants is to map their location and label them as best as possible, depending on the drawing's scale. If the scale is 1 inch = 5 feet (2.5 cm = 1.5 m), it should be easy to label every plant. When working with a scale of 1 inch = 10 feet (2.5 cm = 3 m) or larger, it will be difficult to site and specify each ground-layer plant. Instead, draw a blob and label it as "flowering perennials" or "wildflowers" to provide a sense of what is growing in that spot. Other possible labels include "foliage plants"; "bedding annuals"; "mixed annuals"; "herbs"; and "edibles." It's also helpful to be more specific with labels like "ferns and hostas" or "mixed ornamental grasses." The more specific the better.

The ground layer may also have large areas with just a single species, for example spreading perennials like vinca or sedge, or low-growing shrubs like juniper. In cases like these, the entire planting can be considered a single plant so it's okay to label it that way. If other plants are mixed in, they can be labeled separately.

The final category of ground layer is the lawn. In most residential gardens wherever there aren't any plants, like a hedge or flowers, or where there isn't a structure like a patio or a walk, there is lawn. For lawn, simply place a label "lawn" in any open area where turfgrasses grow. If it's not a lawn, but a field or meadow, or even a patch of weeds, label it as such.

Sometimes there are spots on the site that don't have plants or a structure covering them. It might be a patch of bare ground, or an area covered with mulch or leaves, but it still needs to be labeled so we know what's there. Also, once the plants are located and labeled, draw any bed lines that exist between planting beds and lawns. This includes the shape and size of beds in a vegetable garden.

ANALYSIS

The "analysis" portion of the site survey and analysis is a description and evaluation of the landforms, structures, and plants surveyed, but it also includes a characterization of the site through sensory impressions. The analysis details can be purely practical, for example listing objective attributes like the color of

▶ Your site analysis should describe the impression that the elements of landform, structure, and plants combine to create.

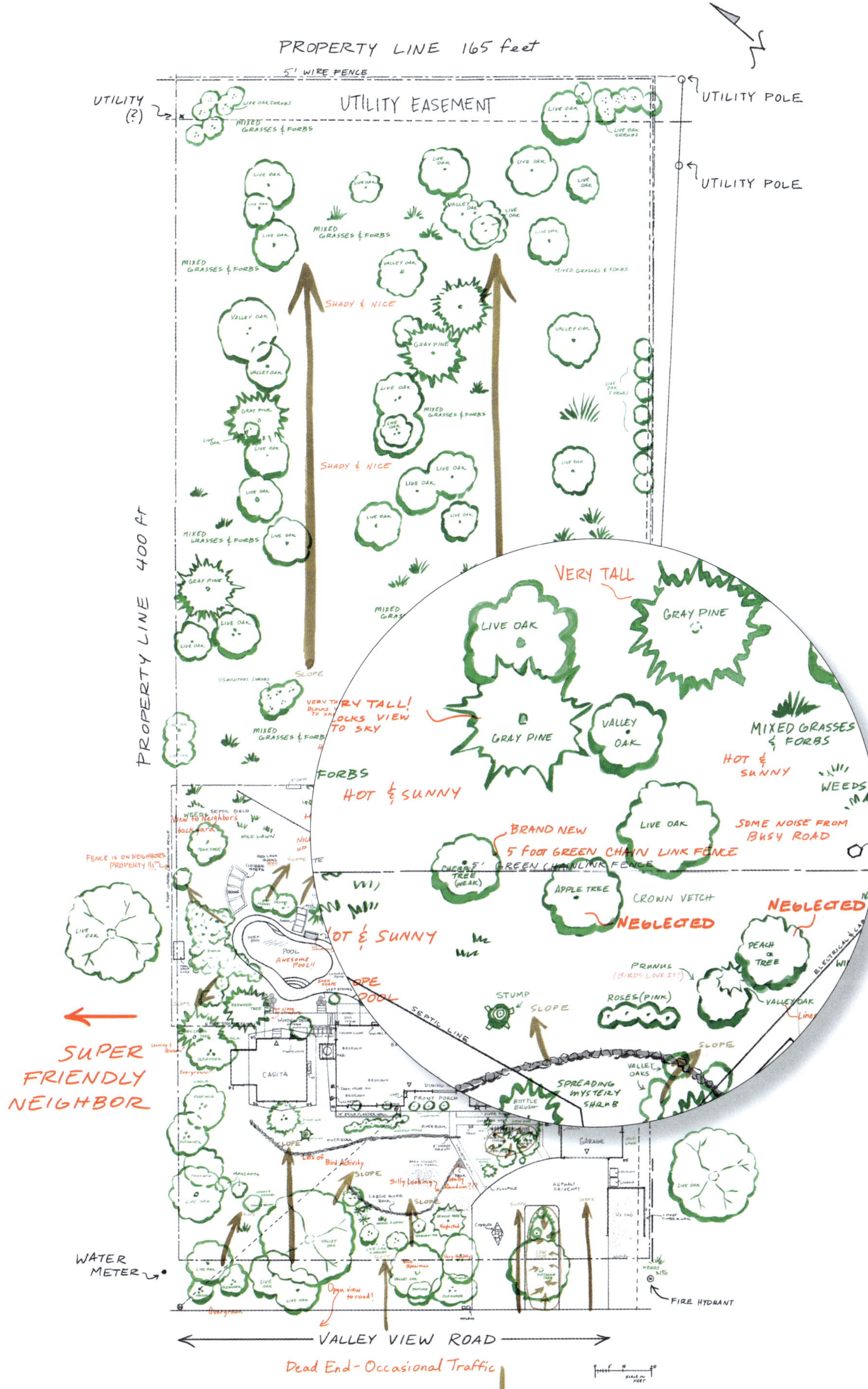

PROPERTY LINE 165 feet
5' WIRE FENCE
UTILITY (?)
UTILITY EASEMENT
UTILITY POLE
UTILITY POLE
LIVE OAK SHRUBS
MIXED GRASSES & FORBS
LIVE OAK
VALLEY OAK
GRAY PINE
SHADY & NICE
SHADY & NICE
PROPERTY LINE 400 ft
SLOPE
VERY TALL
GRAY PINE
LIVE OAK
GRAY PINE
VALLEY OAK
MIXED GRASSES & FORBS
HOT & SUNNY
WEEDS
FORBS
HOT & SUNNY
BRAND NEW 5 FOOT GREEN CHAIN LINK FENCE
LIVE OAK
SOME NOISE FROM BUSY ROAD
5' GREEN CHAINLINK FENCE
CHERRY TREE (WEAK)
APPLE TREE
CROWN VETCH
NEGLECTED
NEGLECTED
PEACH TREE
HOT & SUNNY
PRUNUS (BIRDS LOVE IT!)
STUMP
SLOPE
ROSES (PINK)
VALLEY OAK
SEPTIC LINE
SLOPE
VALLEY OAKS
SPREADING MYSTERY SHRUB
BOTTLE BRUSH
FENCE IS ON NEIGHBORS PROPERTY!!
View to Neighbors back yard
SUPER FRIENDLY NEIGHBOR
POOL Awesome Pool!
CASITA
FRONT PORCH
GARAGE
ASPHALT DRIVEWAY
Lots of Bird Activity
SLOPE
Silly looking
SLOPE
Neglected
Overgrown
Open view to road!
WATER METER
FIRE HYDRANT
VALLEY VIEW ROAD
Dead End - Occasional Traffic

a flower or the building material of a fence, but it should also consist of subjective assessments. The health of a plant, for instance, or the condition of a structure. The site analysis should also include character designations of specific areas on the property, for example places to relax or to work. These impressions and opinions chronicle the essence of the site and help us understand each discrete space within it. On a practical level, the analysis judges what is there, identifying the function and form of all the landforms, structures, and plants as a positive or negative feature. The goal is to find all the noteworthy pros and cons so when we reach the design phase, we can take advantage of, highlight, or enhance the pros and eliminate, diminish, or mitigate the cons.

Usefulness or Mitigation of Landforms

One of the first things to consider when analyzing a site is whether any landform features may limit the usefulness of the space. At the same time, we can look at difficult landforms as possibilities for design. What at first appears to be a problem could become a unique attribute once we find a solution. Steep slopes, a complete lack of slopes, sinkholes, hilltops, or any significant feature must be evaluated. Gentle slopes are easy to navigate, but traversing excessively steep slopes is a different story, bound to affect design decisions. Early recognition of problem landforms may suggest amending the design's goals to match the lay of the land or find creative ways to mitigate them without adversely impacting the design's potential. Labels like "steep slope" "exposed hilltop" or "deep depression" are helpful because the strength of these descriptions makes the magnitude of potential problems clear from the start.

Part of the landform analysis should also include a soil evaluation and a decision by the designer whether they will work with the soil they have or find ways to improve it. This is where a soil test comes in handy to identify potential problems related to texture and fertility (more about this in chapter 4).

Quality and Function of Structures

The evaluation of the structures is next. Basically, it is an ask-and-answer session for each item, be it shed, patio, fence, or flowerpot, to determine its quality and usefulness within the garden. For example, a patio may be in the wrong spot, feel too small, or have multiple broken or heaving stones. Or it could be perfectly placed, just the right size, but made of cheap, ugly stones. The analysis consists of asking eight scrutinizing questions for each structure:

1. Is it necessary?
2. Is it attractive?
3. Is it in the right location?
4. Is it the proper size?
5. Is it the right style?
6. Is it the best material construction?
7. Can it be changed?
8. Should it be removed or replaced?

By answering these questions, we can determine the value of each structure on the site and make the required recommendations for it based on our initial design goals.

Health and Appropriateness of Plants

In addition to a plant inventory, the site survey and analysis requires an assessment of the vitality of the plants. Poor or failing health makes removing or replacing a plant an easy decision, even large canopy trees or other valuable specimens. It's okay to cut down a one hundred-year-old oak tree if it is unhealthy and dangerous. Plants that are weak may be in the wrong sun or soil and might be saved if transplanted or the growing conditions improved. Creating more sun by editing unwanted plants, correcting drainage, or improving the soil around the plant could also help, but if a plant is no good, don't fret. Remove and compost it. Ugly, failing plants are automatic candidates for change. This could call for changing how it is cared for or for some corrective pruning. If that won't work, don't be sentimental, put it out of its misery and compost it.

Plants can also be wrong. Wrong plants are a result of a mismatch between the type of plant and its location. A messy mulberry tree planted next to a walk or driveway is a wrong plant because it will drop fruit and stain everything beneath its canopy. Running bamboo near a house foundation is a leaky basement waiting to happen, and a rugosa rose, though beautiful and fragrant, planted beside a front gate is bound to prick someone. These may be perfectly healthy specimens, but they should be moved or removed to make way for a better plant, or perhaps no plant at all.

Views and Surroundings

Things from outside the site that nonetheless infringe on it must also be noted. This includes views, good or bad, visible from important locations within the garden. What we see and experience from a patio where we may be spending a lot of time makes a difference. Is it a beautiful view, to a lake or a mountain, a nice open field, or a deep wood? Is it an eyesore, like shopping-center traffic, discarded junk scattered throughout a neighbor's lot, or a blinding floodlight at night? What we see from our gardens can be as important as what we see within them, so any view, good or bad, should be noted. A garden next to a farm field looks and feels different from one adjacent to a parking lot. It's as simple as that.

Sun, Wind, and Sound

Sun exposure is a key ingredient to any site analysis and crucial to understanding the garden's potential in terms of what may be grown, but it also affects how people feel. Fully exposed, hot, sunny spots can be uncomfortable, or they may be preferred, influencing what may be proposed for that garden area. Do we need to create some shade for a seating area? Or, will we want to take advantage of the sun for a swimming pool or a vegetable garden? To answer these questions and take full advantage of the property's potential, we must map the site's sun and shade, making note of daily and seasonal changes as well as any extremes, either too sunny or super shady (see Sun Mapping sidebar following).

Identify windy or sheltered spots. Persistent wind can be a problem and require changes to make those outdoor spaces useful. Dead zones, where there is extremely poor air circulation, can also pose difficulties, especially when considering the health and vitality of plants and people. A wind-whipped terrace or a slippery, algae-covered patio are not comfortable places to spend an afternoon.

Sun Mapping

Sun mapping is simply tracking the changes of the sun exposure on a site throughout the day, but it also considers the seasonal changes of the sun's location in the sky, highest in summer, lowest in winter, and somewhere in between during spring and fall. For this reason, we need to perform two sun mappings, one at or near the summer solstice and another time around the spring or fall equinox. This helps establish the range of the sunny and shady spots in the garden.

In some respects, what we are really doing is shadow mapping. The trick is to draw the shadows as they are cast on the ground as the sun moves through the sky and is blocked by tall obstructions on the site such as structures like buildings and fences, and large trees, either deciduous or evergreen.

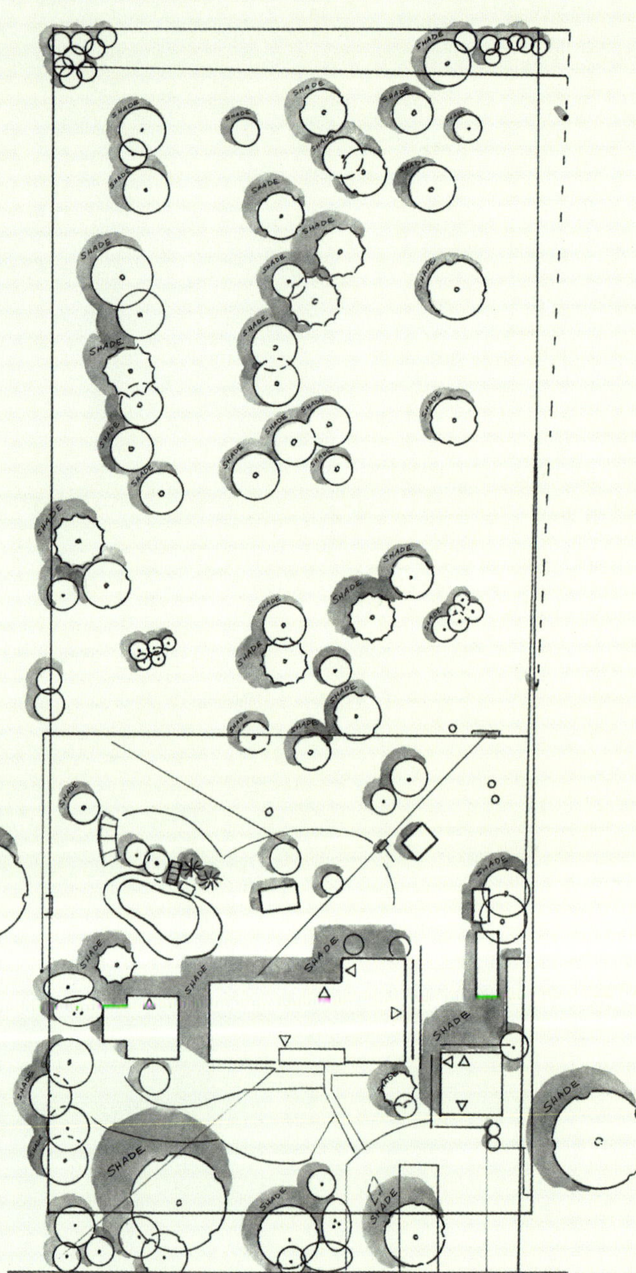

SUN MAP

▶ Although a sun map is just a moment in time, you can use it to illustrate significant sun and shade patterns on the property.

Documenting with Photos

Cell phone cameras are a great tool to document the appearance of a site at the start of the design process. These photos serve as excellent notes when working on the design and are a quick way to verify information on the site survey and analysis, especially if we don't live on the property and can't just step outside to check. These photos also serve as nice "before" shots once changes begin to take place.

When performing photo documentation, stand in key spots throughout the property and take multiple shots from each spot. A small ⅓-acre (0.13 ha) property could require as many as one hundred photos to fully capture what is there. Photos are more useful if they capture a scene, not a single plant or object. Hold the camera at eye level, aiming straight out as if walking and observing the garden. Orient the camera in landscape mode for most shots, and turn it to portrait in tight places, or to capture a tall tree, structure, or some sky. Be careful with the panorama function since it will distort the view. Always supplement panorama shots with a sequence of regular shots to show the view as it really is.

Key Locations

- Across the street, opposite the front entry
- At the driveway entry
- At the beginning of a path
- Along the length of a path looking forward and back
- Looking out from doorways
- Looking out from windows
- From the property lines looking in
- From the property corners looking in
- From the house façades looking out
- From the house corners looking out
- From important seating or gathering places
- From destination points in the existing gardens

Continued ›

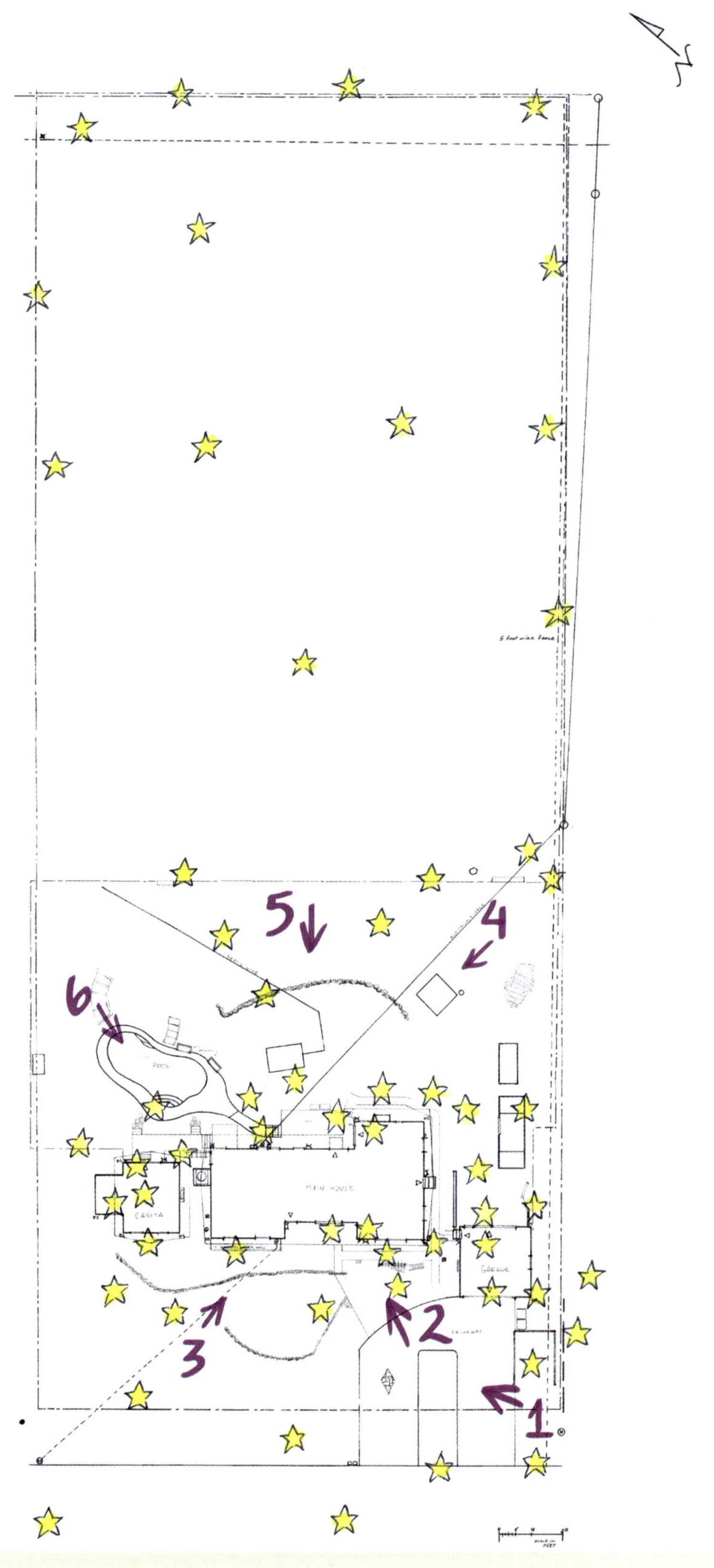

Capture the site's look and feel with multiple photos taken from key locations, or "nodes," throughout the site.

Photo 1

Photo 2

Photo 3

Photo 4

Photo 5

Photo 6

Excessive noise can infiltrate from a distance and detract from enjoying the garden. Determine whether the noise is persistent or intermittent. A persistent drone is often less problematic, as the human ear will, over time, learn to ignore it. Intermittent yet frequent sounds are the worst as they disturb our peaceful enjoyment when outside. Sounds, such as the roll of nearby surf or the twitter and call of birds, can also be pleasing so take note of these as potential benefits to embrace.

Determining Scope of Design

With the site survey and analysis complete, we are ready to determine the scope of the design and establish a program for the design plan. The two main considerations to determining the scope of the design are our needs and desires.

Needs are why we are considering a design in the first place, something about the garden that needs to be remedied in terms of form or function. This can be as basic as creating beauty with pleasing views from the house to the garden or improvements to curb appeal, or a need to improve the usefulness, or function, of the garden. Perhaps some play space for the kids, a vegetable garden to grow food, or a place to relax and connect with nature.

After needs come *desires*. Though the main purpose of a garden design is to address a defined need, good design always considers the fulfillment of our garden desires when meeting those needs. If we are going to the trouble to work on and complete a design, it should provide what we truly desire. This could be anything—from perfect plantings, a party deck or firepit, an outdoor kitchen, a manicured lawn, to even an orchard. Design desires are those amazing things that make all the effort and expense worthwhile and make us excited about the design.

The key to this step is to dream big and keep an open mind. Now is not the time to set limits on a design and discount a great idea due to practical concerns. Although we may not ultimately stay true to a dream desire, it will hurt the design in the long run if we shut down our ideas too soon. The dream of an orchard in a tiny city lot may seem unattainable, but it's not if we understand that it takes only three trees to make an orchard and many fruit trees are dwarf varieties that don't require much space. When it comes to a lot of great design ideas, if there is a will there's a way.

Our scope of design can also be defined by the extent to which we choose to make changes on the site. The most comprehensive approach is to work on a master plan that includes the entire property. This is best because it allows us to plan for the future and avoid doing double work. Even if the plan's implementation may take multiple years to complete, a master plan is extremely valuable.

Sometimes it does make sense to refine the scope of design to specific property areas, such as around the house, or discrete spaces like a front entry or backyard garden. Other discrete spaces include side yards, which are too often neglected, or deck and pool areas. Zeroing in on our scope of design even more, we may focus on a theme-specific garden, like perennial flower beds or vegetable plots.

Brainstorming a Dream Garden

Brainstorming is a useful exercise I always ask of my design students to help them envision the gardens they want. It's an effective first step in the design process performed before or after the site survey and analysis.

Write down, in no particular order, ten object nouns that would be in your dream garden, for example:

1. Greenhouse
2. Palm trees
3. Courtyard
4. Winding paths
5. Stone terrace
6. Sun sauna
7. Citrus trees
8. Succulents
9. Oak trees
10. Hedgerow

Write down, again, in no particular order, ten adjectives (object descriptors) that would be in your dream garden, for example:

1. Private
2. Sustainable
3. Casual
4. Ecological
5. Bird friendly
6. Organized
7. Efficient
8. Memorable
9. New
10. Inviting

In class, we break into groups of three or four where the students share their lists and then choose one noun and one adjective from each list to create a shared dream garden. This is easy if they have similar garden ideals, but sometimes they don't, making for a more interesting result as they are forced to find connections between different outlooks.

We then examine the lists, starting with the nouns. In the preceding lists, certain things stand out, like the greenhouse, sun sauna, and courtyard, as distinct destinations. Then come the winding paths and suddenly a vision of these destinations connected by the paths emerges. Next, we turn to the palm, citrus, and oak trees, which, along with the succulents, begin to line the paths and populate the areas between each destination. Finally, an image of a garden forms, complete with unique and useful structures connected by paths and planted with interesting trees and succulents: a desert garden.

Next, we read the adjectives. "Private" starts the list and "inviting" ends the list. These two descriptors seem counterintuitive, but two others, "sustainable" and "ecological," match up along with bird friendly. Organized and efficient work together and could connect to casual. Finally, we have new and memorable, which also fit if that something new is so new it becomes memorable.

The overall impression of these descriptive words creates an image of a garden, but it now needs to match the image produced by the nouns previously discussed. Palm trees might not be sustainable and ecological on this site, but the oaks are, if they are native species. A hedgerow is certainly bird friendly. The typical result is that some words work together well, and others may pose more questions. However, it could be these same questions that drive the design and make it something new and memorable!

Continued ›

This exercise demonstrates the thought process of design work. We are always striving to find design ideas that free us from purely practical considerations and explore the site's potential. I give this brainstorming assignment to my students because words like these go a long way toward describing what we need and want from our gardens before we even know it. As a professional garden designer, I listen for words like these whenever I meet with a client, but we can also listen for similar words within ourselves. Words like "inviting" and "sustainable" say something about what we want to accomplish. They can even create a sense of what the garden is meant to be.

Making that feeling a reality is the next step. We can't go to the store and buy some "inviting" or a box of "sustainable." Garden designers use things (nouns) to make the descriptions (adjectives) come to life. That's the secret! Gardens are made by selecting and placing objects, but the goal is not simply to gather things. The goal is to create an outdoor space, or place, with character, beauty, and usefulness. We accomplish this by subtracting and adding objects specifically chosen for how they look and how they work by building, planting, and placing them on the site. The result is a manifestation of our dream garden.

Making a Base Map

The base map is simple. Take the refined site survey, redrawn with all the necessary corrections so it is as accurate as possible, and draw it again, but this time leave out everything that will be eliminated or changed, like a broken fence or a dying tree, and include only what will remain or stay the same, like the house or the driveway. Focus first on the landform and structure and include major plants, such as the canopy trees. Make a copy of the clean base map and save it. The empty spaces on the plan are areas for design. Draw directly on the copy of the base map, or use tracing paper, or a digital program to add elements of landform, structure, and plants (more on this in chapter 3).

▲ Label the base map sparingly, as you will need the space to add features to the drawing as the design develops.

Start the Design Using Bubble Diagrams

We're finally ready to design! Though the site survey and analysis process is primarily a record and assessment of the site conditions, it is almost impossible not to be bombarded with design ideas and solutions while mapping out the survey, especially as the site's pros and cons are assessed and recognized. With these ideas for how the garden can be reshaped for new or improved uses in mind, it's a perfect time to employ a preliminary design exercise, called a bubble diagram, to begin assigning the functional program for each garden space.

Bubble diagrams study the outdoor spaces and consider the connections between them by working through several basic use arrangements in preparation for exploring detailed solutions later in the design process.

PET MONUMENT
ELECTRIC & CABLE
SEPTIC FIELD
POOL
PATIO
MAIN HOUSE
CASITA
GARAGE
DRIVEWAY

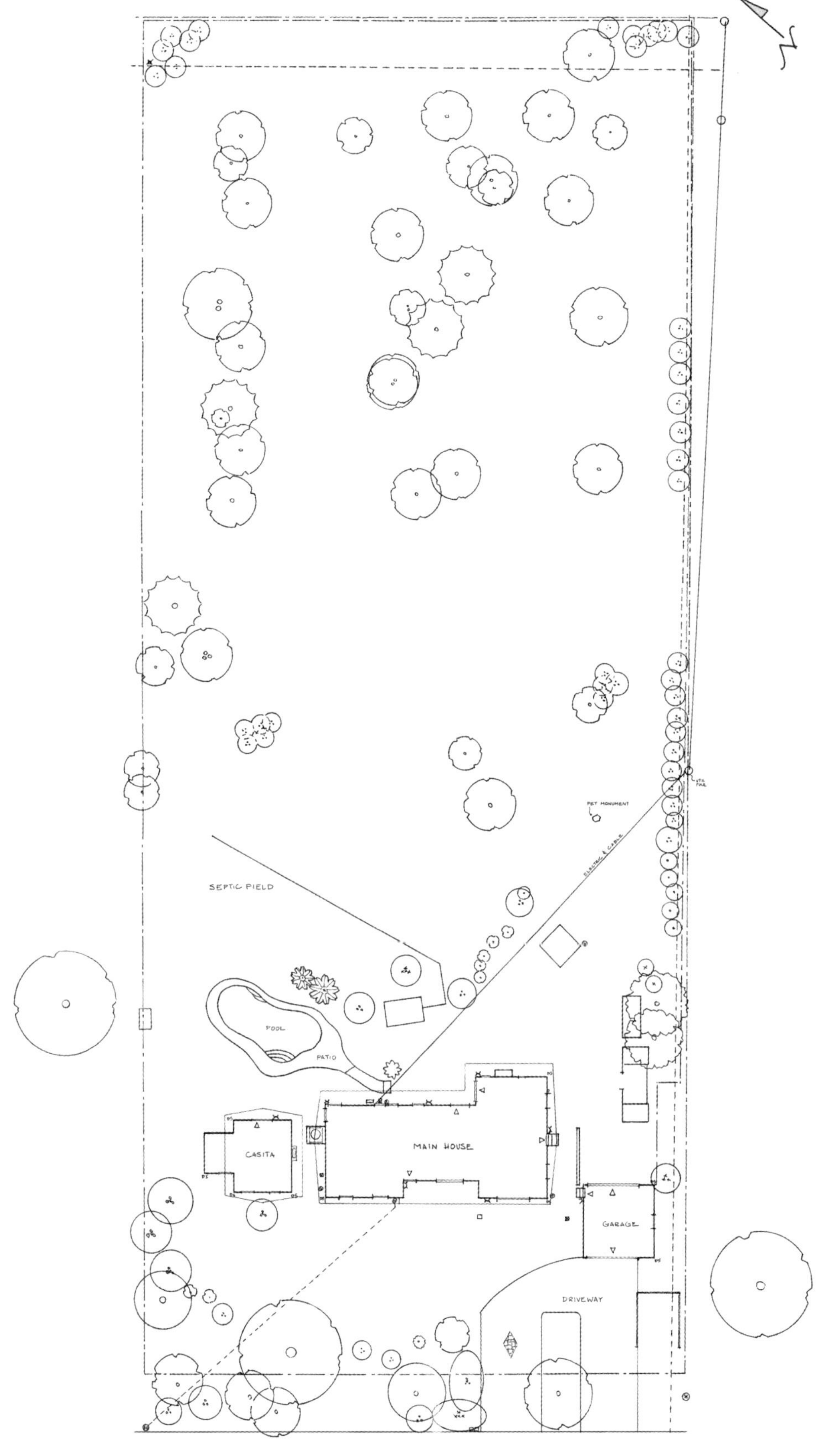

BASEMAP

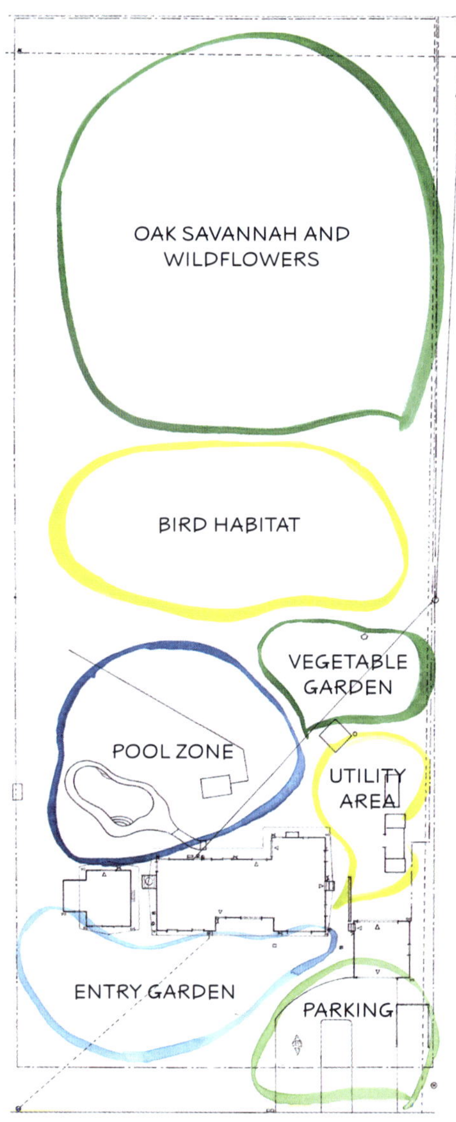

HOW TO CREATE A BUBBLE DIAGRAM

The purpose of a bubble diagram is to explore the relationships between garden spaces, not decide on the details. Details come later. The sketches you will make are just rough, so draw freehand and map things multiple times until the best ideas emerge.

1. Compile a list of general needs and wants to be included in the final garden design.
2. Draw "bubbles" for each element, arranged and labeled on tracing paper laid over the base map.

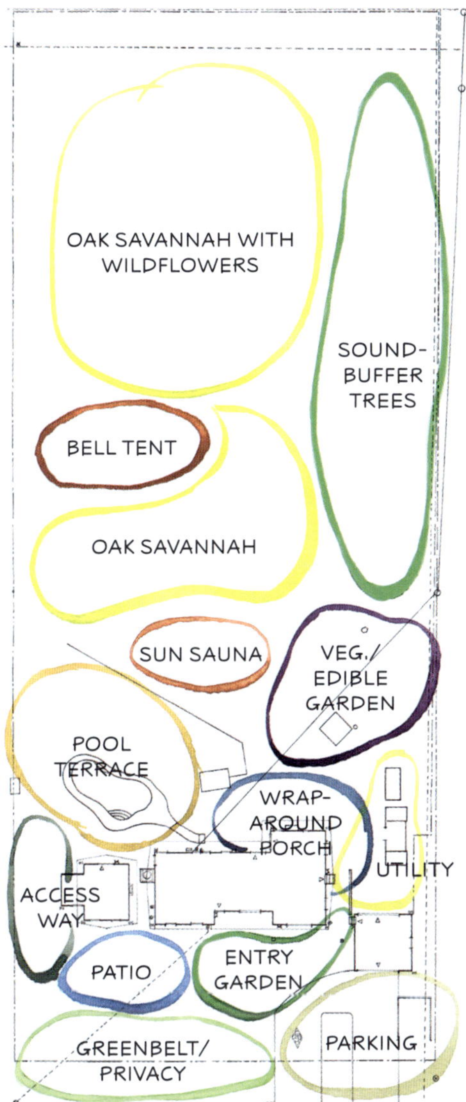

▲ Exploring options with different bubble diagrams

3. Explore options for how these spaces and uses will connect and communicate.
4. Fill the entire site with assigned uses to avoid confusion as the design develops.

CHAPTER 3

Graphics Techniques and Conventions

Primer on basic *hand-drawing techniques* and *computer-aided technologies* that can be used when crafting design *plans* and other illustrations, such as *elevations* and three-dimensional *perspectives* for communicating design ideas.

Graphics as Tools

Design graphics and illustrations are communication tools. Professionals use them to communicate their design ideas to clients, but they also use them to communicate the ideas in their heads to themselves. I have known designers who don't draw, but they always had a way to convey what they saw in their mind's eye. Some designers write it down. Others talk it up. One way or another we must communicate how we intend to shape the landforms, build the structures, and place the plants, and the best way to do it is with drawings. New, inexperienced, or amateur garden designers aren't expected to be highly skilled at drawing designs. In fact, drawings often make amateurs apprehensive because they are uncertain how well they can visually communicate their design ideas. We all remember our kindergarten art class drawings with crooked houses, deformed people, and lollipop trees. Yet our parents praised our work and hung the drawings on the refrigerator because they could "see" what we were trying to draw. That's what mattered then and that's what matters now. Visually communicating ideas is the only goal for design graphics.

I've taught garden design workshops to rank amateurs who didn't know a weighted line from a rendering, but somehow, they were able to communicate the vision of their garden. One student completed their site survey and analysis with pastels and poems. Another pasted photographs cut from magazines on poster board. Others surprised themselves, discovering they had a knack for drawing they never knew about and produced excellent hand-drawn plans. Still more took a tool they knew and applied it to their garden plan. My favorite was a fashion designer who used her software for creating dress designs to lay out a flower garden. The options are endless, however, there are accepted conventions and techniques professional garden designers use, and it's good to learn to use them when we can. Not everyone's drawing skills will match their design ideas, but even a crude drawing can represent an elegant idea, and there is no better way to get better at drawing than by practicing these techniques and training our eyes and hands to work together.

PLAN DRAWINGS

The plan drawing is the first and most important drawing any garden designer makes. Plans are

◂ As garden designers, our graphics skills develop over time but should always demonstrate a level of creativity and artfulness.

two-dimensional representations of the site, seen from above as if floating over the property. How high up we're floating determines the drawing's scale. A site survey, for example, is a plan. Plan drawings are the best way to show how the outdoor spaces relate to one another as well as the location of any landforms, structures, and plants that populate and shape those spaces. Plans are the easiest drawings because we don't have to work with perspectives or a third dimension, though we can add dimensionality to a 2D plan by working with layers, drawing the elements in the plan from the top down so objects become partially obscured by things above them, for example an understory shrub beneath a canopy tree. Plan drawings help us understand and see the whole site, discrete garden areas, and the details within these areas. Designing in plan view is like being a god, shaping the land one way over here, establishing a woodland over there, adding a pond or pool, deciding where the paths people use will be, and what they will see and experience along the way. For this reason, most garden designers design solely in plan view. The plan becomes a working document, where the garden layout takes shape as the designer works through multiple iterations and edits until the best solutions to the design needs and desires emerge.

Another interesting point about plan view drawings is that if the look and feel of the drawing is pleasing, if the shape and scale of the spaces look right on the drawing board, if it appears balanced and well formed, these qualities will translate to the real world. It's true, and it's why good-looking designs become great-looking gardens.

Hand-Drawn Plans

Hand-drawn plans are the best place to start. They can be a simple layout on an 8.5 × 11-inch (21.5 × 28 cm) piece of graph paper, or a detailed design on a 3 × 4-foot (0.9 × 1.2 m) sheet of drafting vellum. All plan drawings begin with a piece of tracing paper laid over the base map. We either redraw the base map onto the tracing paper if it is not too complicated, or simply look through the tracing paper and take note of the elements on the base map and work in and around them. The tracing paper is meant for exploring ideas, trying different locations for elements like structures and plants, as well as deciding how various garden areas will be used, such as an open lawn or a vegetable patch. The designer works out ideas on the tracing paper and, when an idea is good, they keep it, but if a better idea presents itself, they lay a new piece of tracing paper down and try again. During this process we don't erase, we just draw. If a new planting bed looks like it fits, take a new piece of tracing paper and draw it again. If the patio size is off, take a new piece of tracing paper and draw it again. Over and over, until we get it right. Always remember that "trace is for trying," so keep trying until it looks right.

Drawings on tracing paper should be quick, not labored over. Draw it. Look it over. Put down another sheet of paper and do it again. After several iterations, the best ideas will emerge. The curve of a bed may change several times before it looks just right, so draw it several times until it does. Take a small piece of tracing paper and zip out four, five, six, or seven curves without thinking. Then look at them, lay them on top of the

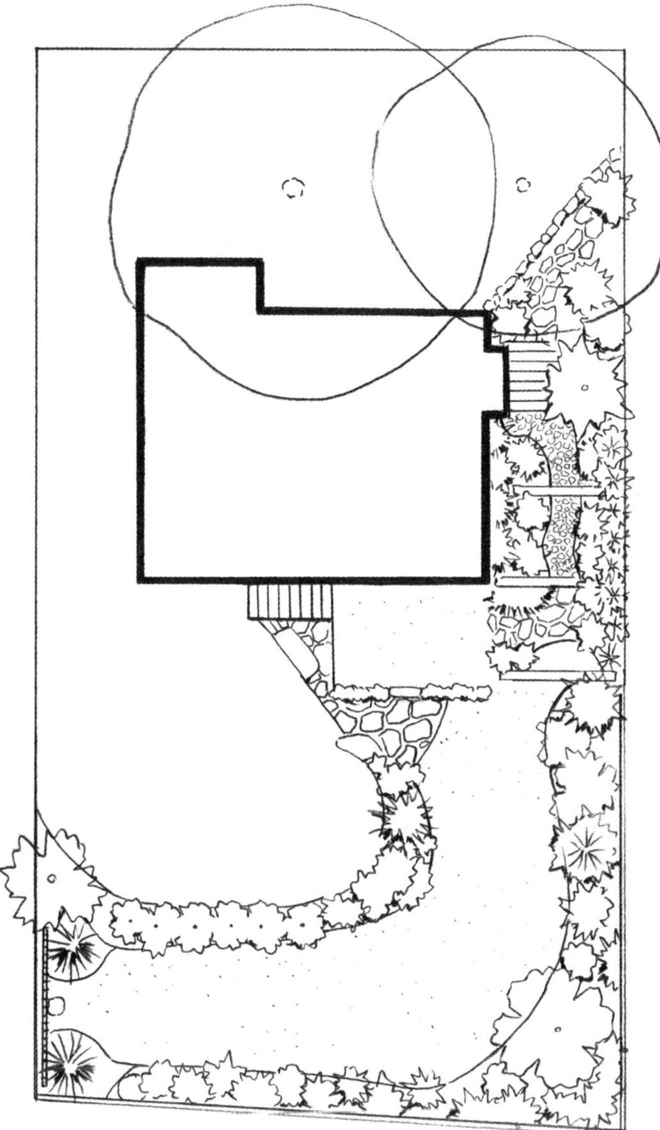

The free-flowing lines of a hand-drawn plan produce a natural look perfectly suited to garden designs, especially within the plant layer.

drawing, and choose the best one. If there isn't one good one, draw some more. Drawing, at this stage, is a verb, not a noun. It's the act of translating what we see in our heads onto the page, or the drawing begins to show us what can be done, revealing solutions to our design problems. We keep drawing until we see it, and when we see it, we will know it.

Work up a landform layer, a structures layer, and finally a plants layer. Once all the best versions of each are on the drawing table and the discarded pieces of tracing paper are scattered on the floor, there should be a plan that resembles a proper design. That's when we take all these layers of tracing paper drawings, stack them on top of the base map, and redraw it all, slowly and carefully on a single sheet of vellum.

Hand-Drawing Supplies

An art supply store will have all the drafting supplies needed for hand-drawn plans. Buy tracing paper or vellum in rolls or sheets, and look for pre-printed title block sheets and graph paper with blue lines that disappear when photocopied.

List of Drawing Tools

- Colored markers
- Drafting board or table
- Drafting tape
- Dusting brush
- Engineer's scale
- Erasers (rubber for pencil, vinyl for ink) and eraser shield
- French curves
- Pencils (graphite, colored, mechanical) and electric pencil sharpener
- Straightedges/triangles
- Technical pens (varied nib sizes: .005, .01, .03, .05, .08 mm)
- Templates (circles, squares, triangles, rectangles)
- T-square

Vellum is like tracing paper, but thicker, and easier to erase on. During the tracing paper phase, it is fine to use marker, pen, or pencil, but with the switch to vellum, switch to pencil. The design process will continue as we make refinements to the shapes and spaces so we may need to erase sometimes to make sure the circles that represent the trees are the right size or that a line meant to be straight is perfectly straight. Straightedges and shape templates come in handy to get things just right, such as making sure a 4 × 4-foot (1.2 × 1.2 m) planter is drawn 4 feet square. Everything must be as close to correct as possible, especially the structures. We can, however, fudge a bit here and there with the landform and plant layers, because an inch or two here or there won't make a big difference.

After the penciled vellum stage, professionals usually take a hand-drawn plan one more step: We ink it. To do that, lay a sheet of Mylar, a transparent, polyester film, over the completed plan and redraw it in ink. During this stage, we can change the line weights of different objects to reflect the density of the forms, such as thick, heavy lines for a stone wall, or thin, light lines for the leaves of an ornamental grass. It allows us to redraw the plants with more character, such as using scalloped circles for a tree canopy or sharp points for thorny shrubs. All of this, of course, can be done in pencil on vellum, but ink allows us to create sharp, distinct drawings that will hold up over time and photocopy well. We use Mylar for ink drawings because it allows a few minutes to erase the ink before it dries and sets permanently if we make a mistake. Ink on vellum or tracing paper can't be erased.

Color rendering transforms a simple line drawing into an artwork.

Color-Rendered Hand-Drawn Plan

Rendering brings plan drawings to life artistically. Drawings can be rendered in black and white using shading to add depth and dimensionality, but color rendering is the best choice for hand-drawn garden design plans. Colored pencils or markers work well, though some designers use watercolors. The key to color rendering is to add a subtle three-dimensionality to the plan with some shading, but mostly it is a way to represent the colors inherent in the design, such as shades of green foliage, flower colors, and hardscape materials like stone of tan or blue. Color rendering adds atmosphere and mood to a design drawing and ambitious designers color render their designs four times, one for each season, to represent how the garden will change throughout the year.

Colored pencils work well on tracing paper or vellum, offering a casual look and feel, well suited for a simple garden design. Colored markers on vellum are especially effective for building layers of color with transparent washes or saturated highlights. Watercolors work the same but take more practice and skill. Color rendering should not be gratuitous. Many a fine line drawing has been wrecked by adding color poorly, thus detracting from the design's quality and destroying the plan's main purpose: to communicate design ideas destined for the real world, not a sheet of paper.

Most of all, rendering turns a simple line drawing into an artwork. If graphics are a communication tool, then a well-rendered drawing goes a long way toward convincing others that the design is a good one. However, some design drawings rely too much on graphics to sell not-so-good ideas: Beware of the pretty drawing but poor design trap. The beauty of the drawing should set the tone for the quality of the ideas it communicates, and while a pretty picture may open the door to acceptance, the elements of the design must deliver.

Computer-Aided Drafting (CAD)

Any computer program used to make a design plan is CAD, or computer-aided drafting. Even the graphics capabilities of a word-processing or slide-presentation program can be used to draw the shapes and locations of plants and structures, as well as labels to explain the design ideas. There are, however, CAD programs specifically for garden designers that come with templates and ready-made figures of trees, shrubs, perennials, pergolas, fences, patios, boulders, and ponds, even slopes as contour lines. The designer lays out the spaces and populates them with these objects, building the design layer by layer, until it is complete.

All CAD programs work with layers, just like the layers of our three main elements of landforms, structures, and plants, but also like layers of tracing paper where elements are added and subtracted, then stacked together to create a final design. The benefit of a CAD layer is that it is easy to edit. Instead of balling up a piece of trace paper when we make a mistake, simply click and delete the offending line or object and start again. It's a time-saver when it comes to revisions and edits, especially when working with textures or the patterns of stone terraces or walls. In a hand drawing, to change the pattern of a patio surface, the whole thing must be redrawn. In CAD, we simply delete one hatch pattern and put in a new one with just a few clicks.

Computer-aided drawing programs do have some drawbacks, most notably within the plant layer. Basic programs lack the subtlety required to represent the living, dynamic nature of plants in a garden design. The structures look great, because they look architectural, and the landform can be represented with contour lines, but the plants' natural imperfections are difficult to reproduce with a digital figure where every tree looks the same. One good trick is to use the CAD program for the structure layer of the design, where it helps the most, but hand draw the plant layer. This produces a drawing with architectural stability and natural expression.

▶ New garden designers typically start out hand drawing, but the convenience of computer-aided drawing programs will enhance your designs.

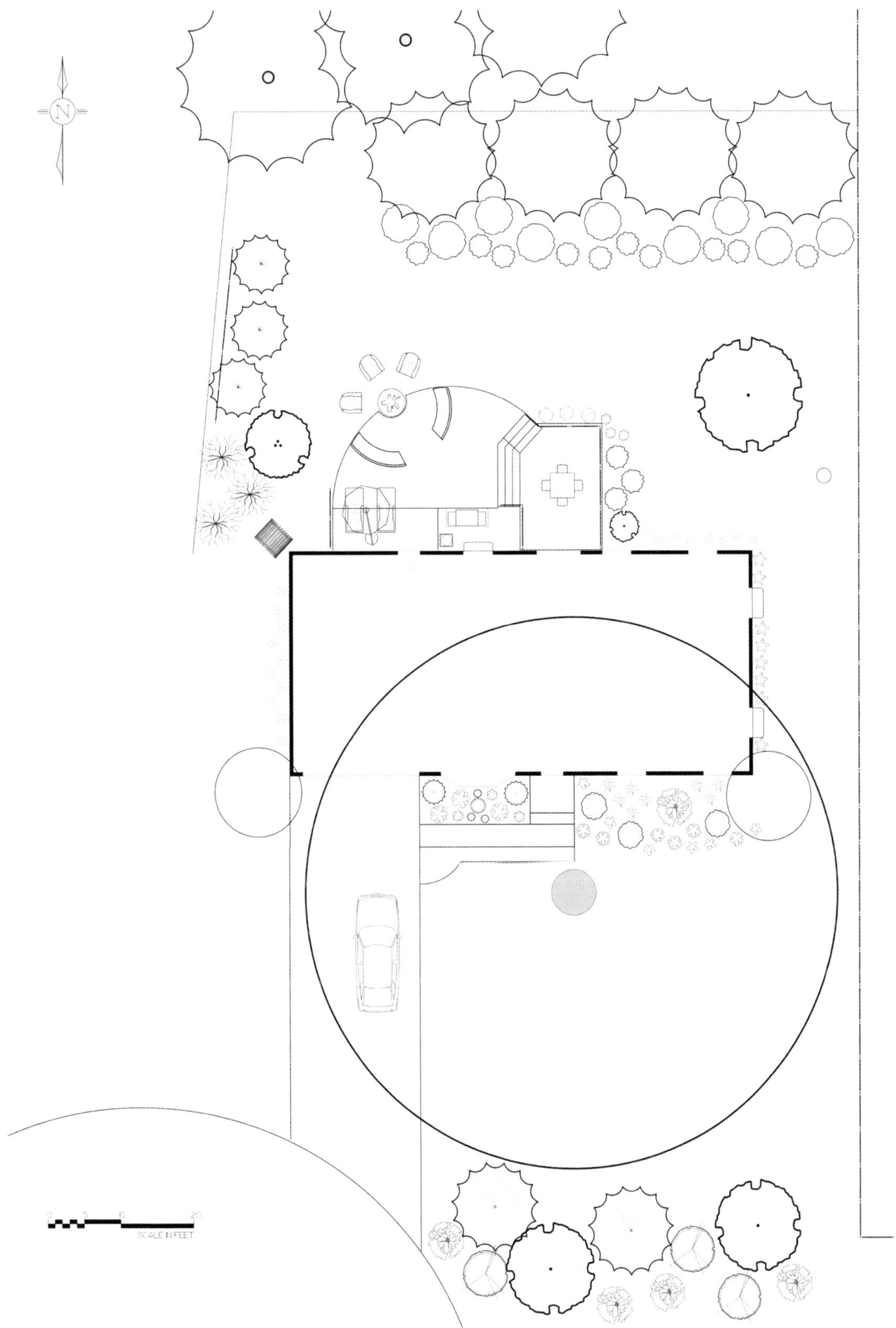
N
0 5 10 20
SCALE IN FEET

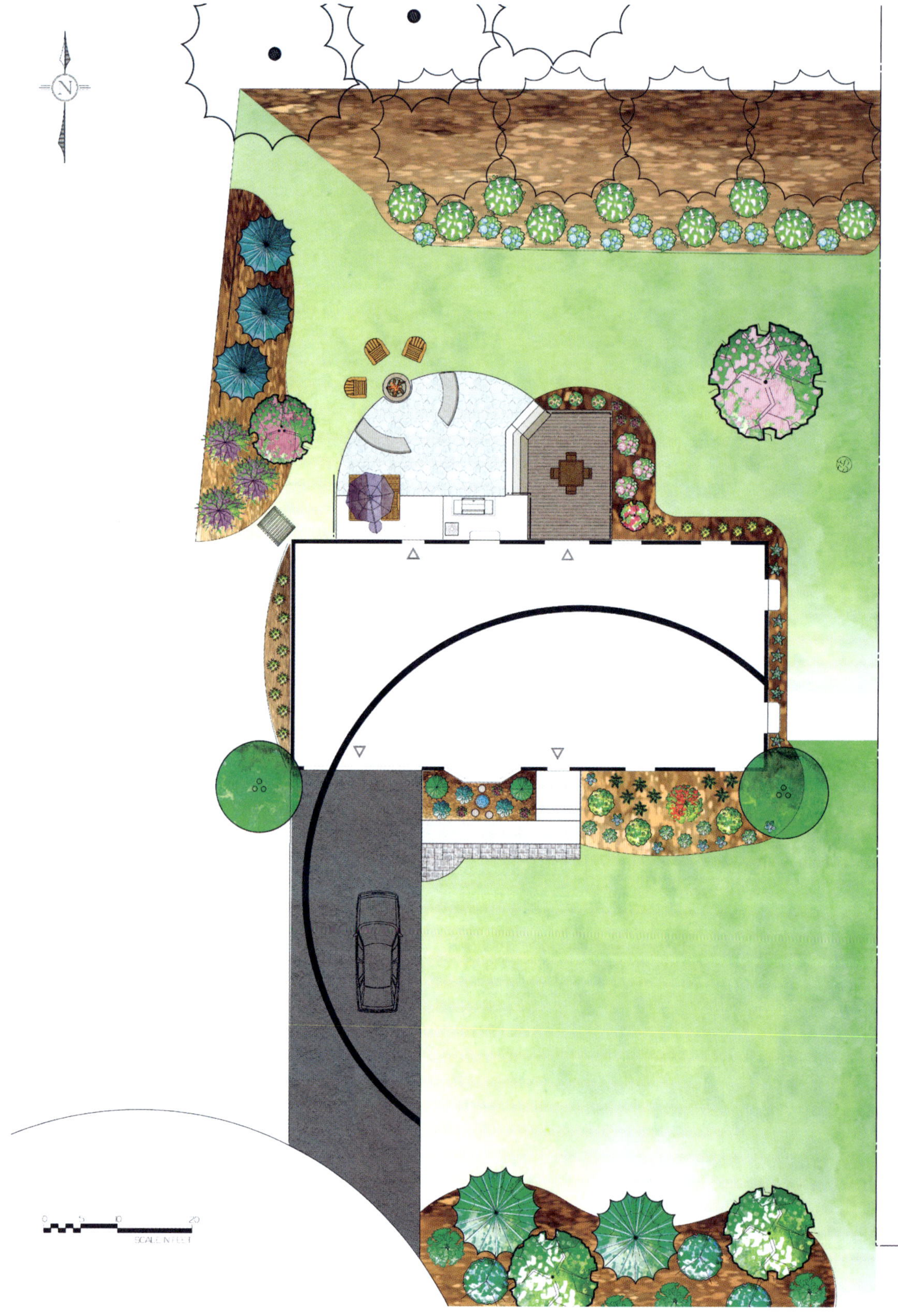
N
0 5 10 20
SCALE IN FEET

Color-Rendered CAD Plan

Color-rendered CAD programs have come a long way, but they're still not perfect. Early versions looked cartoonish, with flat planes of color applied to line drawings, maybe with a little shadowing to hint at a third dimension. But the result always looked fake, and there is nothing worse than a fake-looking garden design. Because our graphics are primarily a communication tool, we got away with it, but it was often better to skip the color and just show the line drawings. That or hand render the CAD drawing with colored pencils or markers to breathe life into the drawing.

In recent years, however, computer rendering programs have greatly improved, enabling designers to create drawings that look almost real, with photographic-quality rendering programs. It takes training and skill to become proficient to use these sophisticated rendering programs, and most garden designers find that a little colored pencil is more than enough to get the point across, though these new technologies are fun to play with.

THREE-DIMENSIONAL DRAWINGS

The primary purpose of a three-dimensional drawing is to allow the viewer to step into the design as it would appear in the real world. As designers, we learn how to make that conceptual leap without a 3D drawing, but for those who find it difficult to translate what they see on a plan drawing into the three-dimensional space it represents, we use 3D drawings. Making 3D drawings also helps designers think three dimensionally as we conceptualize the outdoor spaces in our designs and imagine how it will feel to experience the spaces we create, ultimately determining whether our designs work and fit our purposes.

◄ Color your CAD drawings to highlight significant or special design elements.

Photo Trace Sketch

There is an easy way to draw a perspective. Take a photograph of a garden section that needs a new design, or that is already included as part of a design plan, for example, the front of the house as seen from the yard or street. Make a 4 × 6-inch or 5 × 7-inch (10 × 15 cm or 12.7 × 17.8 cm) print of the photo and tape it onto a table or drawing board. Place a piece of tracing paper over the photo and tape it down as well. Then, trace the structure lines in the image, like the house walls, windows, and roof, as well as any paths or driveways on the ground to establish the perspective view. Next, add some new landform, structure, or plant elements to the garden following the pre-existing vanishing points in the photo. It may take some practice to get the new elements to look right and match the perspective, but it's a lot easier than starting from scratch.

On the same piece of tracing paper, below the perspective drawing, translate it into a two-dimensional plan, locating and drawing the new elements of whatever garden space the perspective shows. It can also be done in reverse order, converting a plan drawing into a perspective by taking a photo of the proposed space and converting the new elements of the design plan onto the 3D image. It's a great way to learn how to see what a plan drawing looks like in real life or try out a few design ideas as quick perspective sketches.

▸ Use this technique to carefully trace the structures and lines to create the true perspective, then rapidly sketch any new design elements, like plantings.

Hand-Drawn Perspective

Perspective drawings are hard. Even experienced artists have difficulty making them look just right, and because we see the world in perspective (assuming we have two working eyes), we can always tell when a perspective drawing is wrong. The benefit of a perspective drawing is that it turns a design idea into a more realistic representation. Suddenly we can see the space as it could exist in the world, not just flat on a sheet of paper, or described in words. It looks almost real, which means we can feel what it will be like to be there. For this reason, perspectives are most valuable as companion drawings supporting the design plan. Just a simple sketch can go a long way toward describing the space and communicating the intention or style of the design.

Computer-Aided 3D Drawing

Different from a perspective sketch, CAD 3D drawings are typically axonometric, which is a type of orthographic projection of the objects from a given viewpoint, but not using perspective. The result is a 3D drawing with accurate measurements. The axes don't converge so all lines remain parallel. Walls don't get lower, and trees don't shrink off in the distance because there are no vanishing points or horizon line. This is how many computer programs make 3D drawings and allow the viewer to move through the spaces, as in a movie. It's neat stuff and getting more advanced every day. But the most important thing to remember about graphics, especially high-tech CAD programs, is that they are still just a communication tool. If the design ideas or the design itself is poor, all the fancy technology in the world won't help when it comes time to make the garden.

GRAPHICS CONVENTIONS

There are specific conventions when drawing garden design plans, and we should learn them so others will understand our drawings. Think of these conventions as the basic grammar of design drawings. Once we know them, we can play around a little, but it's best to follow the rules instead of reinventing the wheel for every drawing, whether hand drawn or CAD.

When it comes to the plants, garden design plans are typically drawn as they will look in ten to fifteen years' time. In other words, we don't draw the plan as it will be planted, with large spaces between young plants, especially trees and shrubs. We draw it as it will look once those plants are established and have begun to claim their space. We also don't draw our gardens the way they will look in fifty years, since that is too far into the future. We want to represent the fact that the plants will grow and change over time; that we are aware of how they will fit the spaces they are in and ultimately knit together. Looking more than twenty years into the future is necessary to pick and place the plants correctly, but it doesn't need to be represented on the design plan. We often choose seven to ten years because it is possible to plant so it looks like that from the start, if we have no budget constraints and can start with large specimens.

Developing a hand-drawn graphics style takes practice and time, and every designer's drawings will look different, which is fine. The tips and conventions that follow are a good place to start developing a personal style with a little less trial and error. But always remember, it's not the quality of the graphics that makes a good garden design. Drawings are just tools, not the real thing.

Advanced CAD programs can convert your two-dimensional design plans into three-dimensional representations. Images and design by *Woodlilys*.

How to Draw Canopy Trees

Draw the canopy trees first because they will be the tallest trees and may block out other things below them. Make a dot, or an X, where the tree trunk stands, then draw a circle with a diameter equal to the existing tree canopy around that spot. If it's a proposed new tree, draw a circle large enough to reflect the mature yet youthful size of the tree, typically at about fifteen years of growth, even if the trees to be planted are much smaller. Use a thick-weight line for dense foliage trees and a thin line for open canopy trees.

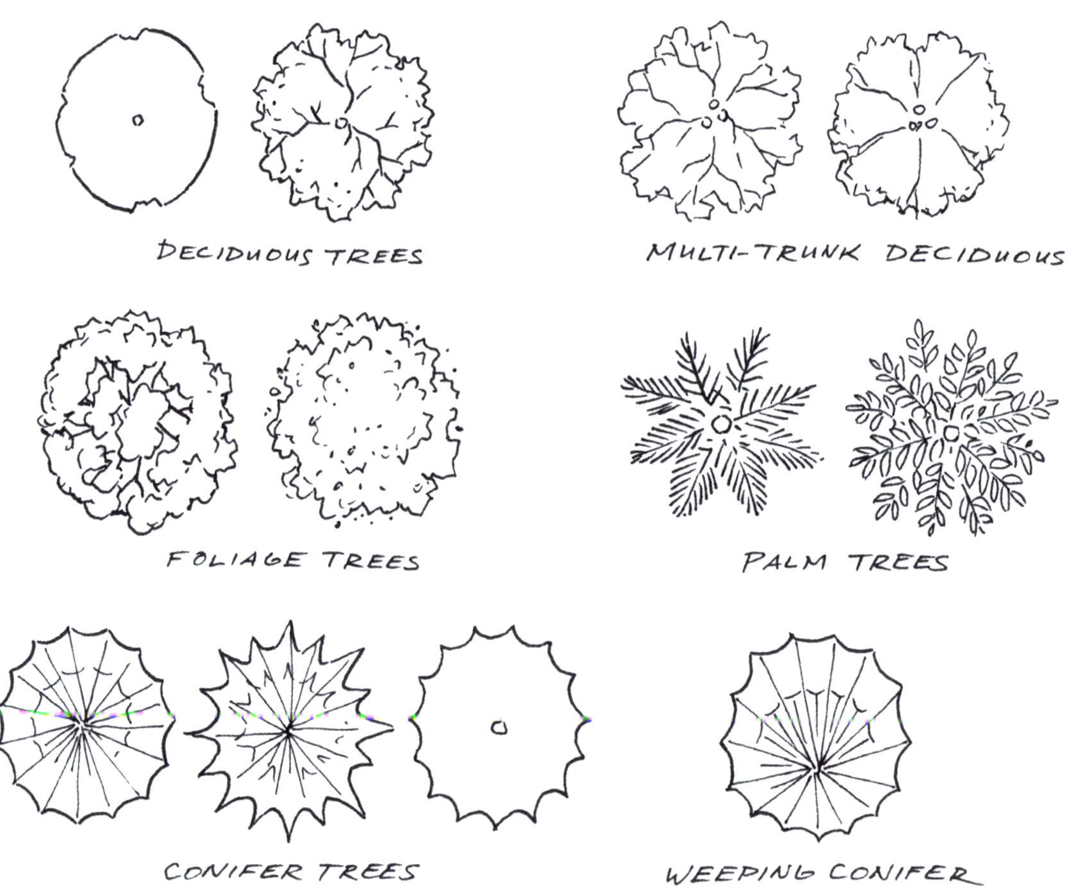

Drawing simple circles for canopy trees is fine, but adding some texture and variety makes your drawings come to life.

Understory Shrubs

Draw understory shrubs the same as canopy trees, with a dot, or X, in the middle and then a circle around it of the proper diameter to show the size of the plant. Use three or five dots to indicate a multistem shrub. (The same can be done for multitrunk canopy trees, like birch.) Overlap the circles if the plants will be placed close enough to grow into each other over time. Draw the understory within the circle of the canopy tree if it is planted there. Use a medium-weight line.

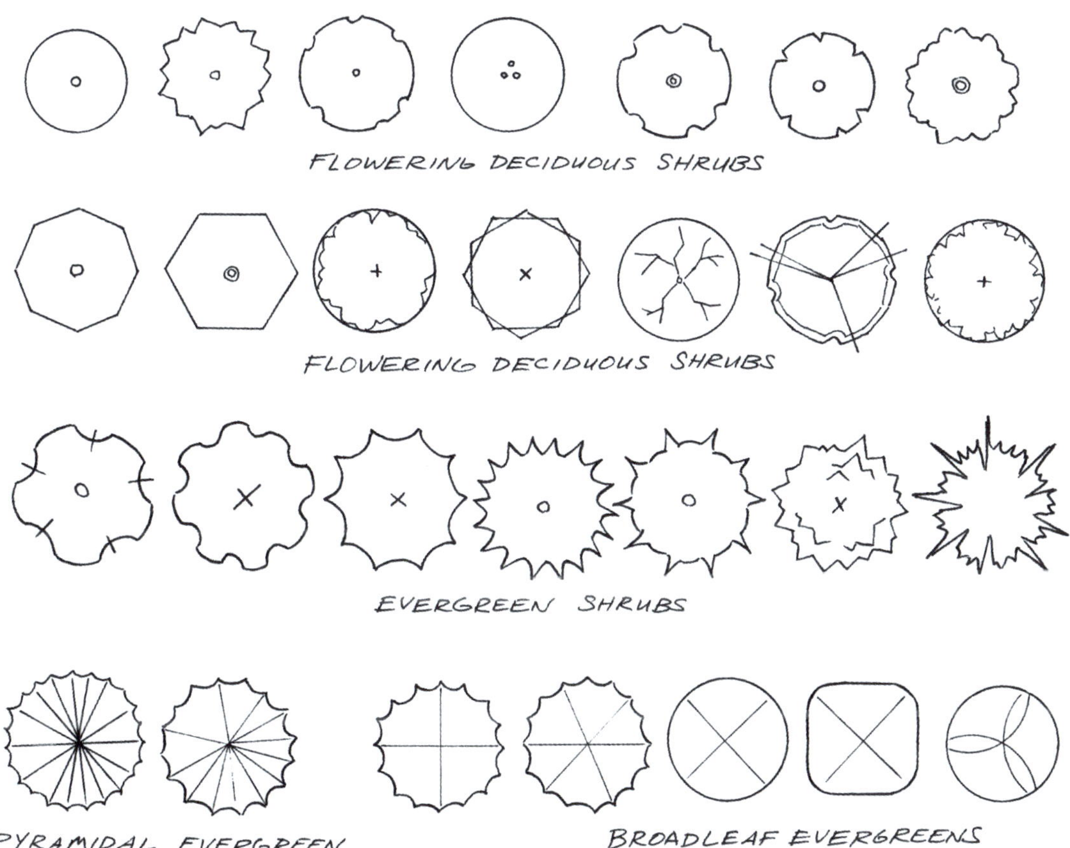

Draw understory shrubs as simple or textured circles with varying levels of detail to suggest each specimen's uniqueness.

Ground-Layer Plants

Depending on the drawing's scale and the size of the drawing sheet, ground-layer plants are drawn either as large groupings or individual plants (individual plants can be drawn as small circles). Groupings can be a collection of small circles but look better as a large blob with multiple dots, or Xs, to indicate the location of each plant. For larger-scale drawings at 1 inch = 15 to 20 feet (2.5 cm = 4.5 to 6 m), simply draw a blob or amorphous figure the size of the planting to be labeled with specific plants, combinations of plants, or a plant category. Use a light-weight line.

▼ Draw ground-layer plants as simple or textured circles with varying levels of detail to suggest the plant's foliage or flowers.

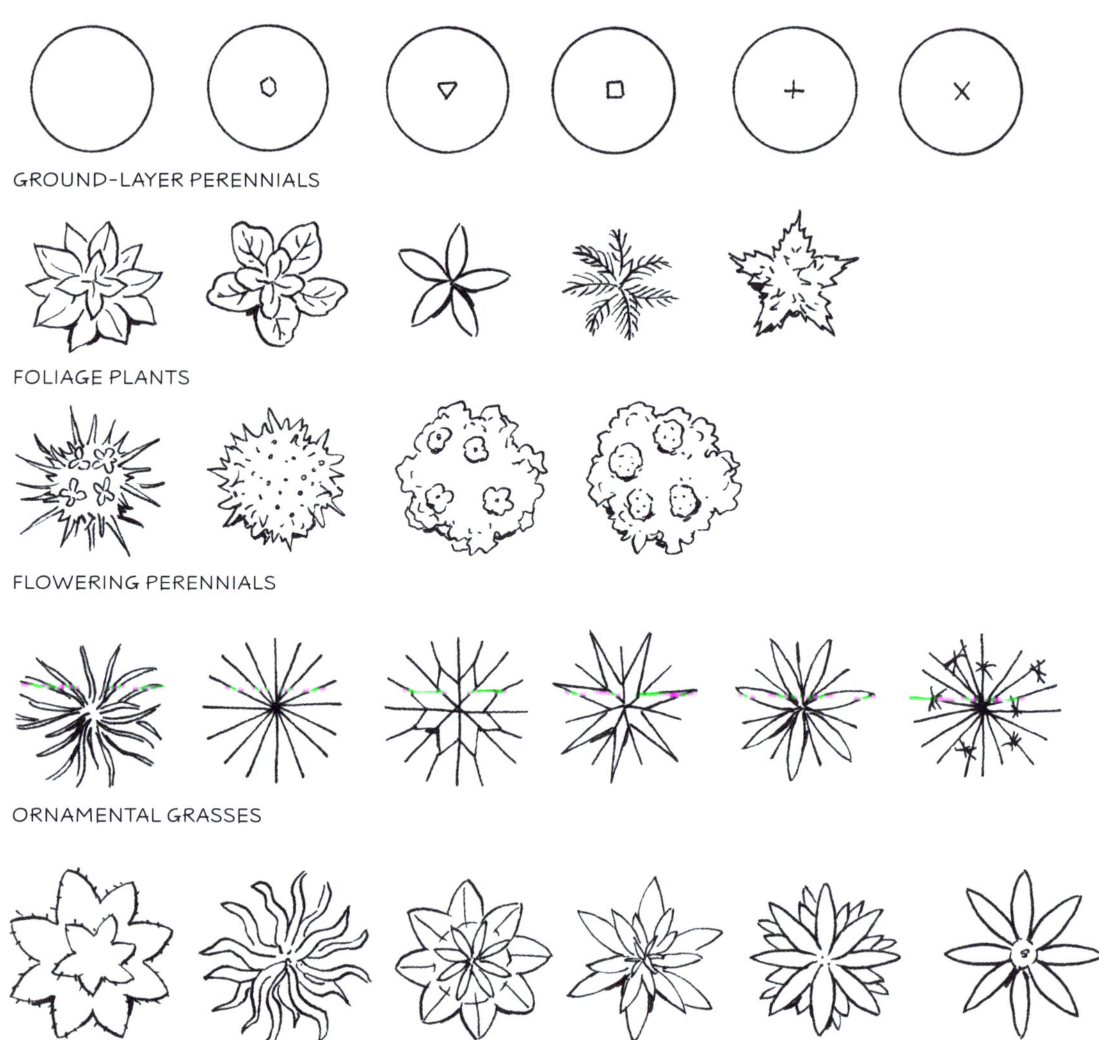

Plant Groupings

Groups of plants meant to knit together as they grow should be drawn as melded, overlapping circles, or as a single amorphous figure, with jagged margins for spiky plants or scalloped margins for rounded plants. It's good to put a dot, or X, to mark the spot for individual plants, or the quantity can be indicated in the label, for example: "Rugosa rose, 9."

Lawn

Don't draw the lawn, simply label empty spaces on the drawing that will be lawn as "lawn." It's easy to extrapolate from there what is lawn, planting bed, or a structure. Use this convention to indicate the location of other extensive planted areas, such as a meadow or field.

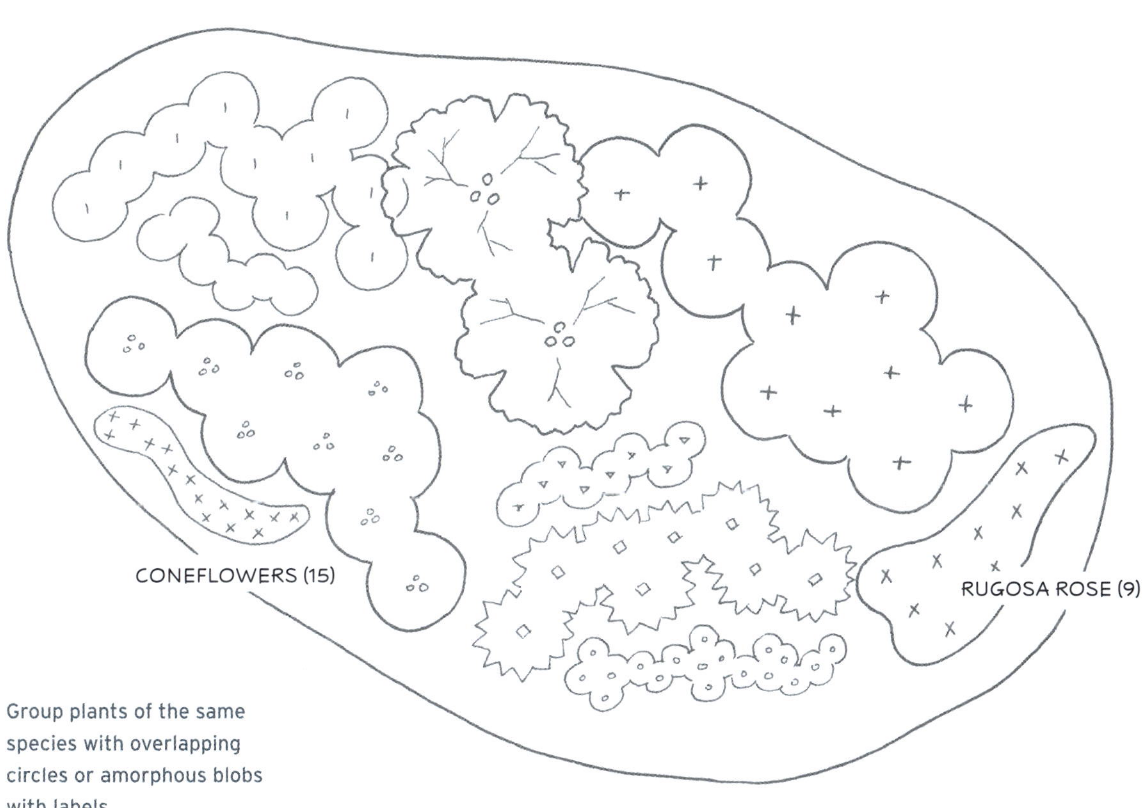

Group plants of the same species with overlapping circles or amorphous blobs with labels.

Line Weights

Line weight, or the thickness or darkness of the lines used to draw objects in a plan, is an excellent way to convey the density, texture, or mass of an object. It takes time and practice to make things look right, and getting it wrong can make a drawing look strange. Using varied line weights along with different margin shapes for plants with different-textured leaves helps convey what the plantings will look like in the real world. Study the drawings of other designers for useful graphics techniques and adopt what you like.

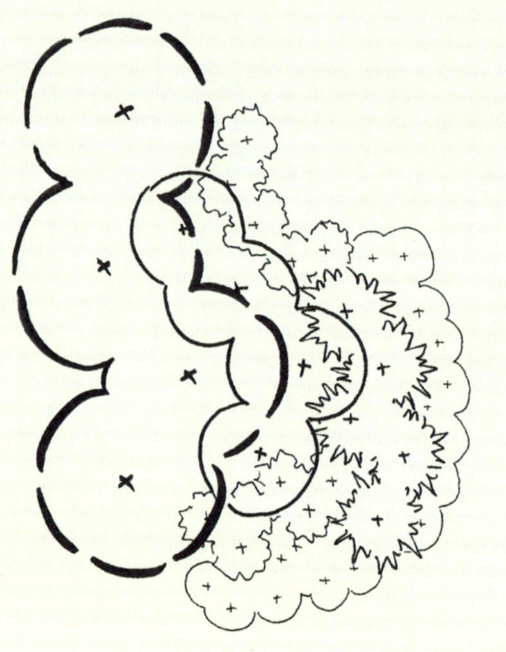

Different line weights help indicate the significance and character of different plants on the plan.

Bed Lines

Draw the bed lines, between planting beds, and lawn areas or hardscape after all the plants are in place. Planting plans look better and more natural if some plants creep over the bed lines, making the edges of the beds start and stop as they come in and out of view. Use a medium-weight line.

Structures

Draw all structures, especially ground-level hardscaping, after the plant layer is in place. This way, any plantings that obscure the structure as viewed from above will be there and the lines of the structure won't cut through the plants. This adds dimensionality to the 2D drawing making it look more realistic. Use heavy- to light-weight lines depending on the density of the structure material, for example light-weight for a slim trellis, medium for a fence, heavy for stonework.

Stonework

Use a heavy-weight line to draw the edges of any stone, such as a wall or patio. This makes it look heavy and solid as compared to plants or lighter objects in the drawings. If the drawing's scale allows, draw the stonework pattern with a medium- or light-weight line. Use circles for field stone, squares, etc., for pavers. Sometimes it's better to just label stonework with a pattern type because drawing the detail can muck up a drawing making it more difficult to read.

Fences

Fences are easy, but it is important to draw them so their location is clear. Simply draw a thin line and place a small X, or dash, every 8 feet (2.4 m) or so to mark the location of a fence post. A dashed line with Xs can be fine, but because fences are commonly located near the property line, which is typically drawn as a dashed line, it's better to draw fences with a thin solid line with the Xs or dashes. Label the fence with its height, material, and type, for example: "6-foot (1.8 m) cedar privacy fence," or "4-foot (1.2 m) chain-link pool fence."

Property or Other Restricted Space Lines

Property lines located within the scope of the design are typically indicated with a heavy, dashed line and labeled "property line." Lighter-weight or dotted lines are sometimes used to indicate the boundaries of special areas, like wetlands or utility easements.

Utilities

These are structures so use a medium-weight line so they stand out on the drawing. There are figure templates for objects like air-conditioner units, gas meters, drains, etc., but simple shapes with labels suffice.

Design Sheet Layout

Title Block

Usually located at the bottom or the right margin of the drawing sheet, a title block consists of several practical elements that help describe the purpose of the drawing:

PROJECT NAME What the design represents, for example: "Backyard Garden" or "Smith Residence"

ADDRESS City and state for sure; sometimes street number and name

SCALE Written scale, such as 1 inch = 10 feet (2.5 cm = 3 m)

DATE Month and year of the design

DRAWN BY Name of designer or firm

DRAWING # Used when there is more than one drawing, for example, "one of two"

REVISION # To indicate if the design is a revision of an earlier design, such as "revision #2"

Orientation

This is a "north" arrow. It is crucial to indicate north on a garden design drawing not just to understand where it may be located on a map but, more important, to know which direction is south because south plays a huge role in understanding the sun exposure on a site and the appropriateness of the plants on the design plan.

Graphic Scale

A graphic scale is a line drawn and labeled with measurements according to the set scales of the drawing, for example at a scale of 1 inch = 10 feet (2.5 cm = 3 m), we draw a 3-inch (7.5 cm) line, labeled "0" at the end, then 5 feet (1.5 m) at the ½-inch (1 cm) mark, 10 feet (3 m) at the 1-inch (2.5 cm) mark, and 30 feet (9 m) at the 3-inch (7.5 cm) mark. A graphic scale allows us to photocopy the plan onto various-size sheets that may change the actual drawing scale. The graphic scale will be enlarged or reduced to show the true scale.

Labels

There are different ways to label the objects in a drawing. Leaders are lines with an arrow that point to the object and refer to the label, such as a plant or structure. Too many leader labels can make a complicated planting plan messy and difficult to read. In that case, use them for important structures only, such as fences and walls, and label the plants with a coded table, or plant list.

Plant Lists

A plant list box should be placed directly on the design sheet so the plan can be read and understood on a single page (see pages 83 and 85). A good way to organize the plants is to start with trees and shrubs, then herbaceous plants. Include the quantity of plant, plant name—common, botanical Latin, or both—and code with letters that refer to the plant name, or simple numbers and/or letters. It's not necessary to include plant sizes yet because there may not be a way to guarantee what size specimens are available (more on plant sizes in chapter 6).

Thumbnails

These are small images that depict a scene, object, or plant included in the design. A thumbnail is a great place to add a traced perspective drawing, as described previously, an image of a desired furnishing, or the foliage and flowers of a specific plant. Use thumbnails strategically and sparingly for more impact.

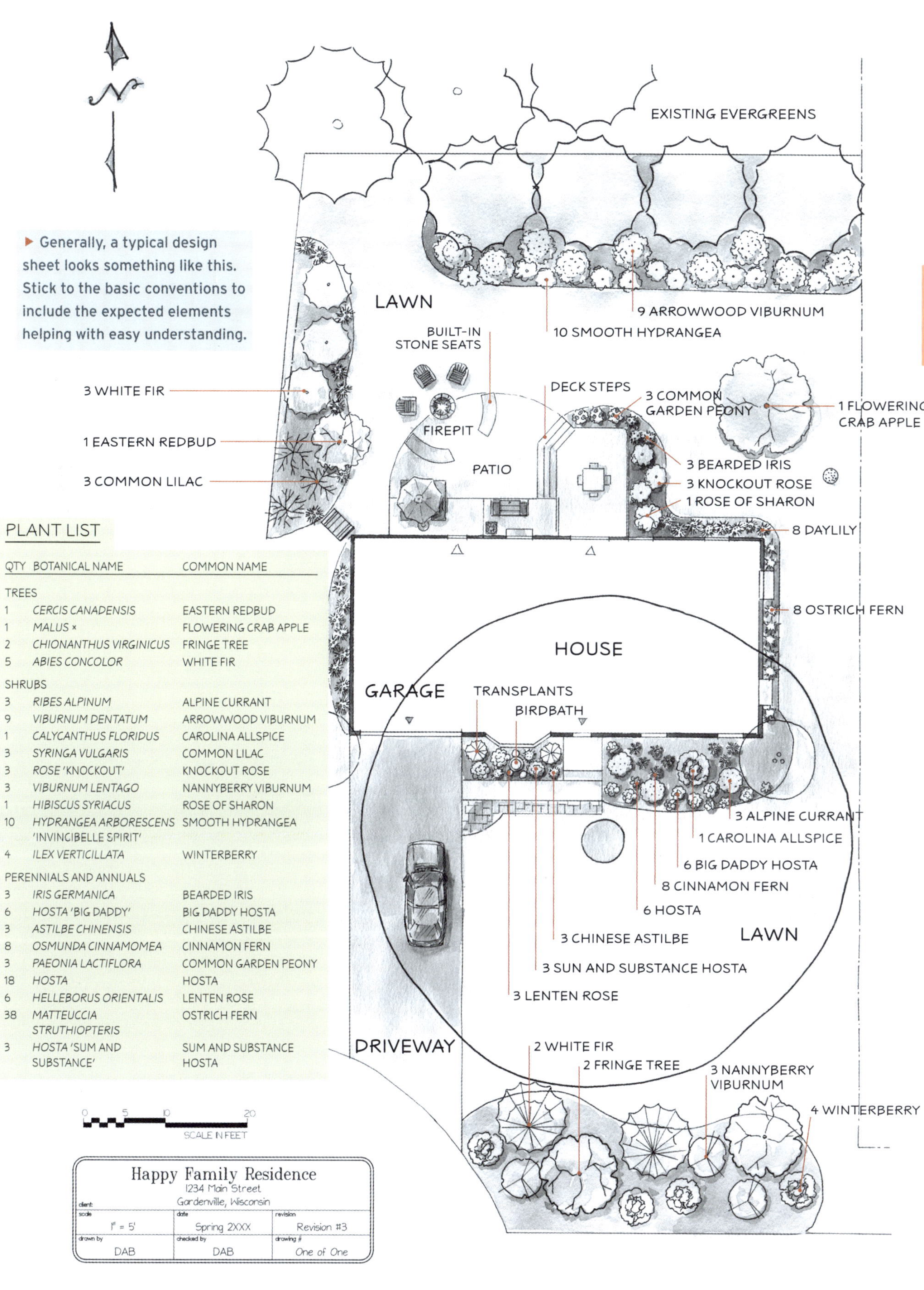

PLANT LIST

QTY	BOTANICAL NAME	COMMON NAME
TREES		
1	*CERCIS CANADENSIS*	EASTERN REDBUD
1	*MALUS ×*	FLOWERING CRAB APPLE
2	*CHIONANTHUS VIRGINICUS*	FRINGE TREE
5	*ABIES CONCOLOR*	WHITE FIR
SHRUBS		
3	*RIBES ALPINUM*	ALPINE CURRANT
9	*VIBURNUM DENTATUM*	ARROWWOOD VIBURNUM
1	*CALYCANTHUS FLORIDUS*	CAROLINA ALLSPICE
3	*SYRINGA VULGARIS*	COMMON LILAC
3	*ROSE 'KNOCKOUT'*	KNOCKOUT ROSE
3	*VIBURNUM LENTAGO*	NANNYBERRY VIBURNUM
1	*HIBISCUS SYRIACUS*	ROSE OF SHARON
10	*HYDRANGEA ARBORESCENS 'INVINCIBELLE SPIRIT'*	SMOOTH HYDRANGEA
4	*ILEX VERTICILLATA*	WINTERBERRY
PERENNIALS AND ANNUALS		
3	*IRIS GERMANICA*	BEARDED IRIS
6	*HOSTA 'BIG DADDY'*	BIG DADDY HOSTA
3	*ASTILBE CHINENSIS*	CHINESE ASTILBE
8	*OSMUNDA CINNAMOMEA*	CINNAMON FERN
3	*PAEONIA LACTIFLORA*	COMMON GARDEN PEONY
18	*HOSTA*	HOSTA
6	*HELLEBORUS ORIENTALIS*	LENTEN ROSE
38	*MATTEUCCIA STRUTHIOPTERIS*	OSTRICH FERN
3	*HOSTA 'SUM AND SUBSTANCE'*	SUM AND SUBSTANCE HOSTA

▸ Generally, a typical design sheet looks something like this. Stick to the basic conventions to include the expected elements helping with easy understanding.

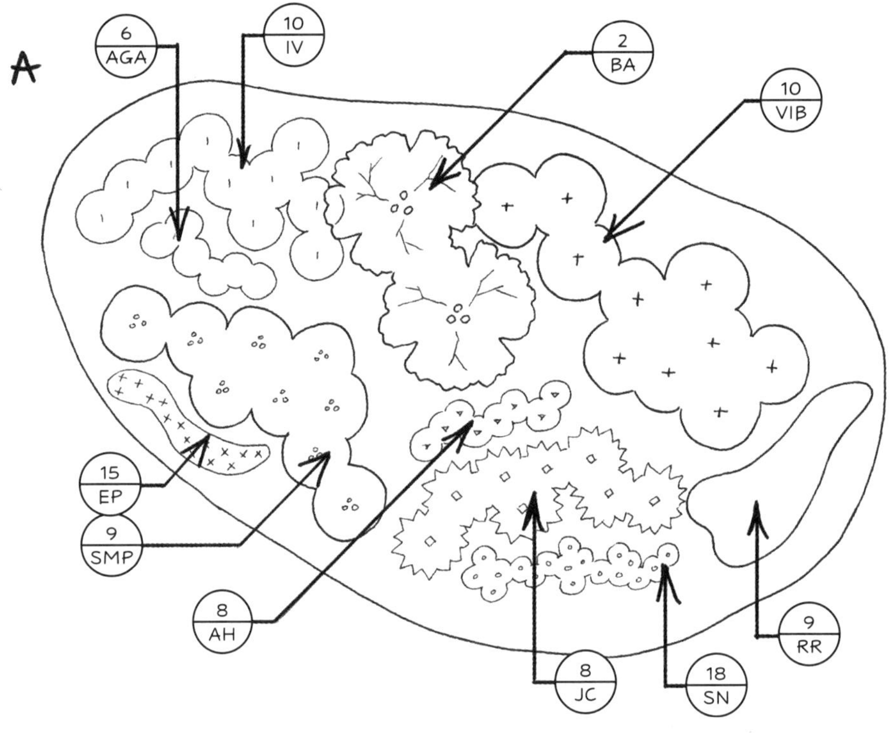

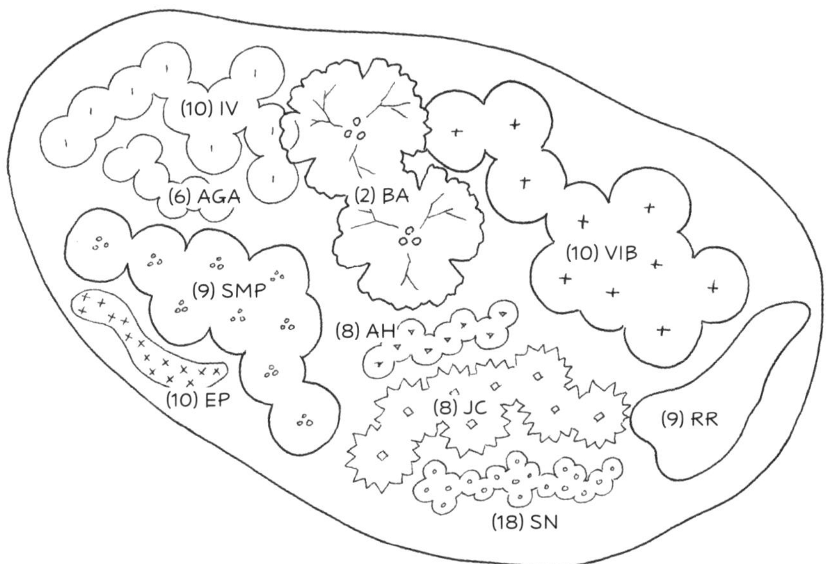

How you label plants is a matter of preference, but always err on the side of keeping the drawing clean and legible.

PLANT NAMES AND QUANTITY WITH LEADERS

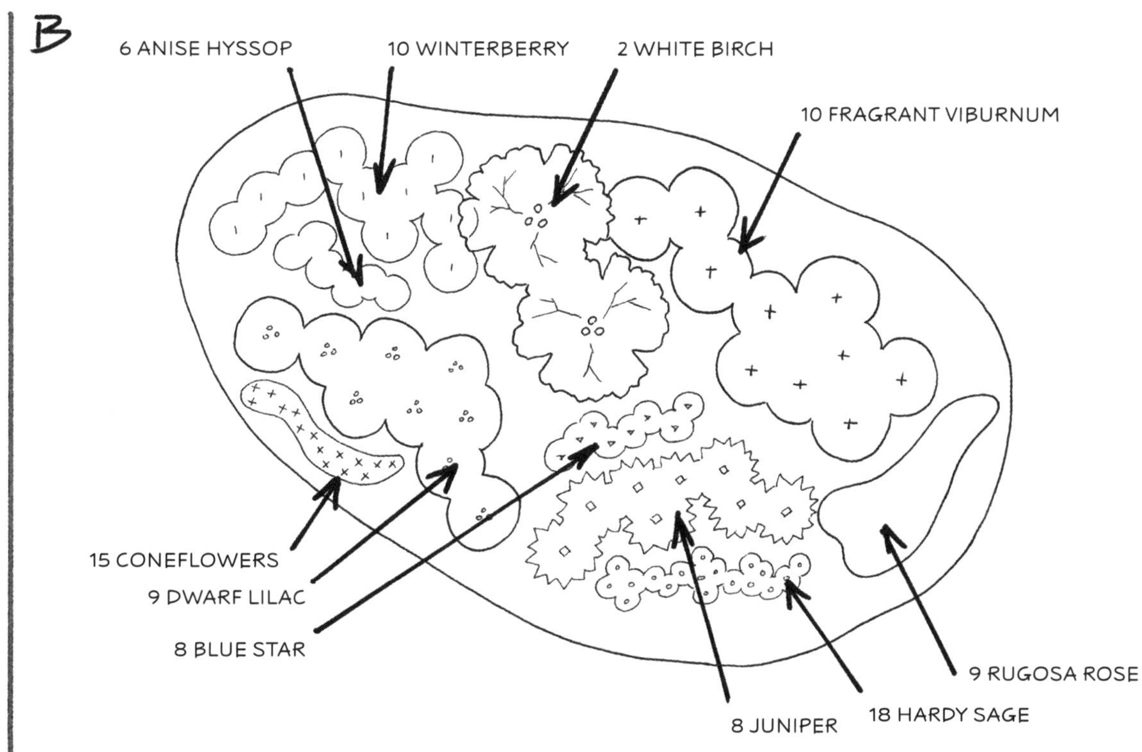

D PLANT CODES AND QUANTITY WITH LEADERS AND PLANT LIST

CODE	QTY	BOTANICAL NAME	COMMON NAME
TREES			
BA	2	*BETULA ALBA*	SILVER BIRCH
SHRUBS			
IV	10	*ILEX VERTICILLATA*	WINTERBERRY
JC	8	*JUNIPERUS CHINENSIS*	CHINESE JUNIPER
RR	9	*ROSA RUGOSA*	RUGOSA ROSE
SMP	9	*SYRINGA MEYERI 'PALIBIN'*	PALIBIN DWARF LILAC
VIB	10	*VIBURNUM × JUDDII*	JUDD VIBURNUM
PERENNIALS			
AGA	6	*AGASTACHE FOENICULUM*	ANISE HYSSOP
AH	8	*AMSONIA HUBRICHTII*	THREADLEAF BLUE STAR
EP	15	*ECHINACEA PURPUREA*	PURPLE CONEFLOWER
SN	18	*SALVIA NEMOROSA*	MEADOW SAGE

A

6 AGA
10 IV
2 BA
10 VIB
15 EP
9 SMP
8 AH
8 JC
18 SN
9 RR

Model Making

Landscape design students are asked to make 3D models of their designs because it is a great way for them to learn to think spatially and understand how the spaces drawn on a plan translate into the real world. Models are good communication tools to help others understand design, but they are also excellent working tools for a designer. It's not uncommon for paths that look the right width on a drawing to suddenly appear too narrow and constricted in a model. Or the quantity of plants in a garden bed on a plan turn out to be too few or too many to fill the space in 3D.

Modeling is also a great way to understand and reshape the landform of a site (more about this in chapter 4). A fun project is to build a 3D model of a contour map using stacked layers of foam core board, with each layer representing a specific elevation. Suddenly the slopes come to life making the site more understandable than it is as a two-dimensional drawing. It's an excellent way to see how the land rolls and slopes and ultimately understand how surface water moves through the site. Landform models like this are often sculpted with clay or carved from Styrofoam.

Models help us *see* what the designed garden spaces and elements of a plan drawing will look like in the real world, though set to a smaller scale. (Design by Zoali Alavarez and Green Day Co.)

CHAPTER 4

LANDFORMING: Evaluating and Improving the Ground

Lesson on how to assess and work with different soils based on *soil texture*, *water-holding ability*, and *fertility* including a discussion on how to control *surface drainage* as well as include *natural landforms* in a design.

During our site survey, we made sure to identify all the remarkable landform features on the property, including any significant slopes, geological formations, and natural water features. The analysis of these landform features consisted of recognizing how they would affect our use of the garden, such as the steepness of slopes, interference of exposed bedrock, or presence of standing water. It was a big-picture assessment of the landform layer. Now we are ready to take things to the next level and think about how we will design within the restrictions of the landforms we've inherited or reshape the land to fit our needs and desires, keeping in mind this could call for creating landforms where there are none. This marks a critical moment when the designer's approach to the landform layer, pre-existing or proposed, is established. It's when we decide to work with the land as it is or begin to shape it.

Equally important decisions will be made within the structures and plants layers, but because the land is, by definition, the foundation upon which gardens are made, how we treat the landforms, as obstacles or opportunities, is fundamental to how we design a garden. This is when we establish our personal land ethic, and if we want to stay true to ideals like conservation, preservation, or regeneration, what better place to practice what we preach than in our personal gardens. I've approached this fork in the road hundreds of times working on client gardens. Early in my career it was easy. We shaped the land and the garden to what we wanted. The land was there for us to use–and sadly often abuse. That was the prevailing ethic at the time, and not so long ago.

Over the years ideals have changed. Garden designers see their role in a different way, as stewards of the land, working hand in hand with all three elements of design, especially the land and the plants. This chapter presents both approaches as well as suggests a compromise between the two because I believe there is a way to achieve what we want and do no harm.

Assessing the Soil

An in-depth soil assessment begins with the design process after the scope of design has been determined. While some basic evaluations are made during the site survey, now is the time to get down and dirty. To touch and smell the soil and ask the questions only a soil test can answer.

◀ *Cells of Life* at Jupiter Artland in Kirknewton, Scotland, designed by Charles Jencks, is one of many inspirational examples of sculpting landform into land art.

The type of soil assessment required depends on the extent of the site under consideration for design, as well as the potential goals of that design, something we don't know until we've worked through our scope of design based on the needs and desires we intend to solve and fulfill. What follows is a sequence of assessments to perform whether we have chosen to work with what's there, change or improve what's there, or potentially heal damage inflicted over the years.

TOUCHING THE SOIL

A soil test can tell us a lot about the ground we're working on. The first criterion is soil texture. Texture refers to the size of the mineral particles that make up the topsoil. These particles range in size, largest to smallest, from sand to silt to clay. Most garden soils have a balanced combination of the three, but it could be the case that there is an excess of sand, even gravel, making the soil fast-draining and infertile, or too much clay, making the soil fertile but difficult to work. Excessively silty soil tends to occur near ponds and streams, making them easy to identify and a category in themselves. It's excess sand and clay that may pose problems so we must find out if the soil texture falls within one of those extremes.

Getting a feel for soil texture is as easy as touching the soil. Take a long-handled garden spade and dig 8 to 12 inches (20.3 to 30.5 cm) deep into the ground. Turn the soil over and break up any large clumps. Then, reach down and grab a handful. Does it feel sticky, soggy, or grainy? Give it a sniff. Does it smell earthy and fresh, like something delicately rotting. (Good, it's fertile.) Or, minerally, like busted-up stone. (Okay, but not too fertile.) Maybe, it's wet and stinky. (Trouble!) Maybe the ground is so hard and compacted it's too hard to dig (big trouble!). Dig, in lots of different spots. Up on a hill. Down in a ditch. Near the foundation of the house and touch each shovelful of soil with your bare hands. Squeeze and sniff it. Get a feel for it. We're checking for extremes, hoping to unearth some decent dirt. Most likely it will be a bit compacted and less than perfectly fertile, but hopefully it won't be anything too problematic. Next step: a lab test.

What a Soil Test Can Tell Us

Gather a soil sample from each spot. If the soil seems the same throughout, mix the samples and send them to a lab to be tested. Most state university systems offer soil testing. Follow their submission instructions and pay the fee and the results will come back with useful information. Top of the list will be a categorization of soil texture. If the word "loam" is in the description, it's okay. Take note if it's a sandy loam or a clay loam to understand where on the texture spectrum it falls. Sandy soil drains fast and is relatively infertile. Clay soil is fertile but often compacted and has trouble absorbing water and allowing roots to spread easily underground.

The test will also indicate general soil fertility including the presence of key nutrients all plants need, such as phosphorus, potassium, sulfur, and iron. More important, it will measure the organic matter content of the soil and its corresponding potential for fertility. Soil fertility is one of those dynamic aspects of gardening, changing over time, getting better or worse depending on how we treat the land.

Another measurement a soil test includes is pH, the acidity of the soil, which influences how plants grow. Like texture, pH is important if it is extreme one way or the other. There is a pH sweet spot, between 5 and 7, where almost anything will grow, so soil pH is something we want to know. If it is extreme, that could affect the design because it will limit our choices for the plant layer or motivate significant amendments to the soil when it comes time to build planting beds. If pH is not extreme one way or the other, it shouldn't have a huge impact on what we choose to plant, though designs can cater to what grows best in soils based on their pH.

Specialized soil tests can tell us if there are any contaminants in the ground, such as heavy metals or other pollutants. This type of test is especially useful for sites in urban centers, though even land in the countryside can be contaminated from long-term commercial applications of chemical pesticides, herbicides, and synthetic fertilizers. A good soil test will also provide some data on the water-holding ability of the soil. This is an assessment of the structure of the soil, something we call "tilth." Soil with good tilth holds water without becoming soggy, allows air to penetrate, and is loose and easy to work. This is different from a soil percolation test, which measures how quickly the soil drains.

Indicator Plants

The presence of existing vegetation can provide clues to the condition of the soil on a site. Certain weed species can signal texture, fertility, or drainage issues, while populations of invasive and native species can tell us which plants will grow well in a particular plot of ground. Together, they may indicate a need to improve the soil, serve as a guide for selecting plants that will thrive on that soil, or a combination.

Weeds

Weeds are excellent indicator plants because they colonize sites with soil conditions best suited to their needs. However, it's important to understand that a few individual weeds don't mean much whereas large swaths dominated by a single species, or a group of similar species, can tell us a lot. For example, field horsetail is an indicator of sandy, droughty conditions, red sorrel is a sign of wet, acidic soil, and lamb's quarters are found in rich soil most likely overfertilized. In addition, perennial weeds that propagate from roots are more reliable indicators than annual weeds that start from seed each season.

Here's a list of common weeds and the soil conditions they may indicate:

- **Bindweed:** Hardpan or crusty surface with light sand texture
- **Canada thistle:** Heavy clay soil
- **Chickweed:** Cultivated soil with high fertility or humus content
- **Chicory:** Heavy clay texture, cultivated with high fertility or humus content
- **Cinquefoil:** Dry soil, often with thin topsoil, acidic or low lime
- **Creeping buttercup:** Wet, poorly drained clay soil
- **Dandelion:** Heavy clay soil, cultivated, acid or low lime, especially on lawns

- **Docks:** Waterlogged or poorly drained soil, acidic or low lime
- **Knapweed:** Acidic or low-lime soil with high potassium
- **Knotweed:** Cultivated soil, acidic or low lime
- **Lamb's quarters:** Cultivated soil with high fertility or humus content
- **Mosses:** Waterlogged or poorly drained soil, acidic or low lime
- **Mullein:** Neglected, uncultivated soil, acidic or low lime, low fertility
- **Mustards:** Hardpan or crusty surface, dry, often with thin topsoil
- **Nettles:** Cultivated soil, acidic or low lime
- **Pigweed:** Cultivated soil, with high fertility or humus content
- **Plantains:** Heavy clay soil, waterlogged or poorly drained, cultivated, acidic or low lime, especially on lawns
- **Quack grass:** Hardpan or crusty surface
- **Shepherd's purse:** Saline soil
- **Sorrel:** Waterlogged or poorly drained soil, acidic or low lime
- **Sow thistle:** Wet soil, neutral or alkaline pH
- **Stinkweed:** Hardpan or crusty surface, high lime

Invasives and Natives

Plants other than weeds are also good indicators of the type of soil that lies beneath. Invasive plants are excellent indicators because they tend to colonize quickly where conditions suit them, making it easy to identify sections of land with the soil type they prefer. On the other hand, a healthy population of native plants is a good indicator of the long-term ecological health of a site and the soil below. I discuss these types of indicator species in more detail in chapter 6.

Surface Drainage

Rainwater doesn't just seep into the soil; it also flows across the surface before finally soaking into the ground. Where it moves and how fast it moves are determined by the extent and extremity of the landform slopes. This is why we pay special attention to identifying existing slopes during the site survey and analysis. Water may move rapidly, or it may sit and pool. Either way, we need to know what it does because how it acts will affect our design plans, and may, if we approach it intelligently, provide opportunities for distinctive design solutions.

Dealing with drainage is often part of the scope of design if problem areas are identified. Water running into a structure, across a walkway or path, or collecting in ill-suited spots are not uncommon on poorly designed or neglected properties. Sometimes water from a neighboring property exacerbates the amount of rainwater a garden must absorb. It's common to find suburban neighborhoods situated on a hillside where the runoff starts at the top and is directed downslope to the adjacent property over and again until the unlucky homeowner at the bottom of the hill receives a deluge of water with no place to go. Hopefully there is a city storm

Building Beds vs. Improving Soil

Building beds is the hallmark of traditional garden design because it allows the garden designer to establish what they want from the start and achieve a garden at peak form in fewer seasons. It requires extensive upfront costs by bringing in large quantities of fresh topsoil mixed with compost to improve the existing soil. These instant improvements mean the designer can work with a plant palette that includes species from different ecosystems from across the globe.

Improving soil is a long-term prospect but with lower initial inputs. A hallmark of sustainable garden design, this approach focuses on incremental improvements to the soil over many years to bring it back to good health and optimal tilth. It starts with a topdressing of compost as part of a comprehensive garden maintenance regimen to promote a living soil. Soil improvement is built into the design plan, allowing time to repair damaged or unhealthy soil. As the soil improves, new species are introduced to the plant layer, and thus the garden design develops over time.

sewer or drainage ditch nearby, but it may not be engineered to accept the volume of flow that has been passed along.

This can lead to intermittent flooding of the gardens throughout the neighborhood, resulting in damage to structures and plantings. It can also adversely affect the health of the soil, which if poorly drained can become overly saturated, unable to support plant life, or cause structures to deteriorate before their expected life span. Good garden designs mitigate issues like these in one of three ways: move the water off the property; capture the water and store it on the property; or develop a design that works with how water flows naturally throughout the site.

MOVE THE WATER

A common practice for garden designers is to find ways to move excess water out of the garden and off the property. Poorly draining soils are usually the culprit. Unhealthy soils are often compacted as their structure has been destroyed over the years from excess applications of harsh chemical herbicides, pesticides, and synthetic fertilizers. Healthy, humus-rich soils tend to hold water more effectively, like a sponge, allowing excess water from storms or outside runoff to infiltrate the ground at a faster rate than it is delivered. However, heavy clay soil can also be a culprit, as clay soils are tightly formed and tend to repel water, forcing a lot of it to run across the surface.

If it has been decided to move the surface water away from structures, low spots, or places it limits our ability to plant, there are a few ways to accomplish this within the purview of a garden design plan. A significant amount of runoff water comes from the rooftops of the house, garage, or other outbuildings. This water is most often collected in gutters and directed to downspouts, which discharge at the base of the building. From there, the water will run off across the surface of the soil or hardscaped area and disperse throughout the property. However, downspouts can be tied into a system of buried pipes running underground that deliver the water where it can be discharged safely away from plantings and structures. On large properties, this could be an open field or woodlot located downslope from the house where water will drain away or seep into the soil naturally. On smaller properties, like city lots, the captured water can be directed toward a city storm sewer or ditch. A less neighborly way directs the water toward a downslope property, as previously described, with the discharge pipe ending just inside the property line.

Catchment drains can also be strategically located throughout the garden where water collects, delivering the excess water to a drainpipe system that takes the water off the property. It may connect to a large system of pipes also attached to the downspouts for a complete property drainage system. Ultimately, the best approach is to identify problem areas and find ways to correct them by planning a comprehensive drainage system in conjunction with the design plans from the start.

Water can also be moved on the surface as runoff. This requires a bit of planning and finesse, but it is less labor intensive and less expensive than installing drainage pipe. It is also less likely to fail or become damaged over time. The idea is to use slopes to move the water. Even a minimal downslope of a 1 percent grade or less will move water, albeit slowly. Steeper slopes will move water more quickly. Either way, water always flows downhill. We can control this flow by shaping the landform, for example building up the soil along the foundation of the house, a patio, or retaining wall. We can also keep planting beds from becoming inundated during or after rainstorms by mounding the soil to raise the grade.

Once the land around any susceptible structures or planting beds is raised, the next step is to direct the surface runoff toward a discharge point on the property. The water moves in sheets on the surface toward a fallow field or woodlot, storm sewer, drainage ditch, or neighbor's yard. This is a useful method because the longer the run of the surface flow, the more water that will soak into the ground and become available for our plants.

Sometimes swales are required to effectively direct surface water to a discharge point. Swales are subtle channels that aim downslope and are shaped in such a way that the surface water stays within bounds as it flows. Swales can be just a few feet wide, or tens of feet wide. The key is that they aim downhill, often quite gradually, so much so they may not be visible to the naked eye, but the water will always flow downhill even if we can't see the slope. Drainage swales can also be designed to be noticed. There is an entire category of garden making that uses something called bioswales to manage water on a site, creating garden spaces, like dry creek beds, arroyos, and miniature ravines.

CAPTURE THE WATER

While the primary function of a drain or swale is to move excess rainwater offsite, these same water moving methods can also be designed to

How to Make a Garden Swale

1. Observe how the water moves through the site.
2. From your observations, determine the best location for a swale.
3. Mark the contour line of the swale's flow with marking paint or a garden hose.
4. Dig a trench along the marked contour line.
5. Mound the soil from the trench on both sides to create a low berm.
6. Add water to test the swale and adjust as needed.
7. Plant the swale and add rocks or other hardscape to hold the soil in place and add interest.
8. Build redundancy into the system where water can collect when flows exceed capacity.

Swales can be subtle. Just the slightest slope will direct surface water runoff where you want it to go.

capture water and retain it on the property to support crops and ornamental plantings or to create designed water features. Shallow, subtle swales can do a good job of slowing the flow of surface water to allow most or all of it to seep into the ground before it gets to the end of its course, but excessive rain events may overwhelm them, especially when water flows from impermeable surfaces like pavement or rooftops. Perforated drainpipes can capture excess water runoff and put it back into the ground as it flows through the perforations, seeping through the gravel base and soaking into the soil. However, during heavy rain events excess water will find its way to a discharge point where it can be captured for immediate or later use.

It's as simple as directing a drain or a swale toward a low spot or depression that can become a holding pond. This pond can be elaborated upon and planted in such a way as to create a rain garden or designed riparian zone. Water that would otherwise be shuttled offsite is now a design feature, captured so it stays on the property where it can be used. This use can be passive, for example collected where water-loving plants can grow, or actively channeled or pumped into an irrigation system in parts of the garden where supplemental water would be beneficial.

French drains and swales can also be directed toward dry wells where water can be collected and allowed to slowly percolate into the ground or harvested as needed. A dry well is basically a deep hole in the ground filled with large rocks and boulders where the water can sit and seep in. Specially constructed concrete dry wells can also be installed, but at a greater expense than simply digging a deep hole and filling it with rocks. However, precast wells last longer and work better. Dry wells are an excellent option if discharging water to the street or a neighboring property is prohibited by city statute, especially in urbanized areas where excessive stormwater runoff floods streets and houses.

Drainpipes without perforations can be used to purposely collect as much water as possible on-site and store it for later use. These drains can flow directly into storage tanks placed above- or belowground. The stored water can then be used later in the season when needed, such as in a Mediterranean or desert climate with alternating rainy and dry seasons. Whatever the method, working out ways to capture the water on the site can create interesting opportunities within a garden design, but they must be worked out from the start, as part of the landform layer during the early stages of the design process.

FOLLOW THE WATER

The least intrusive, hence most sustainable approach to dealing with surface drainage is to follow the water and design a garden that works within that flow, adjusting the plan accordingly. If an area frequently floods and drains slowly after storms, don't put the vegetable garden or firepit there, make it a rain garden, or dig it out and build a pond. If water runs down a slope quickly, eroding the topsoil around some trees or shrubs, solve the problem with a ground layer of fast-spreading plants with fibrous root systems to slow water flow. If rainstorms spawn fast-flowing streams across a pathway, take it as an opportunity to build a small footbridge, or cut the path with an artistic channel design. Where water pools and collects, propose a wetland habitat for native plants and birds. In other words, go with

How to Make a Rain Garden

1. Choose a location where standing water collects after a rainstorm and perform a percolation test to determine the water infiltration rate.
2. Determine the rain garden size and capacity based on the amount of water regularly discharged into it from all sources.
3. Excavate an area large enough to handle 10 to 20 percent more water than expected during a regular rain event.
4. Connect downspouts and drains and wait for a rainstorm to observe how it works and make necessary adjustments.
5. Create an overflow pathway for excess water during exceptionally high rain events.
6. Add a layer of rocks to the bottom of the depression, then fill it with soil.
7. Select and plant water-loving plants.

Rain gardens are the perfect example of how you can transform a difficult drainage area into a garden feature.

the flow. Take cues from how the surface water moves through the landscape and find solutions to perceived problems with creative design ideas. This approach is more difficult, but more rewarding, because the best designs find elegant solutions to difficult problems.

Designing Landform Features

While garden design is primarily a plant-focused pursuit, gardens that include distinctive landform features are always memorable. Garden designers should recognize the potential of any landforms during the site survey and capitalize on them by embracing the challenges or opportunities they present. Landform that is extreme, like a cliff, or non-existent, like a flat, featureless plot, presents problems the designer must embrace and work with, through either mitigation or utilization. Landform decisions must be made early in the design process to be most effective. After-the-fact solutions to landform challenges are often superficial, or cosmetic, adding less value to the plan. The best way to use landform in a design is to embrace what is there and formulate ideas around it. If a property is so steeply sloped that there is no usable, level ground, find ways to make the ground level for those desired uses or stick with the slopes and change the proposed uses to fit the landforms. For example, will a garden on a steep slope become a sequence of terraces or a set of switchback paths?

The choice is not necessarily an either-or proposition, between working with what's there or reshaping it. A garden designer's choices can fall along a spectrum determined by the importance of what is needed weighed against the desire to remain true to the character of the site. It could be that these functions and needs were best addressed before the property was ever obtained, however, this isn't always possible. What *is* always possible is that thoughtful design can make a property more useful and more beautiful. How a designer chooses to use existing landform features as well as introduce new ones can vary for many reasons. What doesn't vary is the foundational importance of landform as an elemental layer in every garden design.

WORKING WITH EXISTING LANDFORMS

The first step to working with existing landforms, be they slopes or geologic and natural water features, is to claim them as part of the design. If there is a pond on the site, include it as a destination or claim it as a view. If there is a running stream, expose it and create a water garden. If there is a hilltop, make it accessible and bring people up there for a reason, perhaps as a unique vantage point. Once a landform has been claimed, find ways to highlight it by making it a useful design element. It's as simple as putting a bench near the pond, a footbridge over the stream, or a fire ring up on the hill.

Taking advantage of existing landforms within a design is integral to creating memorable gardens. We know it works when the design would not work without the landform feature. For example, there might be no bench to sit on if the pond wasn't there or there's no need for a footbridge without the stream, and the fire ring would be less dramatic if not on a hilltop. Note that these examples use structures to claim and highlight a landform. The relationship between landforms and structures is a key to good design because structures make gardens more useful. So, when working with landforms we often introduce a structure element to make the landform feature more useful as well (more on this in chapter 5).

Beyond claiming and highlighting landform features, it is also crucial that our designs connect them to the garden either visually, actively, or both. As described in the examples just noted, we made these landform features destinations, with a bench, a footbridge, or a fire ring. These are active connections between the garden and its visitors, bringing them together in a specific location. This can also be achieved through a visual connection. A view to the pond from the house or from another garden area can also connect the pond with the garden and its visitors. It's a form of visual appropriation, bringing the landform feature into the garden even if it lies outside the property. The same strategy works with slopes and hills. We don't have to climb a hill for it to affect how we feel. It's enough to see the ground rising above us to change our perspective. Or, we can start at the top of the hill and look down, experiencing the surroundings that way. From either vantage point, our vision is shaped by the elevation change of this landform. All of this plays a role in how a garden is experienced with the goal of making each landform better than how it was found.

CREATING LANDFORM FEATURES

Beyond methods of claiming, highlighting, and connecting to existing landform features, our designs can also include creating landforms for similar purposes. "Dig a lake and make a mountain," is an old Chinese garden-making adage, and a perfect description of how to design with landform. We can dig a pond in just the right spot, where we can see it, and visit it easily, and use that soil to build a mound or small hill nearby. We can lay out a water channel and make a stream precisely where it will look and sound best without interfering with other design needs. On a flat plot, we can pile up soil to make a hill. Or if not a real hill, then a nice rise to the ground to add some variety to a mundane plot. Ultimately, when creating landform features, the goal is to make something better than what we started with.

Most landform changes either use what's there or shape something new. The best results typically come from a combination of the two that makes the land useful and beautiful in equal measure. This isn't always easy, but it is always the goal. All too often designers rely on structures that mitigate or eliminate landforms to make gardens useful. This is understandable because structures are so good at solving land use problems. Thoughtful garden designers learn how to approach their designs with landform in mind. We find ways to make the garden spaces useful and beautiful by first shaping the ground before employing structures. This less-architectural approach makes sense when making gardens because we don't build gardens, we make them. There's a difference between building and making, and our approach to landform is where the difference becomes clear.

Build up soil on either side of a walkway to transform your idea for a simple path into a defined garden passage.

Take cues from your landform by nestling trees in low spots or placed within hillocks.

Mounding Soil

Adding soil is the easiest way to make landform where there is no landform, such as raised spaces for seating areas or places with beautiful views. Other options include building berms to raise the plantings higher for more immediate screening, or so plants can be easily viewed from interior windows. Planting on mounds also makes the plants more interesting when viewed from below, allowing us to look up into the canopy of a small tree with unique bark or interesting foliage. Mounding soil on either side of a path nestles it into the landscape so it feels connected to the garden ground. It is also an effective way to build vegetable garden beds for improved production and ease of care. All things considered, mounding soil is a simple, yet effective, way to play with landform.

Defining Low Spots

Unless they are extreme, or filled with water, low spots are often difficult to see due to a camouflaging plant layer. A good design trick is to accentuate low spots by replanting them with ground-hugging plants to define them better. We can also reshape and organize them by adding more depressions to create a pattern, perhaps linked with paths, or tied together with a singular plant, like a grid of trees in planting wells. Low spots are perfect opportunities for rain gardens, as previously discussed, or we can think bigger and carve out a large depression with a central focal point to create a sunken garden. These are all ideas where landform sets the stage for new uses and where reshaping the land introduces an immediate influence upon the space, all of which can be elaborated on during the next phases of design.

Prospect and Refuge

In 1975, British geographer Jay Appleton produced a seminal work known as "prospect-refuge theory," concluding that people have an "inborn desire" for environments that allow us to observe without being seen so we can assess threats from a place of safety. The prospect-refuge theory draws from the assumption that because humans evolved on the African savannah, we innately prefer places with views that provide a safe place from which to survey our surroundings. Over the years, this concept has been applied by landscape designers to create spaces that people will prefer, with a vista (the prospect) partially framed or enclosed (the refuge) to provide a feeling of safety as well as a sense of mystery, or discoverability. As garden designers, we want to make places where people feel comfortable, and this is one way to make that happen.

Shaping Slopes

The simple process of smoothing slopes without using cut and fill is a type of landforming every garden designer can apply. Reshaping slopes to be more pleasing to the eye and feet is a simple way to improve a site. Make slopes merge and meld, fan out where they meet flat areas, or slowly cut into a steeper grade. It's subtle but effective when executed thoughtfully. Refining slopes appears most natural when we employ the concept of the angle of repose. When slopes are reshaped to meet the soil's natural angle of repose, we eliminate the need for structures to hold things in place. It also creates slopes that are comfortable to traverse, climb, or descend on foot. If we choose to work outside the limits of the angle of repose, then retaining walls will be required (more about this in chapter 5).

We can also make slopes where there aren't any simply by adding soil to level ground and shaping it to meet and match different level planes, like patios and walks, lawns, and planting beds. Creating subtle slopes, especially within planting beds, adds an extra dimension of interest that can be useful when we start to design the plant layer. We can lift up smaller plants and sink larger plants, creating mini landscapes within the confines of an individual planting bed. On a larger scale, we can create an illusion of depth with a gradual slope that rises or descends into the distance. Such visual illusions can turn a dull, flat suburban backyard into a diverse landscape ready to accept multiple uses through the introduction of structures and plants in the next stages of the design.

One of the most practical applications of shaping slopes is where structures meet the ground. For example, where the edge of a patio or deck meets the backyard lawn. If the backyard slopes away from the house and we construct a level patio that extends from the house into the lawn, the patio will be much higher than the ground plane the farther it extends into the lawn. Rather than have a slight step down from the patio onto the lawn, it is better to raise the grade to meet the level of the patio, then feather

Raise your patio slightly above ground plane to direct surface water around it and create a prospect, or view, into the surrounding garden.

it into the lawn so it slopes away gently. If the grade change is small enough, there will be no need for a wall or steps to hold the patio in place. We can simply walk directly off the patio onto a comfortable slope of lawn.

Adding Boulders and Rocks

Geologic landform features can also be created by adding or exposing boulders and rocks. We can add interest and dimensionality to a new planting bed with boulders or large rocks to make it feel like it was part of the landscape all along. Rocks and boulders are perfect foils for plantings, adding an element of physical contrast within the greenery of the plant layer.

Exposing bedrock or ledge is another great trick. Natural rock formations are beautiful, but over time can become covered with weeds or lawn. Simply exposing them adds an instant landform element to an otherwise mundane spot in the garden. Take advantage of crevices and cracks in the rocks by adding soil for some plants. If the formations are large, they can serve as backdrops for plantings or structures like seating terraces.

Burying Boulders and Large Rocks

1. Use a sturdy handcart to move and position large rocks and a pry bar to shift them once they are in place. (Large boulders require a backhoe or excavator.)
2. Use a combination of different-size stones, making certain they match the site's scale. Small rocks look silly in large spaces and large boulders overwhelm a small garden.
3. Find the face of each rock before you select it and before you decide where it goes. The face is the most attractive side or facet with an interesting texture, grain pattern, or shape.
4. Dig holes to bury at least one-third of the rock belowground. Dig the hole before you set the rock in place. Rocks set directly on the surface look contrived.
5. When working near existing boulders or ledge, match the direction of the grain of each stone to the grain of any existing bedrock and make sure any new boulders or rocks match too.
6. Arrange the rocks so they look natural by spacing them at irregular intervals, some close, some farther apart. Step back and study the arrangement from a distance and shift the stones until it "feels" right.
7. Use the most interesting rocks as signal stones to indicate an important point in the garden, like a transition from one space to another, an entry to a path, or as a main feature in a planting bed.

▲ Thoughtfully placed and partially buried boulders will help you create a garden setting ready for plants.

CHAPTER 5

HARDSCAPING: Structures that Create Useful Outdoor Spaces

The selection and use of primary *hardscape structures* including walls, walkways, and steps; patios, furniture, and fencing; pergolas, arbors, and outbuildings; firepits, waterfalls, and composters; flowerpots and art objects.

"Hardscaping" is a term used to describe the built structures of a garden, especially those that make the garden more useful, like walls, walks, patios, or fencing. Sometimes referred to as functional elements, hardscaping is a key component to the structure layer of any garden design, and the next element to be addressed in the design process, after landform. Hardscaping falls within one of three categories: specific functional elements needed to make a garden work; featured structures wanted to make a garden exceptional, and outdoor décor that adds originality and convenience throughout the garden.

Hardscape choices profoundly affect the look and feel of a garden so their form is equally important as their function. In many ways, hardscape choices influence the manifest quality of a garden more than any other aspect of the design. Quality of construction and material choice coupled with color, texture, and form can, for example, turn a basic retaining wall into a design highlight. Hardscape features present an excellent opportunity to display taste and style within a design as stone patterns or wood stains affect how a garden looks and feels, and how it is ultimately experienced. Sitting on a camp chair set upon a square concrete patio in a patch of lawn is a world away from lounging on a chaise placed upon a herring bone–patterned brick terrace set into a greensward. Both make an outdoor space more comfortable and useful, but one does it with a bit more flair.

All hardscape decisions fall within the purview of the garden designer and should contribute to their goals for the garden as well as display their design style. The designer may not know how to build these structures, but they must know whether a certain hardscape feature is needed, where it fits within the plan, how it will affect a garden space as well as influence the look and feel of the garden overall. At this stage of the design, planning the actual construction of the hardscape is not necessary. The purpose of this phase is to find opportunities for hardscape and structure features that will make the garden better and provide solutions for principal design needs.

Hardscape "Needs"

The primary hardscape features of the structure layer within a garden design should solve specific problems. As features that make the garden more usable and comfortable, they become key elements of the structure layer that will shape the design. To start, don't worry about the

◄ Level surfaces, nice seating, solid walls, steps, and a privacy fence all contribute to the comfort of this casual backyard garden.

material or style of the structure. Focus on its general purpose and foremost function. From that function, develop its form, settling on a shape and size that works best to ensure that the hardscaping is as useful as possible. Once that is settled, find the best form by working through several versions until it's right. This can take time and practice so follow my suggestions for these frequently used hardscape features. Finally, think about specific material and style choices, understanding that aesthetics and functionality will converge over time as the plan evolves.

GARDEN WALLS

Walls come in two categories: retaining and freestanding. Retaining walls are a natural progression from our work in the landform layer so they are typically the first walls we plan for. Retaining walls are used to create terracing by holding back the soil on slopes and providing usable space above and/or below each wall. Retaining walls are also used when carving stairways into slopes. They hold back soil above the steps and landing areas cut into the hillside.

The most important property of a retaining wall is its strength and ability to hold the earth behind it in place without collapsing. So, getting the size and basic material of the wall right is crucial. A simple rule to follow is, the heavier the wall, the more it can retain, and the best way to make a wall heavy is to make it thick and use large rocks or blocks. A small retaining wall, perhaps a foot high just to hold a slight slope in place, doesn't require much planning, but larger, taller walls do. The garden designer doesn't have to engineer large walls, but we do need to know where they are needed and how significant they should be. Our role is to lay them out on a plan and let a professional mason take it from there.

Once we get a feel for the size and location of any necessary retaining walls, we should think about the kind of wall that will work best, like poured concrete, manufactured block, stacked stone, or maybe a large boulder wall. This choice shapes the style of the garden and will inform future design ideas for plants, such as a rustic wall with pockets where small plants can grow, or a large-scale boulder wall with spaces big enough for trees and shrubs. Planting ideas can come later in the process, perhaps much later, but it's important to recognize how decisions made during the hardscaping phase may influence later stages of the design.

Freestanding walls, unlike retaining walls, are not built into slopes or designed to hold back soil to mitigate landforms. They are, however, influenced by landform. For example, if a freestanding wall is built along a slope, we must decide if it will follow the slope and be built directly on top of it, changing elevation along the way, or will it slice into the slope, keeping the top of the wall at the same level regardless of any grade changes at its base. In the first instance, the height of the wall will remain the same along its length. In the second instance, the height of the wall will change based upon its location along the slope. None of this comes into play, obviously, if the wall is built on level ground.

The primary function of freestanding walls is to delineate space and make garden rooms. They can be tall enough, 6 feet (1.8 m) or more, to completely enclose a space, or they can be low, just 3 or 4 feet (0.9 or 1.2 m) high so they enclose the space but allow views to adjacent areas. They can also be 2 feet (61 cm) tall or less, functioning

Cut a curved retaining wall into a slope to create a defined yet informal space at the base of a hillside.

Carefully consider the size, shape, and color of wall stones to achieve the desired look and feel within your garden.

For a formal look, choose clean brick-work set to a rhythm with alternating sections of pillar and wall.

as visual cues that signal a segregation between two distinct areas. Freestanding walls, therefore, play an important role in shaping outdoor spaces and are a great way to start defining garden rooms.

The shape and material of a garden wall impact the look and feel of the garden room it defines. Whether curved, angled, or straight, form is key. Smooth-topped, crenelated, or capped, all these aspects of a wall's design make a difference and fall within the purview of the garden designer. So too does the material choice, such as concrete, block, brick, stacked stone, or boulders. This also includes colors and textures, like stained concrete, patterned brick, or native fieldstone. These material color, texture, and pattern choices can come a little later in the design process, but it is good to start thinking now about materials and patterns for any proposed walls due to their important role in creating the sense of style of a garden (more about making these decisions in chapter 8).

At this point, the location, shape, and size of these walls is what counts and should be included in the design plan. Approach it as an opportunity to experiment with multiple versions. Play with different geometries, like straight lines versus curves. Think about how the wall will change the shape and size of the space it encloses as well as the shape and size of adjacent areas outside the wall. It may become evident that a wall is not needed, or that more walls are required. Whatever the case, this is the time to get creative and have some fun exploring ideas in search of the best solutions.

WALKWAYS, STEPS, AND RAMPS

Walkways are hardscape surfaces built on the ground to provide ease of movement through the garden. Garden steps are walkways that go up a slope, though a walkway going up a slope could also be a ramp. Walkways and steps make moving through the garden easier. Their solid surface accommodates wheels and high heels, keeping feet clean and dry, and preventing slips and spills. Even more important, walks and steps should provide the best route to get from place to place. For example, lead us to the front door from the sidewalk or take us from the front yard to the backyard. Once the need for a walkway, steps, or ramps is determined, garden designers work out different options, understanding that the most direct path may not be best.

The most important aspects when designing walkways are location and size. Walks are typically placed where they are most needed, but during the design phase we can create new garden spaces using walks that make these spaces more accessible. Walkways can also shape garden rooms and establish how they will be experienced. A garden with comfortable paths is totally different from a wild space with no paths at all, and a nicely designed walkway is a great way to lend an air of formality to any garden. When it comes to hardscape, we are focused on structural walks, not casual paths, though formal gravel paths are considered hardscape, especially when kept in bounds with stone, brick, or metal edging.

Add curves along a walkway to create simple moments of mystery as we wonder what might be around the next bend.

Use quality materials and try different patterns within the design to make good-looking walkways that work well.

Employ a permeable walkway using flat stones set within a gravel field to create a relaxed yet clean contemporary feel.

Walkway width depends on the proposed use of the walk. A 4- to 5-foot (1.2 to 1.5 m) minimum width allows two people to walk abreast comfortably. Wider widths, 6 feet (1.8 m) or more when space permits, and the walkway begins to function like a gathering place or patio. Single file is fine for narrow walks if space is tight, or if the garden we're passing through is meant to be experienced that way.

The length of a walkway also matters. Excessively long, straight walks become boring unless their surroundings make it interesting, for example as an allée leading to a distant view. The longer the walkway the more likely the need to break it into sections. This can be accomplished by changing patterns or materials, varying widths, adjusting the geometry, or adding accessories like benches and potted plants in key locations. The design goal should be to turn a potentially long slog into a pleasurable stroll, turning the pure function of moving through the garden into an interesting experience.

Stairway length, especially the number of steps between landings, is a key consideration. Start by working within the constraints presented on the ground that make steps necessary and strive to design something that makes the garden work and look better. See it as an opportunity to solve a problem that also enhances the design. Rather than force folks to find their own way up a slope, a well-designed stairway can deliver them in style, setting the tone for their arrival in the next part of the garden.

Ramps allow us to climb a slope without steps. Often part of an ADA (Americans with Disability Act)-compliant design, ramps are a great way to make gardens accessible to all, but they can also provide a bit of interest and fun to an otherwise traditional garden plan. Well-designed ramps let guests flow through elevation changes in subtle ways using twists and turns. They also work well as discrete, or hidden, transitions between terraces. Follow the same width, length, geometry, and material choice guidelines discussed for walks and steps when designing ramps.

PATIOS AND DECKS

Patios and decks are the most effective way to make a garden space useful and comfortable. As perfect transitions from the architecture of the house to the garden outside they are essential features within the structures layer of a design. Patios are best for areas with flat ground, out the back, side, or front doors of the house. Front-yard patios are also an option if there is no workable, level space in back. Decks are raised structures, commonly used to provide a more immediate transition from the house to the garden, but they can also serve as raised walkways and landing spots within the garden. Patios, by definition, are made from stone, concrete, pavers, or bricks set on a base dug into the ground, while decks are made of wood or composite materials built aboveground on a support structure with posts and footings set into the

Add a sense of historic charm to a garden stairway by choosing rustic stones laid out in simple curves.

Set steps within plantings and establish a garden passageway to guide guests up a slopeside.

Try clean-cut, wide treads and low risers for a set of casual steps with modern appeal.

Construct an area of solid, level patio hardscape to provide ground space to enjoy the outdoors in comfort.

Design and build your deck so it is married to the house and garden equally.

Combine decks and patios to create a variety of functional garden spaces right outside your house.

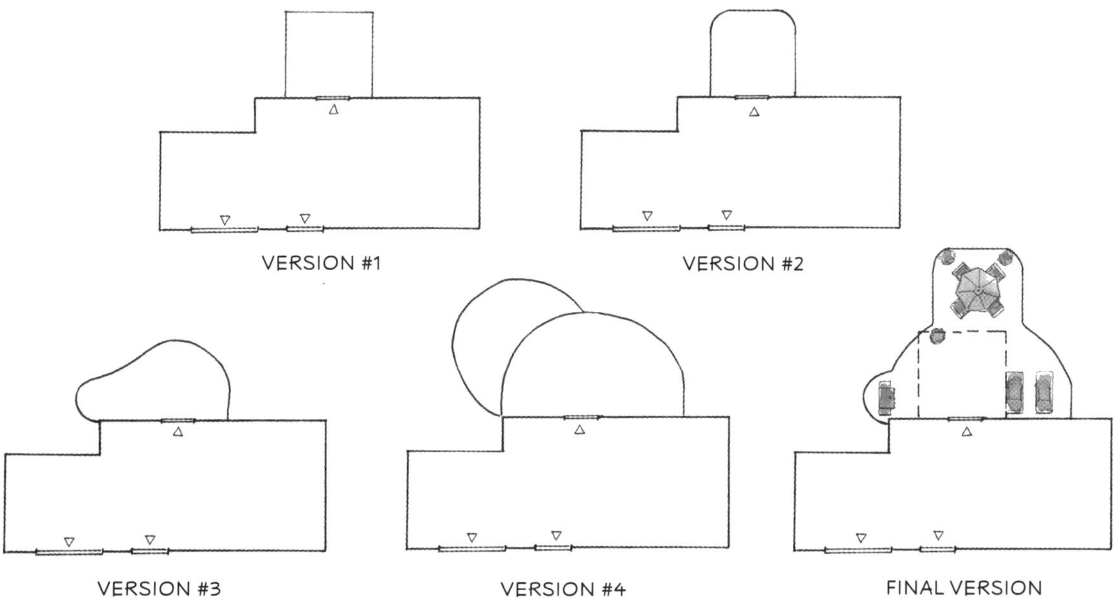

Play with the shapes that make up your patio and deck designs until you find the perfect, pleasing geometry.

ground. Decks, however, don't have to be raised. They can be built as low platforms. An excellent design idea is to use patios and decks together, with a raised deck close to the house transitioning down to a patio at ground level.

As with other hardscape features, the most important attribute of a patio or deck is its size. Any area less than 10 feet square (100 sq. ft., or 9.2 sq. m) should be considered cozy or functioning as a pass-through space within a larger scheme. Twenty or 25 feet square (400 to 625 sq. ft., or 37.1 to 58 sq. m) is enough room for a table and chairs plus other furnishings, like a barbecue grill and potted plants. Larger patios and decks have room for multiple uses, like outdoor kitchens and furnished seating areas. Sometimes size is limited by the surroundings so make sure the intended use of the patio or deck fits the size of the available space. Remember, design is a process of working within limitations yet finding solutions for success.

Second to size is geometry. Patios and decks allow for a variety of design choices, applying different curves and angles, incorporating overlapping forms to create multiple layers of interest. When laying out a new patio or deck, try multiple approaches. Start with something simple, such as a square or rectangle. Then add some curves or arcs to soften the shape. Start from scratch and try again with free-form shapes. Next, play around with some circles and tangents. Then, combine two or three ideas and keep experimenting until the best version reveals itself.

Thoughts About Porches

Open porches are architectural features that function like decks and patios with a rooftop. Because the porch is directly tied to the house, a new porch may require consultation with an architect or a contractor so the result suits the house and is assured to be structurally sound. The garden designer, however, can and should decide whether a new porch is needed and propose where it will best serve as an enhancement to the garden. A well-built furnished porch thoughtfully matched to the landscape provides a beguiling sense of being both indoors and outdoors, yet firmly ensconced in the garden.

Because it establishes the floor of an outdoor room, the location and configuration of a patio or deck will profoundly affect the further development of the design plan. Pay attention to how people are likely to gather on the patio or deck, and how they may traverse it to get to another garden area. Good hardscape designs serve more than one purpose so think beyond the obvious and consider all the places a patio or deck can prove useful, such as a cozy seating area in the vegetable garden, or a discrete deck in a field of wildflowers. Ultimately, patios and decks are safe spots to "land" in the garden, providing a special place to spend some quality time.

FENCES AND GATES

They say good fences make good neighbors, but when it comes to garden design fences do a whole lot more. Fences define spaces, functioning as walls to garden rooms, but to varied degrees, as visual screens, or physical barriers. Like freestanding walls, fences can be tall enough to completely screen the view into and out of a garden, or short enough to segregate the gardens yet allow views between them. As space-defining features, both tall and short fences can effectively inhibit movement from space to space, controlling how people move through the property.

Property line fences are typically tall, solid structures built to keep intruders out, pets in, and create privacy between neighbors. They also provide good buffers to sound, like from traffic, especially when used in conjunction with screening trees or hedges. Sometimes, however, a property line fence can function as a visual cue to mark a boundary, for example a split-rail or corral fence. Different heights and styles of fence can be used along different property lines, depending upon what is on the other side of the line. Whatever the case, a good property line fence should effectively mark the boundaries of the property no matter how tall or see-through it is.

Use a simple picket fence to define your garden and as a complement for casual plantings.

Define your property line without blocking the view with a well-built split-rail fence.

Create subtle screening and support for climbing plants in tight spaces with a trellis fence.

A trellis is cousin to the fence. It screens views and creates enclosures just like fences do, but is also designed to support plants, especially vines. A trellis can be conceived as an open-grid fence, with plants growing up and over it to fill the gaps and provide the screening desired. Some call them green fences, or botany walls, but ultimately, it's just a trellis with vines.

Fences also keep whatever is inside them safe, especially plants. Vegetable gardens usually require fencing to keep critters like rabbits, deer, and groundhogs out, which often means the fence doesn't just go up, it may also extend partially underground. Fences are also used to keep dogs on a property or penned inside certain garden areas. Some gardeners install 8-foot (2.4 m)-tall black wire fence along the entire property line to keep deer out. This can be an expensive prospect, so most gardeners specify limited areas within the garden to fence off so they can grow whatever they want inside the protected area.

Aside from size, the design and material of a fence are key considerations. Designs run the gamut from prefab panels fastened between posts to stick-built designs made from scratch. Material choices range from different types of wood, composites, PVC, and metals such as wire, aluminum tubes, or corrugated sheets. With so many materials, colors, styles, and patterns to choose from, fencing can contribute to the look, feel, and style of any garden.

Even more important is the location of the fence and how it affects the garden space it surrounds. Part of this determination is deciding where the fence starts and stops and if there are any other structures to which it can be attached to complete the enclosure, like a garage or corner of the house. This is often the case when we decide to add extensive deer fencing, or when trying to find the least intrusive placement for a swimming pool fence. Figuring out where fences like these belong on the plan forces us to begin to make some design decisions, devising ways to hide fences, or make them somehow attractive yet functional. Always remember when proposing a fence that certain areas of the property will become less accessible depending upon the fence's location, though access can always be solved with gates.

Most fences have a gate or two, but not all gates need to be part of a fence. When planning the placement of a new fence, take note of where gates will be necessary or convenient. Long spans of fencing without a gate can cause access problems. Fortunately, gates can be added to an existing fence, but it is best to determine where they belong beforehand. Put gates in key spots—near the house along a path where people will frequently come in and out or anywhere regular access is desired. For long stretches of property line fence, always add a secure gate somewhere along its length, for example at the corner of the property or across from a convenient entry point to a neighboring property. These gates can be locked and are as secure as the fence but prove handy when access is needed. Identify where a wide or a double gate may be helpful, for example as access for large equipment like a commercial lawnmower, excavator, or tree lift. This is especially important if there are plans for more work on the property after the fence is installed. A double gate 10 to 12 feet (3 to 3.6 m) in width is adequate for most large machinery.

Gates are doorways, and as such are perfect for guiding visitors through a garden. A gate is a signal that leads to another garden space,

Add a well-built arbor gate to your design for a definitive transition between garden rooms with a distinctive style.

and while most gates are attached to fences, a fun design trick is to place a gate between two spaces to signal the transition. A 4-foot (1.2 m) gate is enough to do the trick. When standing on one side of it, we are in one garden room. When we pass through, we have entered another. It works best if there is a walkway connecting the two gardens, because then the gate really feels like a doorway.

Any gate transition that will be used frequently should have a threshold stone set into the ground where the gate swings open and closed, especially if there isn't a path leading up to and through the gate, such as a gate located on a fence in a lawn area. Frequent foot traffic through the same spot will wear out the lawn, leaving a muddy patch. A threshold stone will prevent that and serve as a nice marker for the gateway. Even if the gate is located along an existing walk, it's a nice idea to change the walkway slightly to signal the transition. This can be done by changing path material, like switching from brick to stone, widening the walk at the gate, or changing the pattern of the walkway material. All these techniques will work as strong visual cues to mark one garden room from the next.

DESIGN RULES FOR PROPERTY LINE FENCES

There are a few design rules when it comes to property line fences. All too often homeowners position the fence directly on the property line. This is not the best idea, because then the fence is technically owned by both property owners, regardless of who built it. This may become a problem if one neighbor decides they don't like the fence or want to change it. A better approach is to set the posts for a property line fence a foot or more inside the property line. (If uncertain where that line is, pay for a survey to be sure!) It's also wise to install a "good neighbor" fence, a fence with two "good" sides that look finished, as opposed to a fence with one finished side and one that shows fasteners, etc. Barring the use of a "good neighbor"-style fence, the best thing to do is face the good side out and the less attractive side in with plantings to obscure it.

PERGOLAS AND ARBORS

Pergolas are remarkable garden structures for their ability to create the impression of a ceiling within an outdoor room. Constructed from parallel rafters set upon a post-and-beam framework, pergolas cut the sun's intensity by one-third or more, depending upon the spacing of the rafters and whether there is lattice added on top. They can be attached to another structure, like a house, or freestanding on a terrace. Pergolas are perfect for creating sheltered, cozy spots for outdoor seating, dining, or kitchen areas. While the partial shade provided by the rafters and lattice makes it comfortable to sit beneath a pergola on a sunny summer afternoon, a pergola is the perfect addition to an outdoor space by creating the impression we're in a room with a ceiling open to the sky.

Like pergolas, arbors also make outside ceilings, though often with more significant side structures, and are generally located along a path or walkway. A short arbor, in conjunction with a gate, is an excellent way to create a garden doorway. Even without the gate an arbor will signal a transition between gardens. Long arbors built along the length of a wide walkway, or driveway, make a bold statement by fashioning a tunnel space. The construction of the arbor determines how it feels to pass through it. Light metalwork suggests a floating ceiling whereas wide wooden beams better define a room.

Location and size are key to using these two hardscape elements effectively. The scale of a pergola must match the scale of the space, either the size of the patio floor it is set upon, or within the larger context of the garden. On large terraces, a pergola can shelter a section and define an area for a particular use, like dining or grilling. Pergolas also make nice transitional shelters outside of entryways into a house or other building. They signal a transition from inside to outside by creating the impression of an outdoor foyer. When designing with pergolas always consider the space beneath them as a separate outdoor room. The same is true for arbors, but in this case the room is a hallway, or entryway, so think of arbors as connectors between gardens. Both pergolas and arbors, of course, can be planted with climbing vines to soften their structure and add to their charm (more on this in chapter 6).

Hardscape "Wants"

Garden "wants" are, for the most part, optional, but they are also aspects of a design that make it unique and memorable. Good design strikes a balance between form and function so a design that provides only what is required for the garden to be useful, without any aesthetic interest or charm, is bound to disappoint. Fulfilling these "wants," especially within the structure layer, makes a garden more than just the sum of its parts. They are features that truly define a design. While some "wants" may reside in the landform and plant layers, distinctive structural objects are best at pushing a design above and beyond pure function to create something special. Most structures discussed here aren't strictly necessary when designing a garden, but it's the role of a designer to decide whether something is truly a "want" or if that "want" may indeed be a "need."

WANTS WE NEED: THE CROSSROADS OF A GARDEN DESIGN

There will be a moment, sometimes many moments, as we design our gardens when we come to a crossroads and must make decisions that set the project on a trajectory we cannot change. Such decisions occur most often when defining the goals of the garden, invariably shaped by our needs and wants. As previously discussed, needs address problems that must be solved through design. They come first. But what about the wants, features of the garden that will fulfill our idea of what makes a garden special? This is our opportunity to look beyond the basic function of design and make it serve our personal motivations for making the garden in the first place. This is when we realize there are ***wants we need*** to fulfill to make it all worthwhile.

The boundary between needs and wants is a slippery slope. Take, for example, a greenhouse. Does a casual home gardener really need a greenhouse, even though it would be awesome to have one? Or do they just want a greenhouse? Well, maybe they don't want to be a casual gardener anymore. Maybe they want to get serious about propagation or overwintering tropical plants. Maybe they need to fulfill this want. Suddenly the design takes on a whole new purpose because if this want is ignored the garden will disappoint and perhaps be followed by regret. So, when we arrive at a crossroads when a want becomes a need, the best advice is to go with it. Design a garden that fulfills. Find a way, even if only on paper in the design plan. If it proves to be impossible to achieve when it's time to make the garden a reality, so be it. The dream can live on, even if only in the plan, because what's the point of designing a garden if it doesn't fulfill a few dreams.

OUTBUILDINGS

Outbuildings are any architectural structure that isn't the main house. Some may have been mapped during the site survey, but there could be additions needed, or wanted, as part of the garden design. Now is the time to figure that out and include them in the plan. Garden-specific outbuildings, like greenhouses and sheds, should be considered first because they will be important to the overall organization of the garden areas.

Greenhouses must be sited based upon sun exposure and access to utilities like water and power. While they can be attached to the house or stand alone in the garden, there are specialized considerations as well, such as will it be a hothouse (heated through the winter) or a cold house (unheated), or both? Will there be a cold frame or root cellar attached? Perhaps it's meant to be a conservatory space filled with potted plants, doors open to the garden in summer and closed tight in winter. Maybe it's an orchid house, or a propagation house. Whatever it is, it must be located where it will be convenient and receive the proper amount of sun. At this point, there's no need to fully design the greenhouse, just determine its shape, size, and orientation.

The same is true for sheds and barns, whether a storage shed or a proper potting shed, but unlike siting a greenhouse, more leeway is allowed with these structures, though orientation still plays a role. First, decide how big it should be based on its use and purpose, and then choose a location where it will fit and be convenient. Next, imagine how these new walls will shape the garden spaces around them; how the building, positioned in relation to the house, might create a courtyard, protected from winter winds but open to the sunny south in cold climates, or sheltered from the harsh summer sun in hot regions. It might be a good idea to place the structure close to the property line where its bulk functions as a fence, or let it stand alone in a woodland or meadow as a destination within a new garden room. Think each option through by drawing each version on the plan and study how the surrounding garden spaces will be affected until the best solution emerges.

Garages and barns are significant outbuildings. If an existing garage is being expanded, or demolished and rebuilt, now is the time to decide where it will be located. A new garage will profoundly affect any adjacent outdoor spaces so figure it out now. Same with a new barn. Where will it go and how will it be used? For animals? As an artist's loft? A guesthouse, or an extra entertainment space? The purpose, location, and size of these outbuildings are key. The garden designer doesn't have to design them, but needs to know where they go, how big they will be, how they will function, and how they link to the garden, either as views through their windows or access through doors.

Smaller, specialized outbuildings like saunas, playhouses, doghouses, and chicken coops are easier to site, but should be included in a garden plan to ensure they don't interfere with other garden goals. Saunas are nice outdoor amenities best placed near a back door with a comfortable walkway for easy winter access. Playhouses should be close to the house but not so close that the kids shouting at play will disturb others. Treat these structures like every other building

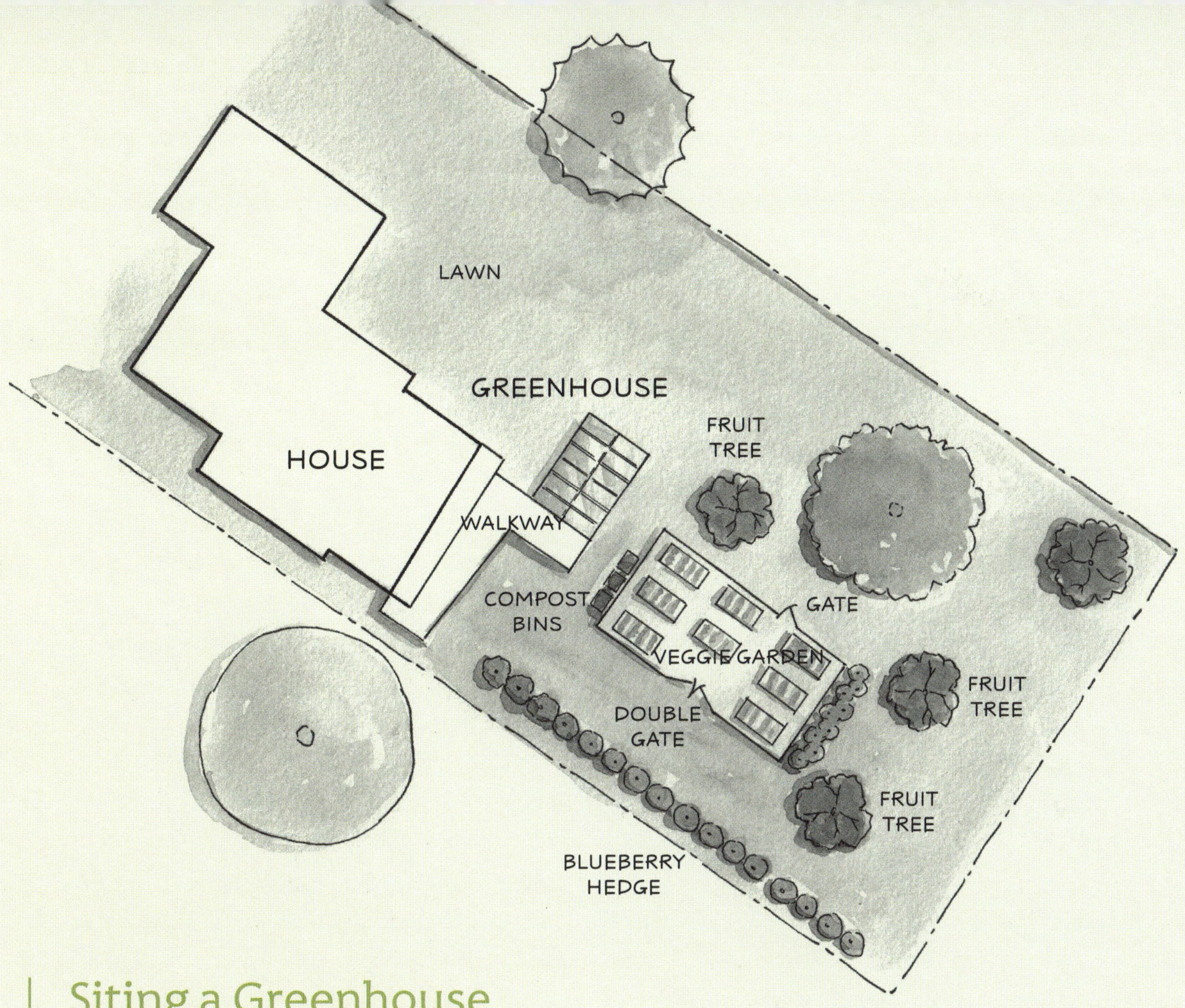

Siting a Greenhouse

Follow these guidelines to find the best spot for a greenhouse, focusing on maximum sun exposure and protection from frost pockets and cold winds.

1. Stay away from large shade trees that block light and drop branches. Leaves and insects can stain the glass and tree roots can damage the foundation.
2. Put the structure as close to the house as possible to make daily visits easy and convenient. This makes the greenhouse a nice destination within the garden where the plants can be enjoyed inside.
3. Avoid slopes to save on construction costs for things like retaining walls and keep the greenhouse away from the bottom of hills where frost pockets develop naturally, making it more expensive to heat.
4. Orient the structure east-west to maximize light during winter. A north-south orientation is best for summer growing because it provides equal sun exposure throughout the house.
5. Keep 4 feet (1.2 m) of space clear all around the greenhouse to allow access when panes or covers need to be replaced or cleaned. Keep it clear of other structures that may cast shade or disrupt ventilation.

▲ Carefully consider the context of the entire garden when choosing the best location for your greenhouse.

Is It a Gazebo or a Summerhouse?

A gazebo is another garden structure that, if done right, contributes to the utility and beauty of a garden. A gazebo should be a destination, not an afterthought. This destination may include a view to a lake or seashore, proximity to a koi pond, or be something as simple as a sheltered spot for a picnic table. A gazebo as a destination, complete with electricity, furniture, and things to make it nice and cozy, then becomes a summerhouse, a teahouse, a writer's retreat, a yoga room, or a meditation space.

on the site, paying attention to location, size, and surroundings. Make a garden around the playhouse so it is in a nice setting, maybe beneath a large shade tree. Put the doghouse or chicken coop in a safe, sheltered spot where the animals will be comfortable on hot days. Consider adding a dog run area near a doghouse or kennel so the pups can get outside and exercise.

SWIMMING POOLS AND SPAS

If there are any plans for a swimming pool now is the time to think it through. Again, size and location are key. Work closely with the pool company to decide the location. They will want it in the easiest place for them to build it, but we want it where it will look best in the garden. Think of a swimming pool area as a garden room. This includes where people will sit poolside or get in and out of the water. Leave space for decorative plantings to make it look and feel like a garden. Some people want the pool close to the house for convenience. Others want it farther away. Either way, pay attention to nearby canopy or understory trees. Large trees can shade areas of the pool and the adjacent pool deck, which may be okay on hot summer days, but might limit the pool's use when plunged into shadows. Deciduous trees that drop their leaves or flowers can also pose problems. Evergreens aren't as messy, but they still drop needles, cones, and lots of pollen. If there are any young trees nearby, understand they will grow over time and may become a problem later. Also, think about privacy screening from neighboring properties or the street, and don't forget about where the pool equipment will go as it will include pumps that can be loud and unattractive. All these criteria should be considered when deciding the best location for a swimming pool.

Spas, or whirlpools, are often built as part of a swimming pool, but sometimes they are stand-alone in-ground or aboveground. Portable spas can be placed on decks and patios, in-ground spas should be sited by thinking it through the same way we do a swimming pool. Consider ease of access, sun and shade, privacy screening, and, most of all, how it fits within adjacent garden areas or maybe as part of a garden room itself.

FIREPITS AND KITCHENS

Outdoor kitchens are the epitome of a designed garden room. They can be quite elaborate, with grills, stovetops and ovens, refrigerators, beer taps, cocktail stations, work counters and comfy chairs. Or they can be super simple, with just

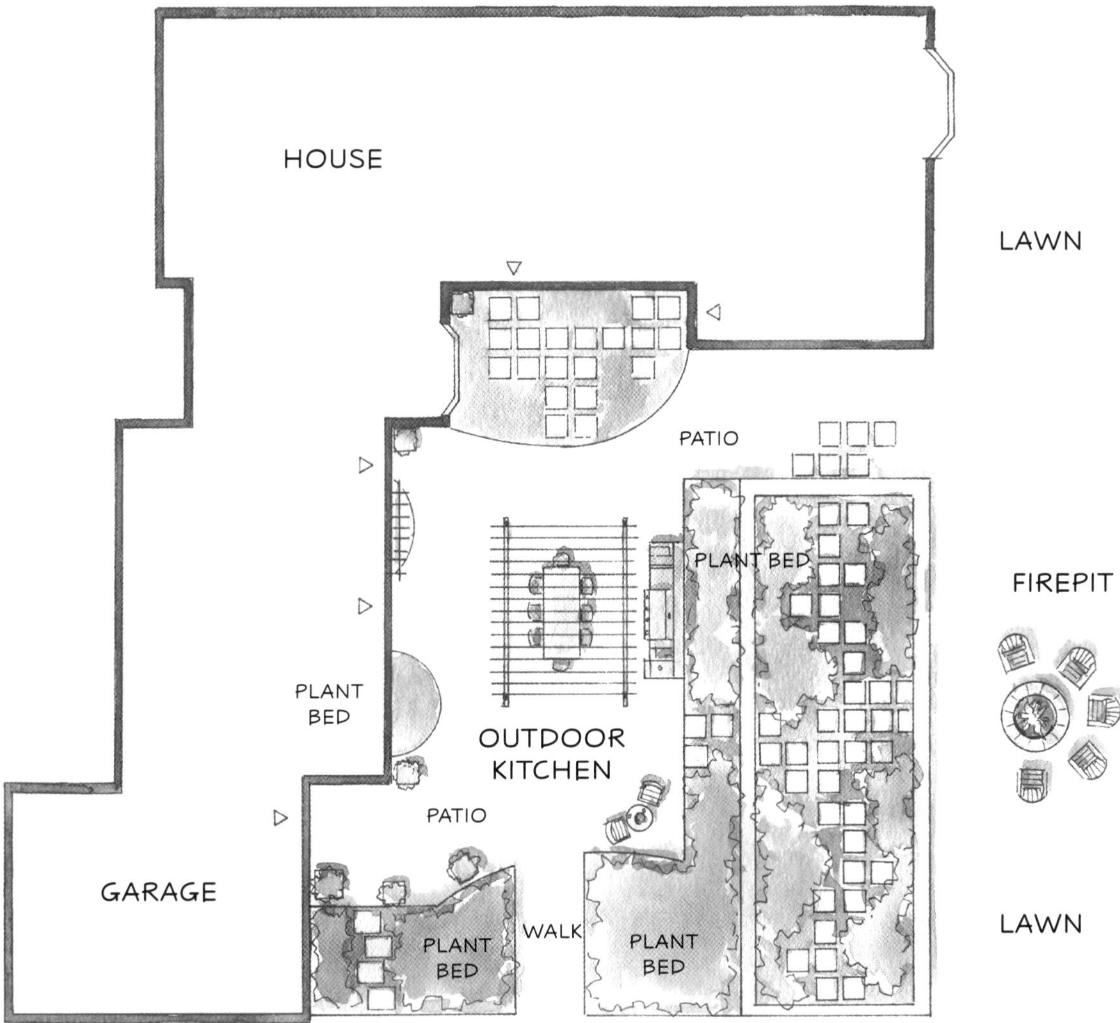

Design outdoor kitchens and firepits as singular gathering points set within the garden landscape.

enough space for a grill and a cooler filled with drinks. Either way, outdoor kitchens are useful spaces that can be a prominent feature of a new garden design. They are usually located within the patio or deck space, but it's important to work out the best spot based on ease of access from the house, gathering places like swimming pools, or proximity to an herb or vegetable garden. In most cases the kitchen should be close to the house near a door leading to the interior kitchen. The size of the outdoor kitchen depends on how it will be used and how much space there is available where it will be built. Make sure there is room to work and room to eat. Determine what type of equipment and accessories are needed, like grills, pizza ovens, coolers, bar stools, etc., and find a location that will accommodate them all, then draw it on the plan. Pay attention to sun exposure and include shading features like umbrellas or pergolas.

Firepits are a fun hardscape feature that can instantly light up a garden room. They come in many shapes and sizes, even actual outdoor fireplaces, complete with a chimney and storage space for firewood. The most important criterion is location. Firepits that are part of a larger outside terrace or entertainment area are often self-contained and fueled with propane gas with easy-to-light switches. Larger woodburning pits should be located farther out into the garden, open to the sky and designed as a gathering place complete with chairs or a seating wall. The choice is based upon how the firepit will be used, as a source of light, as an entertainment feature, or for warmth on chilly nights. Most important, find a place away from flammable objects where the heat from the flames can rise safely into the sky, clear of overhanging canopy trees, and so prevailing winds don't send the smoke into the house or toward the neighbors. Also, provide enough room adjacent to the firepit for guests to gather 'round. Once the size and location of the pit is determined, think about a style suited to the garden design such as a rustic ring, a sleek stone square, or an iron bowl, among many available options.

FOUNTAINS AND WATERFALLS

Be wary of water features, like fountains and waterfalls, that require plumbing. Consider a self-circulating fountain that just needs power to run the pump, though it is more convenient if there is a refill mechanism to ensure the water reservoir doesn't run dry, but that means plumbing. The same is true for constructed waterfalls, which rely on a reservoir pond or tank to collect the water and a pump to push the water back to the top. Naturalistic waterfalls also need skimmers and filters to keep the water clean, resulting in ongoing maintenance concerns. Leaks in the pipes, basins, or reservoirs are additional complications. Fountains and waterfalls are, however, interesting features that work well as focal points in the garden. A fountain should be placed in a special spot, centered in a space or, if it's a wall fountain, at the end of a walkway where it will be noticed. Waterfalls look best if they are built on a pre-existing slope rather than constructed with piled stones to provide an elevation change in a flat area. Elaborate waterwalls are often part of a designed stream and pond system. We can put these on a plan, but like the construction of many other hardscape features, such as greenhouses, swimming pools, or outdoor kitchens, these complex hardscape projects are best built by a practiced professional working in conjunction with the garden designer.

Create a classic mood in your favorite garden room by including a central fountain seen easily from several vantage points.

Accentuate the echoes of flowing water in your garden as it spills out of a wall and into a basin below.

Make your garden beautiful and useful long past nightfall with the drama of thoughtfully planned night lighting.

LANDSCAPE LIGHTING

A landscape lighting plan is an important feature for any garden design, especially if the outdoor spaces will be frequented at night or if they are transition spaces from public and semi-public areas like sidewalks, driveways, and front walks. While the main function is to guide guests through outdoor spaces safely, landscape lighting also makes less useful spaces more useful and adds ambiance to garden settings at night. The garden designer should plan for where lighting is wanted and required, for example to illuminate paths and steps, light up a work or play area, or highlight plantings or garden structures. There is an art to landscape lighting, often best provided by experts, but with a little basic knowledge of the different types of lighting features, anyone can devise an effective lighting plan. Landscape lighting is typically offered by irrigation companies since both types of work involve running electric wires underground, but DIY landscape lighting is also an option thanks to LED technologies that allows for low-voltage lines, eliminating the need to hire a licensed electrician.

THE ART OF LANDSCAPE LIGHTING

There is an art to landscape lighting, and it is good for garden designers to understand these techniques so they can specify how they want to light the garden when designing a lighting plan. The following list includes common landscape lighting techniques with a brief description of how each works and where it is best employed.

- **UPLIGHTING** is a way to add light at the bases of trees, statues, or architecture to encourage mystery and intrigue by showing off forms from below.
- **DOWNLIGHTING** is a method for accenting planting beds or garden features from above, mimicking natural light by installing fixtures that cast light down on walkways and steps.
- **FLOODLIGHTING** casts a wide, strong, bright beam of light to illuminate large areas by placing fixtures on the ground, or raised and attached to a structure.
- **HIGHLIGHTING** is used to illuminate the shape, color, and form of interesting objects by placing floodlights or spotlights at the foot of the feature.
- **SHADOWING** creates a shadow on the wall or hardscape behind a garden object, like a plant or sculpture, with a spotlight on the ground several feet in front of the object to be shadowed.
- **SILHOUETTING** is like shadowing and is used to highlight dramatic shapes by placing spotlights or well lights behind an object or plant that isn't as noticeable during the day to light them up.
- **GRAZING** is a technique applied to walls and shrubs to display their texture by creating shadows with well lights aimed upward and that "graze" the surface of the object with an indirect angle of light.
- **MOONLIGHTING** is a technique that uses soft spotlights positioned high in trees angled downward to create the effect of moonlight bathing the area below in a subtle "moonglow."

IRRIGATION

If irrigation is going to be used anywhere in the garden, the design phase determines where and what kind. Thoughtful planting plans should not require supplemental irrigation (more on this in chapter 6), though irrigation can help establish new plants or support special-use areas such as traditional lawns, orchards, and vegetable gardens. First, identify if the water source will be city water, well water, or pumped from a pond or stream. Then map out where buried irrigation pipes and control or valve boxes may be located to ensure they are easily accessible. Plan to pre-install underground conduit so irrigation pipes and wiring can be installed beneath hardscape elements like walkways and patios to reach isolated garden beds or lawns. A comprehensive irrigation plan can be part of the design, if only to keep the option open for a later date. Such a plan also includes the location of new hose bibs, or spigots, above and beyond what may already be attached to the house, providing access to where hoses can be attached for hand-watering garden beds and potted plants.

COMPOSTERS

Creating compost from kitchen and garden waste is a key component of any organically grown garden. (Refer to chapter 2 for a lesson on soil building.) All our plants, not just the edible ones, will be healthier and happier when grown in good organic soil. Soil building is part of gardening, and because compost is needed to improve and maintain the soil health over time, designating an area for composting within the design is the first step toward achieving this. Many garden plants produce a lot of detritus, in the form of pruning clippings, autumn leaves, deadwood from trees, or just the basic cleanup that comes out of a flower or vegetable plot. All this material can and should be recycled back into the garden soil after it is composted so we need to find space to set up composters, bins, and piles.

Large piles for lawn clippings, brush, and autumn leaves are best located in out-of-the-way places where they can break down over several seasons. If there are plans for a large vegetable or herb garden, plan for a three-bin composting system nearby. This makes it easier to haul plant material to the bin and bring the completed compost back to the garden. Barrel composters and tumblers are best for kitchen scraps and should be placed close to the kitchen door for easy access. Some gardeners incorporate composting techniques as features of the design, using key-hole gardens, or growing plants in straw bales. There are also attractive structures, like trapdoor, beehive, or stacked pot composters, which can make composting a decorative feature within the design.

UTILITIES

Garden designers often need to hide existing utilities, like electric and gas meters, air conditioners, wellheads, power lines, and poles. Simply screening utilities with rows of plants or fencing is the lazy way. A better idea is to draw attention away from them by creating an interesting view that turns heads in a different direction away from the eyesore. That said, sometimes screening does work best, but it must be done so it blends into the design or transforms the eyesore into an interesting backdrop as a well-conceived artistic screen. When designing a screen around a utility, always maintain good access to any equipment for repairs or service. Don't plant woody shrubs near utilities. The shrubs may be damaged or may need to be removed to repair or replace the unit. A better idea is to plant fast-growing perennials, like ornamental grasses. These can be cut down to the ground if necessary but will grow back quickly afterward.

In the case of new construction or when remodeling a house or adding outbuildings, placement of utilities can be part of the garden plan. It's a great opportunity for the garden designer to place utilities where they will be less intrusive within the landscape. No one wants to listen to the air conditioner kick on and off while trying to enjoy a peaceful morning in the rose garden, so the garden designer should enter this conversation with the architect or builder early in the game and press their point. Contractors look for the easy way and rarely consider future enjoyment of the outdoor spaces and gardens. In many cases utility equipment can be regulated to a single location where it will be less intrusive overall. This includes identifying utility areas within a garden plan, such as places for garbage and recycling bins as well as dedicated behind-the-scenes work areas like potting tables or plant nurseries.

Décor

Garden décor elaborates on the style of a design using accessories like furniture, planters, pots, and art objects. As furnishings are used to fashion interior designs, so too can distinct décor elements play a similar role in garden design. From whimsical to classic to chic, décor items ultimately express the gardener's personal taste and should be chosen based on personal preferences, not unlike choosing the material and style of other structures. We choose and use what we like. It's as simple as that, though sometimes garden trends play a role in what we like at a given point in time. The best way to approach the selection and use of outdoor décor is the same way it's done indoors, turning to pleasing colors, textures, and forms that match the style goals of the garden rooms. Try to stick to an overarching theme or style, such as traditional or contemporary, or go eclectic, which means anything goes.

FURNITURE

If garden design means making outdoor rooms, then furnishing these rooms is part of the design. Seating areas automatically make outdoor spaces useful, but the type of furniture used in a garden is as diverse as the goals of the design and the preferences of the designer. On a practical note, a good garden design considers the space and place for specific furniture. This often begins with the patio table and chairs. A design may simply indicate the location of a table for four, six, or eight, depending on the

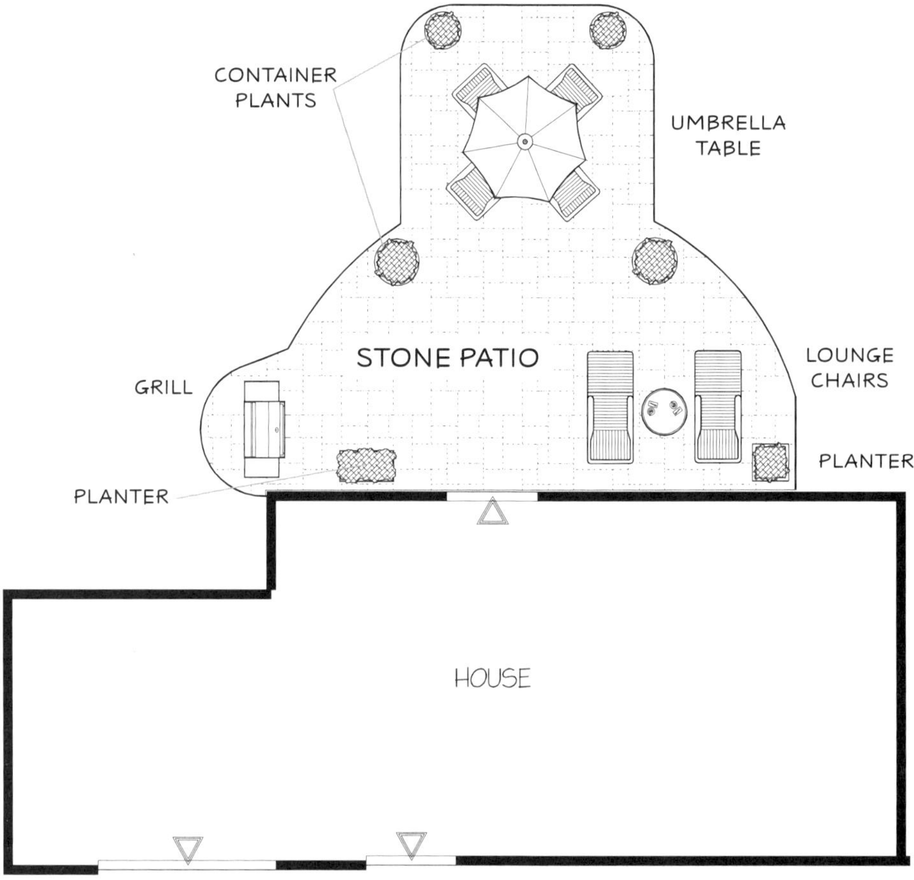

Furnish your patio or deck as you would an interior room, with the added benefit of including container plantings.

expected needs, with the actual choice of style coming later. The same goes for other furniture, like lounge chairs, picnic tables, hammocks, and sectionals. Half the fun of designing a new outdoor room is planning the furniture layout that will work best for the space and the people meant to enjoy it.

CONTAINERS AND PLANTERS

Some of the best garden décor is the containers we use for potted plants. These can range from small clay pots to antique urns and large teak boxes. A comprehensive garden design should provide opportunities for potted plants, whether on a wall, grouped along a stairway, or as focal points at the ends of garden paths. Container plants expand our plant palette to include plants that may need to come inside for winter, and they also work well as featured players in a garden, placed on hardscape, lawns, or even in planting beds. The design phase should accommodate the addition of potted plants over time as well as establish key locations for large containers and built-in planters for every season.

Always combine art in the garden with plants as it sets the scene for something special.

As another layer of interest we can add to the developing design, it is best to consider the extent and location of containers and planters during the planning phase.

ART OBJECTS

Including art in the garden is a great way to add interest and flair to a design. Some art is created specifically to be displayed in gardens and some gardens are designed specifically for the display of garden art. Either way, the placement of an art object should be carefully considered. We must decide if it will work as a stand-alone central feature in a garden room, as a focal point leading guests from one garden to another, or encountered unexpectedly. It's best to fall in love with a work and then decide if and how it can be included in a design or create a garden that needs a piece and then take the time to find it. As some art aficionados suggest, "Let the work of art find you." Always remember that the term "art" does not mean an object must be expensive or rare. There's a range of fun folk art and local crafts that fit the bill if they are suitable for the garden and the tastes of the designer.

CHAPTER 6

SOFTSCAPING: Designing with Plants

Lesson on *how to build a plant palette* based on the design concept of creating layers of canopy, understory, and ground plants presented with sections focused on designing with trees; designing with shrubs; designing with perennial flowers, including annuals, tender perennials, and bulbs; as well as how to pick plants for a beautiful and bountiful edible garden.

The Art of Designing with Plants

Gardening is all about growing plants and garden design is all about which plants to grow and where and how to grow them. The most important thing to remember when designing with plants is that they are alive and change over time. That's what makes garden design special, the fact that these essential elements are dynamic, living things. It's also what makes garden design difficult. All artists need to learn how to approach and apply their medium. Painters blend paints, musicians play notes, sculptors understand stone, and garden designers grow plants. In some instances, aspects of design, like balance, harmony, contrast, and scale, come naturally to those with inherent talent (more about these aspects of design in chapter 8). Garden designers with this intuition have an advantage over those without it, but they still need to know plants, and that's the tricky part because plants, unlike paint, notes, or stone, possess veritable life forces. Plants will grow without us and transform over time. The same isn't true for the medium of other arts or design.

The best way to know a plant is to grow a plant, and that puts us in an exciting place if we love to learn. Designing with plants requires that we understand the roles they play in the garden, refining these roles as they interact within the plant layer until we distill the purpose of each plant down to its purest essence of influence. We can create a design on a basic level and refer to plants as "shade trees," "flowering shrubs," or "ornamental grasses," and the plants will still play their important roles. But as we learn how individual plants perform their part—how a tree contributes to the canopy, how a shrub provides habitat, and how perennial flowers fill gaps on the ground—our appreciation for plants grows. Our knowledge of all types of plants begins to blossom into a working plant palette, our go-to species list. What each genus or cultivar brings to a design—its color, form, size, and life span—can be learned in a book. Books are a great place to start, but we truly know plants when we actively choose, use, and grow them over time.

◀ The best place to find healthy, unique plants is at your local gardener-owned and -operated nursery or garden center.

The Importance of Botanical Latin

Botanical Latin isn't for showing off, it's for getting it right. Garden designers should learn a little botanical Latin and use it because it allows us to specify the precise plant we want in our designs. You don't want to say "pine" for every evergreen. You don't want to just say "pine" (*Pinus*) when it's actually a limber pine (*Pinus flexilis*), and you don't want to just say limber pine when it's a weeping limber pine (*Pinus flexilis* 'Pendula') you want. It takes time to learn and remember botanical Latin names, but as you build the plant palette for your designs and become more familiar with all the different plant species and cultivars available, certain ones will stick in your head and, before you know it, you've learned the botanical name.

There is a moment in every garden designer's life when plants become partners in design. When a deeper, botanical understanding of what they are and how they live takes shape, marking the moment we graduate into garden makers. Our designs come alive as we blend, play, and carve our designs from the plants we have chosen as our collaborators. It's a joining of forces between living things. Between us, the plants, as well as the animals and insects they support, but it's the garden designer who sets things up and keeps them going, practicing the art of designing with plants.

Canopy Trees

When designing the plant layer, start from the top and work down to the ground, planning the canopy first because it will influence what can be grown beneath it. Work within the canopy layer may start with editing trees. Not every tree in a landscape is beneficial or a positive influence on a design. Diseased or dying trees are prime candidates for removal, as are poorly formed or inappropriate trees, especially nonnative invasives, like Norway maple in the eastern United States or eucalyptus in the West. Both trees are fast-growing weeds that inhibit habitat, making them difficult to work around. Edit the canopy for horticultural reasons first, then consider its impact on the design. If a tree is appropriate to the site and healthy, the first option should be to adjust the design to include the tree, rather than remove it to make way for something new. However, if nothing can be accomplished without editing the canopy, such as in a small city lot with an overgrown shade tree, eliminating that tree may be a necessary first step toward a whole new garden.

Once any editing is identified and done, the next step is to plan and plant a replacement canopy, if one is wanted. However, there does

BUILDING A PLANT PALETTE

The first step to designing with plants is to build a plant palette by compiling a list of go-to plants commonly used in your designs. This list can be built from outside sources to start but should become a list that grows through experience. Designing straight out of a book is dangerous because the plants in that book or magazine article may not be available in the nursery trade, or they may be limited or small. So, unless the design concept is to create a garden 100 percent from seed (which would be a fun challenge!), select plants that are available at a local plant nursery or garden center. Go there! Walk the aisles and take notes. Better yet, land a part-time job at a garden center and get paid while learning about plants.

Another place to start is with the plants you have experience growing. There may be trees or shrubs you know and like. There are probably perennial plants you are familiar with. Odds are, if you know them, you can find them, and they can be included in your designs. So, start building that list, which at first may seem limited and not too exciting, but it will grow over time. In just a few years of compiling plants, your plant palette will become more detailed, with different varieties and cultivars discovered along the way.

A good plant palette for a sunny temperate garden might start out something like this.

- **TREES:** Sugar maple; white fir; quaking aspen; flowering dogwood; saucer magnolia
- **SHRUBS:** Common lilac; blue hydrangea; Japanese boxwood; creeping juniper; fragrant viburnum
- **HERBACEOUS PERENNIALS:** Purple coneflower; garden phlox; hardy sage; stonecrop; lamb's ear

Continued ›

Plant Palette Full Sun

TREES

1. Sugar maple (*Acer saccharum*)
2. White fir (*Abies concolor*)
3. Quaking aspen (*Populus tremuloides*)
4. Flowering dogwood (*Cornus florida*)
5. Saucer magnolia (*Magnolia* × *soulangeana*)

1

2

SHRUBS

6. Common lilac (*Syringa vulgaris*)
7. Blue hydrangea (*Hydrangea macrophylla*)
8. Japanese boxwood (*Buxus microphylla*)
9. Creeping juniper (*Juniperus horizontalis*)
10. Fragrant viburnum (*Viburnum carlesii*)

6

7

FLOWERING PERENNIALS

11. Purple coneflower (*Echinacea purpurea*)
12. Garden phlox (*Phlox paniculata*)
13. Hardy sage (*Salvia nemorosa*)
14. Stonecrop (*Hylotelephium telephium*)
15. Lamb's ear (*Stachys byzantina*)

11

12

3
4
5
8
9
10
13
14
15

not have to be a canopy in the plant layer. For example, there may be tall trees on the neighboring property that provide a sense of canopy and so there is no need to establish one in the design. If that is the case, jump right to the subcanopy or understory, or even straight to the ground-layer plants. While there is no rule that there must be a canopy in a garden, it is good to remember that the more diverse the plant layer is, the more interesting and ecologically balanced it will be. In the best cases, we inherit an established canopy, but that is not always the case, and if we need a canopy, we must plant those trees first because they will take the longest to establish and grow to a significant size.

DESIGNING WITH TREES

When selecting trees for the canopy or subcanopy, we must envision what each tree will become in time. Most will never reach full maturity in our lifetime, like oak or beech, but we still plant them. So, we need to think about how they will contribute to the garden as they grow, not just what they will become. Trees have juvenile and mature forms, and it is important to know how a tree will change over the years. Pine trees start as bushy cones, but then drop their lower limbs to form tall trunks and open crowns. A young maple tree will start with a slim, smooth trunk and an oval canopy, but in a few decades the trunk will grow thick and ridged as the branches above expand into a wide crown. Garden designers that understand how trees grow through time are more likely to pick the right tree and plant it in the right place for the best effect from the start.

Shade Trees

Shade trees are the largest specimens in the canopy, ranging in size from 30 to 100 feet (9.1 to 30.5 m) or more. These are deciduous trees grown for their size, form, and foliage. They are the ones that can support an old tire swing our grandchildren or their children will play on someday. Designing with shade trees requires that we plant them where they have room to grow into mature specimens over many years. That means planting them out in the open, far enough from houses and outbuildings so they will not grow into or loom over them. The canopy of a mature sugar maple can grow 50 feet (15.2 m) wide, which means it should never be planted within 30 feet (9.1 m) of a house. It's okay, and in fact looks good, if a mature canopy reaches a little bit over a rooftop, but it should be just the canopy edges, not the main limbs. In a case like this, the shade tree may start out in the lawn all on its own. As the shade tree grows, the shade it casts increases, effecting a change in the plants that thrive beneath it, slowly transforming the lawn into a shade garden. This natural succession will take place over many years and should be planned for.

Deciduous shade trees can be planted on the south side of a house to keep it cool during the hot summer months and then drop their leaves, letting sunlight reach the house in winter. For the same reasons, they are also useful near patios and decks, but not too close. The extensive root system of a large shade tree, especially those with shallow roots, like maple and beech, can lift and heave patio stones. Shade trees should not be planted in small gardens where, over time, they will overwhelm the space. While predominantly selected for their form and foliage, some shade trees, like horse chestnut and hawthorn, sport showy flowers (see the Recommended Plant Lists appendix for a list of great shade trees).

Ornamental Trees

These are the 15- to 30-foot (4.5 to 9.1 m)-tall, flowering decorative trees popularized in landscape plans. Garden designers use them to create a lower canopy, or as a colorful highlight in places where a large shade tree will not fit. Almost all ornamental trees feature showy flowers that can emerge in earliest spring or at the beginning of summer. The best also have desirable attributes like interesting bark or a unique form. These are the trees we plant closer to the house, though still 20 feet (6 m) or more away to keep their branches off gutters and rooftops. Their flowers can be messy when they fall so do not plant them too close to swimming pools or water features. In an open area, the petals will all fall within a week, making an interesting color carpet on the lawn or terrace.

Ornamental trees work well singly as a feature specimen or as a low canopy within a flower bed. They also work well in groupings, on the lawn, along a walk, or a driveway. If grouped out in the open, maintain proper spacing to allow their canopies to fill in and retain their natural form. Actual spacing depends on the tree species and design goals: planted with enough room so each tree has open space around it and the sun can slip in; close enough so the edges of the canopies just touch, creating a loose screen; or even closer so the branches intertwine to form an aerial hedge. Keep maintenance like pruning in mind, which can be managed over time or initiated early on, such as pleaching to create a tree canopy tunnel.

If space allows, plan for several species of ornamental trees to provide a sequence of blooms. It is easy to have a flowering tree from earliest spring into summer starting with magnolia, followed by pear, dogwood, cherry, crabapple, snowbell, and finally stewartia. All these trees make excellent focal points in the garden, positioned at the end of a walk, or adjacent to a patio or planting bed. Their flowers are a highlight but last only a week or two so look to trees with more than a single season of interest. Fall foliage can come in many colors, from clear yellow to bright orange, scarlet red, and dusky purple. Distinctive bark color and texture can also add interest throughout the seasons as will the branching pattern and form unique to each tree, whether baked into its DNA or maintained with skilled pruning. Treat them as sui generis representatives in the garden, contributing color, form, and texture through their flowers, foliage, trunk, limbs, branches, and twigs, keeping in mind that the trees we choose for a design will shape the spirit of the garden over time (see the Recommended Plant Lists appendix for a list of great ornamental trees).

Patio Trees

These trees are for tight spaces, like courtyards and small plots, and should max out at 15 feet (4.5 m) tall and 10 feet (3 m) wide. Anything larger crowds the space, making it difficult to grow other plants. The best patio trees have light, airy crowns that let sunlight filter down to the ground. Sometimes the only thing that distinguishes these trees from shrubs is their single trunk, though a small clump, with three or five trunks is still a tree. The opposite is true too. Traditional shrubs, like hydrangea or lilac, can be trained to grow on a single stem that will work well as a patio tree. The idea is to create a canopy in miniature that fits the allotted space yet allows for a matching understory and ground layer. These trees can also be treated as sculptures, planted on their own, or with a low groundcover carpet underneath, featured as a centerpiece in a small garden room.

Dwarf varieties of popular ornamental or shade trees also fit the bill. Bred to grow slowly, they will stay in bounds. Nondwarf varieties of ornamental trees can also be good patio trees if kept to size with strict seasonal pruning. This becomes an opportunity for the gardener to display their skills and, over many years, create an in-the-ground bonsai-style tree. Of course, if the pruning master abandons the garden, a tree like this will become a problem (see the Recommended Plant Lists appendix for a list of great patio trees).

Screening Trees

Screening trees are what the name implies, trees planted to screen a view, from or to, areas adjacent to the garden. They also block sound, wind, and sun. We use evergreens for four-season screening, but there are situations where deciduous trees work, such as around swimming pools or summer gardens. There are three ways to arrange screening with trees, planted in a row, in a zigzag pattern, or as groves.

1. A single row of screening trees can do the trick, and although it may eliminate visual intrusions upon the garden, like streetlights or neighbors, a single row of identical evergreens is less capable of blocking sound. It's also uninteresting.

2. The zigzag arrangement helps fill gaps between the first row of trees, building more depth to block sound, sun, and wind. By and large it's always better to make the screening deeper and denser, and if space is limited, build depth with a double row of narrow, columnar-form trees planted in a zigzag pattern. Still, zigzag planting is basically just a fat row.

3. If we want to create an interesting screen, start thinking "groves."

Grove screening looks more natural because it employs variable sizes and irregular spacing. Seeds don't fall from trees and land in a perfectly straight line and germinate all at the same time. Grove-style planting mimics natural dispersal, as if the trees sprouted randomly and grew at different rates. Groves typically require more trees but produce a more natural-looking scheme. For example, covering 180 feet (54.8 m) with single-row screening would require twelve 10-foot (3 m) spruce trees planted in-line 15 feet (4.5 m) apart, whereas a grove screening would use 15 to 20 trees of various sizes—10-foot, 8-foot, and 6-foot (3 m, 2.4 m, and 1.8 m), and perhaps a few 12-footers (3.6 m), arranged in groups with variable spacing between 8, 10, 12, and 15 feet (2.4, 3, 3.6, and 4.5 m) apart; some pulled forward and some pushed back to form groupings.

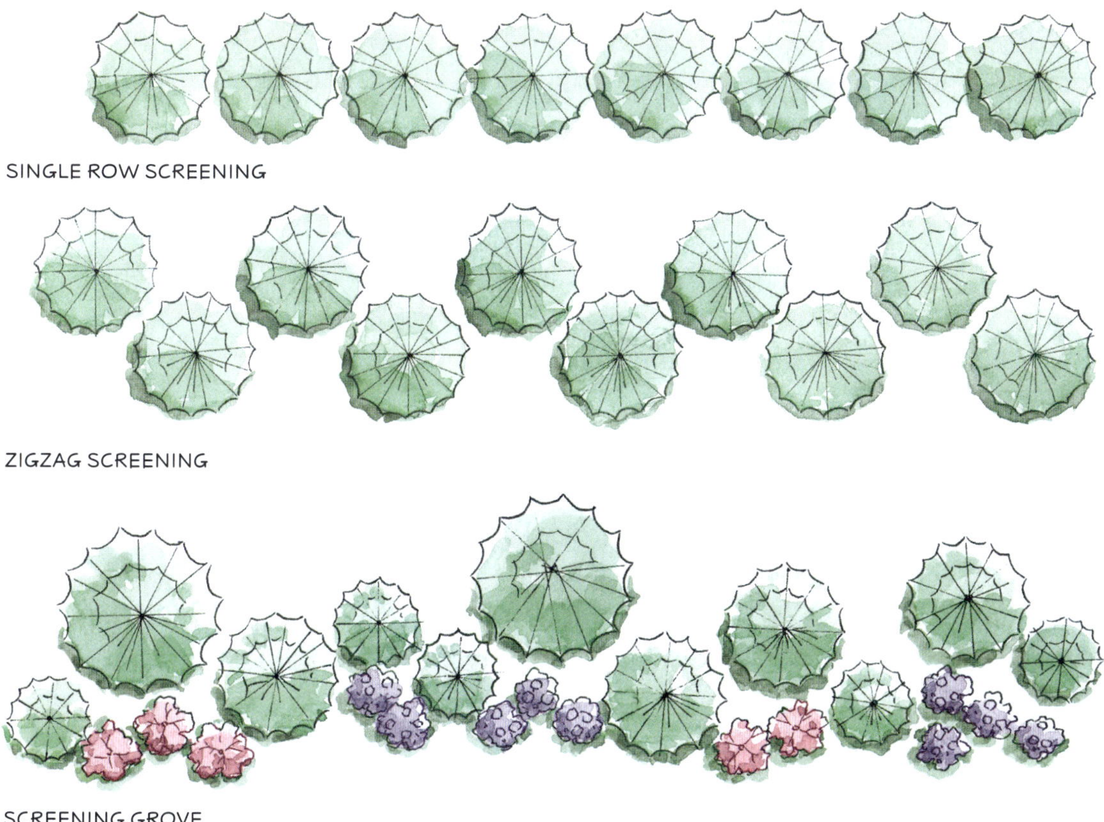

The size, type of tree, and how you arrange the trees are all equally important when planning a screening planting.

The grove arrangement automatically creates depth, serving as a better sound buffer than a single line or zigzag pattern. With this depth come pockets between the trees that are perfect for ornamental subcanopy trees, taking advantage of the evergreen backdrop. These pockets can also be planted with understory shrubs and ground-layer plants. This is good design, transforming a purely functional screening into an opportunity for a community of plants with trees, shrubs, and flowers.

A final rule for designing groves is to stick with the same species. In the wild, trees grow in groups, sharing nutrients between their roots, and preferring the same soil and sun. Nonetheless, a sequence of groves of different species can work by starting a screening with a spruce grove in the sun and ending with groves of fir trees in part shade (see the Recommended Plant Lists appendix for a list of great screening trees).

Why Not the Traditional Pine Trees (*Pinus genus*) for Screening?

Pine trees are notorious for dropping their lower limbs, making them a poor choice as a screening tree, especially if arranged in a line or zigzag pattern. Their low cost and fast growth make them a popular choice among developers and builders looking for a quick fix, but they should always be underplanted with evergreen shrubs to plan for the inevitable loss of the lower branches. Pine trees can be used as a fast-growing backdrop to a screening grove or in concert with other evergreen trees and understory shrubs that fill the gaps that develop over time.

Specialty Trees

Aerial Hedge

Any dense-canopy single-trunk deciduous tree can be trained into an aerial hedge to provide screening. The trick is to find a specimen with a tall trunk, 4, 5, or 6 feet (1.2, 1.5, or 1.8 m) from the ground to the first set of limbs, and plant them in a tight row, close enough so as their crowns expand, their branches will overlap and intertwine forming a dense screen. We then tip prune them along the top and sides to create a regular shape and increase the density of their crowns. This works great when planted in front of a wall or fence that screens the bottom few feet, allowing the trees to take over above. Excellent choices for an aerial hedge include:

- American beech (*Fagus grandifolia*)
- East Asian cherry (*Prunus serrulata*)
- Fringe tree (*Chionanthus virginicus*)
- Hawthorn (*Crataegus crus-galli*)
- Japanese crabapple (*Malus floribunda*)
- Red Maple (*Acer rubra*)
- Snowbell (*Styrax japonica*)
- Stewartia (*Stewartia psuedocamellia*)

Espalier

An espalier is a tree trained to grow flat, with a single trunk and distinct side branches trained perpendicular to the trunk. Espaliers are often planted against a wall, but they can also be grown into self-supporting specimens able to stand on their own and form a perfect low screen. For a denser screen, they're trained into multiple-trunk espaliers and supported with trellising until they grow stout enough to hold their own. Excellent choices for espaliers include:

- Apple (*Malus domestica*)
- Cornelian cherry dogwood (*Cornus mas*)
- Hornbeam (*Carpinus betulus*)
- Japanese maple (*Acer japonica*)
- Pear (*Pyrus communis*)
- Southern magnolia (*Magnolia grandiflora*)

Try an aerial hedge if you want a formal look, but only if you are willing to maintain it.

Show off your pruning skills and give your garden an air of sophistication with an espalier.

The weeping willow you plant today at the edge of a pond will provide an iconic scene for years to come.

Water-Loving Trees

Attention must be paid to the trees we choose when planting along the edge of ponds and streams or anywhere intermittent or seasonal flooding may occur. Some trees hate to have wet feet (roots) and should never be planted near water, or where the water table is close to the surface. Other species love these conditions. There is always something that can be planted almost anywhere, even directly in the water.

- American larch (*Larix laricina*)
- Bald cypress (*Taxodium distichum*)
- River birch (*Betula nigra*)
- Silver maple (*Acer saccharinum*)
- Swamp white oak (*Quercus bicolor*)
- Sweet bay magnolia (*Magnolia virginiana*)
- Tupelo (*Nyssa sylvatica*)
- Weeping willow (*Salix babylonica*)
- Western cottonwood (*Populus fremontii*)

Understory Plants

Understory plants are woody shrubs. They range in size from 2 to 15 feet (60 .9 cm to 4.5 m) tall and wide and may be deciduous or evergreen, flowering or decorative. How we employ them in the plant layer beneath the canopy determines the character of the middle ground of our gardens. Understory shrubs can be arranged as single specimens in the landscape, as mixed masses in borders, or members of hedgerow habitats but, most important, they establish a plant layer just above and below eye level. While the canopy layer hovers well above our heads, the understory shrub layer presents itself differently. A stand of trees appears as a distant mass that, upon approach, becomes a sequence of trunks we might navigate around. The understory is more likely to block our way, literally and figuratively, because it can be tall enough to screen a view, and it can prevent us from moving through even if we can see over it. The understory can also thrive on its own, without a canopy, as a garden hedge, a foundation planting, or a stand of native shrubs in a meadow or flanking a stream.

DESIGNING WITH SHRUBS

Shrubs are relatively undemanding plants requiring a modest investment that will be repaid over many years in the form of flowers, foliage, and stems. When designing with shrubs, we must appreciate their influence on the other two parts of the plant layer: the canopy and the ground plants. Shrubs bridge the gap between the two. They are the size of humans and so live closer to us than the trees overhead and the ground plants underfoot. This makes shrubs more companionable. Although they primarily reside at eye level, shrubs can also break the middle plane and encroach on the other two plant layers; when used effectively, they can provide more significant masses of flowers and foliage than trees and ground plants combined. The main difference between a shrub and a tree is that a shrub is a multistem plant whose stems do not die down to the ground in winter, distinguishing them from most ground plants. As a result, shrubs contribute to the winter garden, and even if they lose their leaves after the first frosts, the stems and branches persist, serving as refuge for overwintering birds and providing captivating forms beneath fresh snowfalls.

Shrubs are effective as hedges and screens, trained against walls or fences to create a backdrop for a planting bed or to enclose a garden room. They also work well on their own, as visual anchors among other plants, along a curve in a path, or placed discreetly beside a garden shed. Low shrubs can mark the boundaries of a walkway or define the geometry of a border with in-line rows or curves. Masses of shrubs are perfect for holding together a slope, quite literally as their roots keep the soil in place, as well as visually, providing a tapestry of colors, textures, and forms carpeting the hillside. Most shrubs start the season with blooms of white or shades of pink, red, blue, purple, or yellow, then transition into summer with verdant foliage ranging from chartreuse to deepest green, and finally passing into autumn displays of burnished gold, orange, and scarlet. Many shrubs also sport silver, purple, red, gold, or blue foliage, amplifying their embellishment of the garden in all seasons (more on designing plant tapestries like this in chapter 7).

Choosing the right shrub for a particular use in a garden design requires forethought and understanding the cultural needs of the plant: its potential for vegetative growth, flowering, and fruiting; its contribution to the senses of scent, taste, and touch as well as how it may create habitat, especially for birds. Size and location are key, but so too are character, impression, and discernment, so think of shrubs as companions that hold a place in the garden in all four seasons, cycling through spring, summer, and fall on into winter. They grow larger, laying more claim and consequence with each passing year. Or they may be artistically sculpted into maturity, trained by pruning to hold a preferred shape and size. But, before we add any shrub to our designs, we must envision the future of what it will become, transforming from a collection of insubstantial twigs in a 5-gallon (18.9 L) nursery pot into an architecture of branches blanketed with leaves and seasonally draped in blossoms.

Flowering Deciduous Shrubs

Most flowering shrubs are deciduous, and almost all bloom in spring. There is, however, a range of bloom times among them, making diversity a key for extended flowering, though color doesn't come just from flowers. Foliage also provides shades of summer chartreuse, purple, gold, and variations of every shade of green. These all arrive with a multitude of textures, large and small, on a variety of forms, such as mounding, rounded, vaselike, or weeping. Nonetheless, with all these attributes in mind, our first consideration when selecting shrubs should be size.

Large flowering shrubs, 6 to 15 feet (1.8 to 4.5 m) tall and wide, are a mainstay in gardens large and small. In small spaces, they can dominate, setting the stage in a garden bed with companion plants shining nearby, or as sentinels, next to a patio or porch, where their bower of blooms returns every spring followed by unfurling leaves that provide summer shade and seclusion. In large gardens, large shrubs fill space and cover the ground in mixed groupings. When sequenced properly, a combination of shrubs will provide blooms for months in a row. However, one species planted en masse can memorably overwhelm the senses for a week or two before receding into the background.

Medium and small flowering shrubs, 2 to 6 feet (60.9 cm to 1.8 m) tall and wide are often companion plants among their larger cousins, the trees, or ground plants. They play a supporting role, just below our sight line, knitting together larger planting schemes or filling space between specimen trees or structures like paths and patios. In a small garden room, a medium-size shrub can act like a large shrub, able to enclose or screen a space, or hold its own as a singular specimen. Small shrubs, less than 3 feet (0.9 m) tall, always work best in groups no matter the garden size, unless they are part of the ground-plant layer, serving as punctuation and winter interest among a collection of perennial flowers. In formal gardens, the smallest shrubs are used to line paths and borders or enclose parterres (see the Recommended Plant Lists appendix for a list of great flowering deciduous shrubs).

Parterre

Aptly defined as a level space in a garden or yard occupied by an arrangement of flower beds, parterres play an important role in formal gardens, providing a geometrical framework within which riots of colorful plants may be restrained. Typically formed by tightly planted mini hedges of broadleaf evergreens with dense foliage, like boxwood and Japanese holly, or subshrubs like rosemary or heather, parterre gardens can be extensive or diminutive, depending on the scale of the garden room where they reside.

Get fancy and find a spot in your garden for a formal parterre planting.

A Note on Invasive Shrubs

Many popular landscape shrubs, like burning bush, Japanese barberry, and glossy buckthorn, have fallen out of favor among gardeners because they are inclined to "jump the fence" and seed into the wild. Once free, they spread, unhindered by indigenous insects or foragers, quickly outpacing the growth of native plants. Whole swaths of woodlands and fields have been swallowed up by these pernicious invasives. Some intransigent gardeners continue to grow them, thinking they can keep them contained, but we know better and so most of these plants are banned from sale in multiple states. Each had their day in our gardens, burning bush with its striking scarlet fall foliage, barberry for its immunity to browsing deer, and buckthorn for speedy growth in subpar soils. Thankfully, there are other options to choose from, such as blueberry (*Vaccinium* spp.) for scarlet fall foliage, American barberry (*Berberis canadensis*) to discourage deer, and black chokeberry (*Aronia melanocarpa*), which grows in poor soils. Some other familiar shrubs considered invasive and best avoided include bush honeysuckle, butterfly bush, nandina, privet pyracantha, and Russian olive.

Evergreen Shrubs

Evergreen shrubs are excellent anchors in winter gardens because they hold their leaves through every season. Evergreen doesn't mean they never drop their leaves or needles (note: A needle is a leaf!); they just never drop them all at once. This transition provides a moment of interest with decorative conifers when as many as a third of their needles change color, often a nice contrasting yellow or gold, and hold awhile. Unlike conifers, broadleaf evergreens sport showy flowers like their deciduous cousins, but the blooms are set off among masses of dark, shiny foliage rather than clinging to spring stems. Use large specimens of either type for privacy screening, and small ones as fancy features, jewels of needle green or blue-black leaves in mixed borders filled with flowers (see the Recommended Plant Lists appendix for a list of great evergreen shrubs).

Decorative Conifers

Typically, dwarf cultivars of cedar, cypress, fir, hemlock, pine, and spruce, decorative conifers are best used as stand-alone sculptures in clearings or as punctuations within large planting schemes. Employed in masses or groups, they lose their individual charm, though small varieties work together well in the ground layer. They come in all shapes, sizes, and colors. Globes and pyramids are excellent visual anchors, whereas weepers work wonders perched on a rock outcropping or above a wall, and spreading forms can carpet the ground or scramble over walls. Dwarf varieties hold at 2 to 10 feet (60.9 cm to 3 m) tall and wide but given forty years or more they can grow as big as a bus. Colors range from every shade of green to blue, silver, yellow, and gold, with white variegations thrown in for good measure. Their needles can be short or long, stiff or soft, fat or slim, twisted or straight. Then there is the bonus of their cones. They come in all shapes and sizes, and eye-catching hues of blue, brown, green, purple, and silver.

Flowering Broadleaf Evergreens

With sizes ranging from very large to very small, flowering broadleaf evergreens provide a unique opportunity to grow shrubs blanketed with blooms in spring or summer that won't become a scaffold of sticks come winter. As evergreens, they can effectively enclose a space singly or in groups, and as flowering shrubs they add color and charm above and beyond the typical evergreen hedge. Care must be taken to give them sheltered locations, as winter winds can desiccate their foliage and stunt the flowers, most of which are formed the previous season. Give them space to grow and leave them unpruned so they can develop their natural form. Excessive shearing may keep them to size, but they will weaken over time or form dense, bushy tops that shade lower limbs resulting in a leggy plant. Most of these are shade lovers, meaning they are perfect understory plants happy to grow near dense canopy trees. The trick is getting them started early by planting them with the trees so they all grow up together and learn to live side by side. (See the Recommended Plant Lists appendix for a list of great evergreen shrubs).

Traditional Hedges vs. Habitat Hedgerows

Traditional hedges typically consist of one species of plant lined in a row, but there are other ways to create hedging. One is to think in terms of a hedgerow. Hedgerows are messier rows of shrubs, often of mixed native species, that function as a traditional hedge but with the added benefit of providing the potential for a sequence of blooms throughout the spring instead of a bloom period of a single species. A diverse hedgerow's distinct advantage as bird habitat comes from different densities and branching layers for nesting along with seasonal berries and seeds for foraging. Planting a hedgerow is a more casual affair than a traditional hedge and does not need pruning once established. Spacing should fall somewhere between the mature span of each shrub. For example, if the stated mature spread is 6 feet (1.8 m) wide, plant it 4 feet (1.2 m) from its neighbor to ensure they will grow together. But don't plant too close, or the relaxed look of the shrubs in combination will be lost, and too much density will result in poor air circulation, leading to fungal diseases.

HEDGING

Hedges are garden walls made of plants, but it takes a special kind of plant to make a hedge. Hedge plants must exhibit dense growth to create an adequate screen but, more important, they must respond well to shearing so they can be kept tidy and to size. When planting a hedge, it is important to get the spacing right and plant them tight. The idea is to encourage the plants to intertwine and grow together, as if they were one long plant, because that is what they will become. Planning for size is also key. Some hedge plants grow tall and wide, some stay small, even without excessive pruning. A good idea is to envision how high of a hedge wall is wanted and select a species that will hit that height in five years' time or sooner, whether it's a narrow, 3-foot (0.9 m) hedge designed to segregate but not fully enclose, or a 12-foot (3.6 m) hedge for complete privacy (see the Recommended Plant Lists appendix for a list of great hedging shrubs).

You can clip your flowering hedges into formal shapes, keep them pruned to size, or allow them to grow wild.

Hedging Shrubs with Flowers

There are several flowering shrubs that can be used for traditional hedges because they respond well to pruning. However, regular pruning often stunts flower production, which is their real charm. Nonetheless, all the following shrubs are often used in hedging applications:

- Common lilac (*Syringa vulgaris*)
- Forsythia (*Forsythia xintermedia*)
- Japanese camellia (*Camellia japonica*)
- Nannyberry viburnum (*Viburnum lentago*)
- Oleander (*Nerium oleander*)
- Red tip photinia (*Photinia robusta*)

VINES

Vines are specialty plants that can climb to great heights in trees or creep along the ground, but they are most often used within the understory layer to scramble up pergolas, arbors, and walls. The key to designing with vines is to understand how they grow and what they can accomplish over time. Vines can become a flower-laden bower supported by stout branches, twining tendrils reaching their way up a lamppost, or a blanket of suckering stems covering a brick wall. Vines are perfect plants for small urban gardens or anywhere ground space is limited. Their main stems can slip between other plants, with roots nestled in tight spaces, and still produce a bounty of blooms or a lush foliage screen or ceiling. Another great option is to support a vine growing in a planter or pot with a trellis or tuteur (see the Recommended Plant Lists appendix for a list of great climbing vines).

GROUNDCOVER SHRUBS

Shrubs that grow low and spread across the ground are useful as a transition from understory to ground layer. Many shrubs hug the ground naturally, never rising more than a foot or two above the ground, though some with arching habits will reach 3 feet (0.9 m) or more as they advance through the garden. Use them as fillers between larger shrubs, as a uniform carpet nestled among the trunk of a canopy tree, or as cover companions for tall ground-layer plants. Choose among evergreens, both conifer and broadleaf, as well as deciduous types that provide profusions of flowers and distinct fall foliage. Mass them close so they knit together quickly. A nice trick is to underplant groundcover shrubs with spring flowering bulbs, like daffodils or tulips, that poke through, bloom, then fade away (find more ideas like this in chapter 7; see the Recommended Plant Lists appendix for a list of great groundcover shrubs).

Understory Fragrance

Because shrubs tend to be at or near eye level, they are perfect candidates to introduce fragrance into the garden where it will be best appreciated. However, we need to be patient when planning for fragrance from shrubs, even if we include those known for their strong perfume. It takes time for shrubs to grow large enough to produce sufficient blooms for a fragrance that is noticeable in the landscape. For this reason, focus on shrubs with flowers that have strong, not-subtle scents, knowing full well that even these will take time to provide a significant outdoor aroma.

Superfragrant Shrubs and Vines

The following list of shrubs and vines are all superfragrant, meaning they will make an immediate aromatic impact in the garden and, as they grow larger, they will become so fragrant at peak flowering season their aroma will pervade the garden.

- Abelia (*Abelia xgrandiflora*)
- Carolina allspice (*Calycanthus floridus*)
- Common honeysuckle (*Lonicera periclymenum*)
- Common lilac (*Syringa vulgaris*)
- Fragrant viburnum (*Viburnum xcarlcephalum*)
- Gardenia (*Gardenia jasminoides*)
- Honeysuckle bush (*Lonicera fragrantissima*)
- Mock orange (*Philadelphus coronarius*)
- Star jasmine (*Trachelospermum jasminoides*)

Ground Plants

The ground layer is the most diverse sublayer within the plant layer at large, providing countless opportunities for color, texture, and form from a multitude of herbaceous species. Despite the name, ground plants can range in height from less than 1 inch (2.5 cm) to 6 feet (1.8 m) tall or taller. This layer also consists of several layers, including perennials, annuals, bulbs, and tender plants, all combined and well timed for when each will emerge in spring, flower, set seed, then fade into fall. This diversity allows us to design layers within layers, marking the moment when true complexity enters our designs. Basic planting plans will include canopy, understory, and ground plants, but too often with plant palettes that are limited for simplicity's sake or in an effort for easy elegance. This is fine, and a smart way to design, however, true diversity within the ground-plant layer opens a world of opportunity to transition and blend within a lushness unattainable from any other garden design element, or for that matter, any other plant layer. The ground-layer plants are what propel designs beyond mere landscaping, or outdoor planning, into living, breathing gardens.

Designing with Herbaceous Perennials

Herbaceous perennials come in a multitude of shapes, sizes, and colors and their role in the plant layer is to tie together everything, between the trunks of the canopy trees and the masses of understory shrubs. In a garden, on any exposed soil, wherever there isn't hardscape, there must be plants, and if those plants aren't going to be weeds, we need to decide what will grow there, plant it, promote it, and let it take hold. Naturally developing wild landscapes do this on their own. The forest trees slowly infiltrate an opening, along with understory shrubs, but still a ground layer of just a few pioneer species of plants grows first, covering the soil and protecting it, building a base upon which the future ecosystem can establish. If we are designing a self-sustaining garden, or practicing regenerative gardening, that is exactly how we establish our plant layer, but in most cases, we want to have a little more fun and fill it out with a variety of herbaceous perennials for a "better than nature" look. That's true garden design.

SUN-LOVING PERENNIALS

The first thing to consider when choosing the plants that will make up the ground layer is the sun exposure on the site. Full to part-sun conditions allow us to use a variety of plants, but we need to know if it is truly full sun, meaning six, eight, or more hours of direct sunlight per day. Or is it partial sun, meaning less than six but more than three hours of direct sunlight. This is where it gets tricky because, often, under the canopy, there is a range of exposures so we need plants that perform well in both sun and partial sun. This requires plant research, but experience and experimentation are our best resources, and another reason the best way to build a plant palette is to include plants we have grown before.

Choosing the right plants from the start is crucial when selecting woody plants for the canopy and understory, but we can get away with trial and error in the ground layer because herbaceous plants are easier to adjust. We never want to replant a tree or shrub because it's in the wrong spot, for sun, shade, or any other reason, but herbaceous plants are easily transplanted. In fact, we should expect the herbaceous ground layer to require editing over time. Some plants will thrive and spread. Others will weaken and die, depending upon changing growing conditions or simple bad luck, like a summer drought or harsh winter.

As the canopy and understory layers grow, the ground-layer conditions will change. Larger tree canopies cast more shade, affecting the sun exposure on the ground plants. Understory shrubs will encroach on ground plants, meaning those that start in sun, filling the gaps between new shrubs, should be considered placeholders that will slowly die out as the shrubs grow in size. In cases like this, we should plant what will fill in fast and act as a living mulch while the understory knits together, keeping in mind that the design's plant layer, especially the ground plants, will evolve continually. With or without canopy or understory companions, we can expect the ground layer to change as these plants compete and adapt, or we may decide to add to or edit what we planted in the first place.

Sunlight powers all plant growth so sunny perennials typically grow fast and can get big if they are genetically predisposed to do so, though there are plenty of low-growing, diminutive sunny perennials. While height is a major consideration when selecting a plant for the ground layer, spread also matters. Some plants grow in clumps and expand slowly. Others propagate via underground stems and can colonize quickly. The trick is to understand each plant's growth habit and plant them where they fit best. Sunny perennials often have smaller leaves more suited to growing in hot sunny spots. Small leaves help them release less water through transpiration, making some plants drought-tolerant, like santolina or blue star. A preponderance of small foliage plants affects how we combine them with others. Too much of the same thing tends to get lost, making the planting plans for sunny spots difficult to design (more on how to work with different plant textures in chapter 7; see the Recommended Plant Lists appendix for a list of great sun-loving perennials).

SHADE-LOVING PERENNIALS

Plants that prefer shade are useful especially when the garden canopy is already established and there is plenty of shade from the start. It's usually a bad idea to try to change the sun exposure beneath a large shade tree, though it can be accomplished by thinning the canopy to allow more sun to reach the ground. But don't make the mistake of removing the lower limbs (limbing up) hoping to find more sun. Limbing up wrecks the tree's natural form and leaves a telephone-pole trunk with a lollipop canopy. Besides, there are plenty of plants we can use in shady spots. Shade plants prefer less than four hours of direct sunlight per day, and some do just fine with almost no direct sun at all. Dappled shade is the best kind of shade, since the shade lover is never stressed by a blast of full sun. Shade plants tend to have larger leaves because they need more surface area to collect sufficient sunlight to grow. This provides the opportunity to create lush plantings in the shade, though in general, shady plants take a little more time to establish and fill in. So, it is a good idea to plant them closer together than their recommended spacing.

Shade-loving plants typically have less showy flowers than sunny perennials, but they still have their moments when the blooms are impactful. Once again, it is all about the power of the sun. Shade perennials tend to put more energy into making roots and leaves. Although there are plenty that have beautiful flowers, like hellebore and turtlehead, we need massing to make it work. A single plant may make only a single bloom, but multiple plants mean multiple flowers, producing a better effect, especially in larger spaces. Single specimens may stand out in a tiny, shady spot where each can be appreciated individually, but that's a special circumstance. Instead, create a combination of three, four, or more species that look good together with or without flowers (see the Recommended Plant Lists appendix for a list of great shade-loving perennials).

BLOOM PERIOD

An important part of choosing plants for the ground layer is providing seasonal or year-round interest in the form of flowers. Most trees and shrubs bloom in spring, often early spring, but there are many perennials that bloom in summer or fall. In fact, the range of bloom times among perennial flowers runs from early spring, like creeping phlox and dianthus, into summer, with astilbe and coneflower, all the way through autumn with windflower and asters. Truly, there isn't a time during the growing season when there isn't a perennial that could be in bloom. The thing many new garden designers struggle with is finding enough plants to provide a sequence of flowers throughout the season. It's easier to pull off in a large garden, where lots of plants can be grown together so something is always in bloom. However, even this can be limiting, since most perennials bloom for just a few weeks, making adequate overlap a challenge. There are some, however, that bloom much longer, for a month or more, like Russian sage and black-eyed Susan, and others that can be cut back or sheared to provide a second flush of flowers, like catmint and coreopsis.

A simple way to design for three-season flowering—spring, summer, and fall—is to build a plant palette with three diverse species, one that blooms in spring, one in summer, and another in fall. Because most familiar plants come in many different varieties, or cultivars, with different bloom colors, but still bloom at roughly the same time of year, we can have some variety within each season while sticking to a single species. For example, iris in spring, astilbe in summer, and asters come fall. Another option, best for larger properties where there is more room for more gardens, is to set a season for each garden or planting bed. For example, design a specific "spring garden" replete with flowers from early April into May and June—the time when that garden room is the place to be. Then find another location for "summer borders" where the blooms peak from June through July and August. Then, make an "autumn garden" where late-season flowers and ornamental grasses steal the show until frost arrives (learn more about seasonal gardens in chapter 9).

FOCUS ON FOLIAGE

Early on, practiced garden designers learn the mantra "flowers are fleeting; foliage is forever." If there is one key ingredient to designing within the plant layer, and especially with ground-layer plants, it is to focus less on flowers and rely more on foliage. Of course, everyone loves flowers, and they will always play an important role in our designs, but the reality is that most perennials have relatively short bloom periods. However, we get season-long impact from their foliage long after their flowers have faded. Leaves come in many shapes, sizes, and even colors, primarily green. But there are many shades of green. In fact, there can be a vast difference from plant to plant, such as the pale green of a hardy sage compared to the almost black green of Lenten rose. On top of that, there are plants sporting leaves of blue, gold, purple, silver, and yellow as well as with white stripes, blotches, and dots, and other variegated patterns. Think of flowers as bonus moments in the plant's life cycle and put more thought into the foliage.

INCLUDING ANNUALS

While the bloom time of perennial plants is limited, annuals will bloom all season long, making them key contributors to ground-layer designs. Adding a layer of annuals to our planting plans

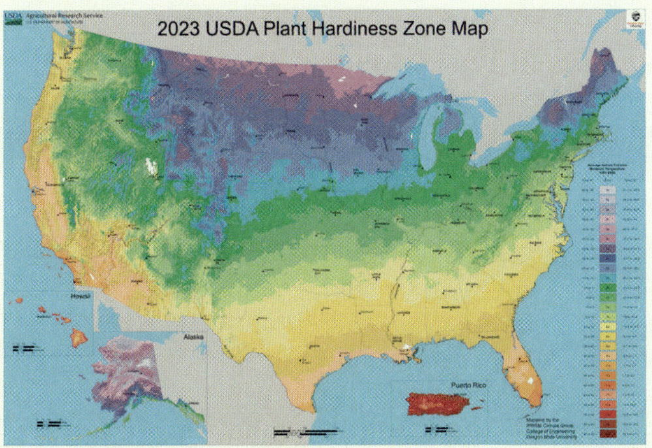

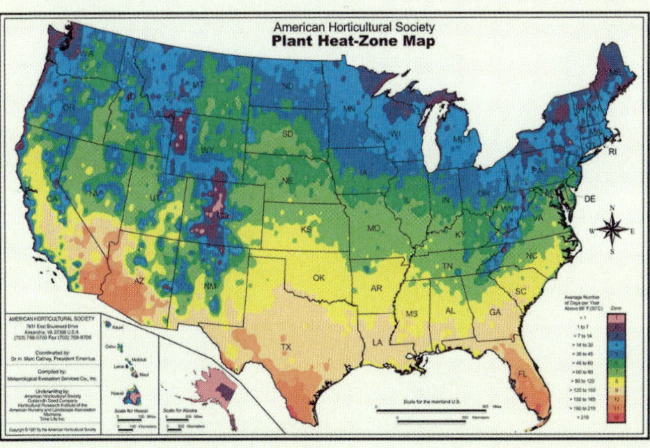

Make sure the plants in your plant palette match the hardiness zone of your garden.

Summer heat also makes a difference, so find out which heat zone your garden is in.

A Note on Hardiness Zones and Heat Zones

Winter hardiness is a measure of the average low temperature experienced in a region each year. It is designated by a number, from 1 to 13, with 1 being coldest and 13 warmest. All plants possess a winter hardiness range, for example Norway spruce, with a range of 2 through 7, meaning it will survive just fine from northern Minnesota, south through Missouri. This matters most for trees, shrubs, and perennial plants because they are meant to survive the winter and come back year after year. Annuals, on the other hand, by definition, live a single season.. However, most of our ornamental annuals are perennial plants, but with a high winter hardiness number, such as 11 or 12, meaning they are indigenous to places close to the equator. Still, we can grow them in our temperate gardens during the warm months until winter sets in.

There is another aspect of plant hardiness we may need to consider, and this is related to summer hardiness. A heat-zone map, developed by the American Horticultural Society, indicates the average number of days each year above 86 degrees Fahrenheit (30 degrees Celsius), designated with a number ranging from 1 to 12, with 12 being the most consistently warm. Recognizing heat zones is especially important where summers are challenging, like much of the western and southwestern United States. In these dry summer regions, winter is when plants can relax and enjoy cooler temperatures with regular rain. Working within hardiness and heat-zone challenges is one more argument for the use of indigenous plants in our designs because what grows natively near our gardens is likely to grow happily within them.

can make up for the limitations of woody plants and perennials as short-term bloomers. This can be accomplished in a few ways. First, using annuals as bedding plants in formal spaces. In this instance annuals are planted en masse, either in beds of their own where they can pack a colorful punch, or in groups beneath trees and alongside shrubs. This could be where early spring ephemerals like trout lily and trillium have faded and the annuals can flower until frost. Bedding annuals are typically lower-growing plants that fill in quickly, and while some, like geraniums or petunias, need weekly deadheading (removing spent blooms to encourage more flowers), others, like impatiens and begonias, won't, as they naturally drop their blossoms and keep making more.

Another way to use annuals in garden beds is as companions to the perennials. These specialty annuals fill the gaps for the first few seasons as new perennials are establishing, or provide season-long flowers that bridge the bloom times between established perennials. The trick is to slip them between the perennials throughout the bed using varieties that grow large enough to hold their own among the perennials they are with. Mealycup sage and spider flower are two excellent sun-loving examples. Then again, some annuals self-seed and come back the next season on their own. This can be a happy accident or planned. Plants like nasturtium and violet are excellent self-seeders and will often pop up in places we never expected them, surprising us year after year (see the Recommended Plant Lists appendix for a list of great annuals).

WORKING WITH BULBS

Bulbs are ground-layer plants included too often as an afterthought, when in truth they can contribute significantly to the ground layer and should always be included. The reason garden designers sometimes forget to include bulbs is because bulbs are typically planted in fall, long after most gardeners think about putting new herbaceous plants in the ground. Savvy designers build planting plans with bulbs in mind, then set aside some time and money to order and plant them come fall. Some spring bulbs emerge early, like snowdrops and crocus, well before any perennial plants, and well before it's safe to plant annuals outside, making them the only blooms in the garden during those late-winter and early spring weeks. Bulbs look great growing in groups in a meadow or lawn but can also contribute to planting beds before the summer perennials emerge. However, because the foliage from bulbs looks messy as they finish, a good technique is to plant them among perennials that will camouflage the finishing foliage as it recharges the bulb for the following season.

Summer-blooming bulbs, like ornamental onions and lilies, add another layer to ground-layer plantings, with blooms that float on tall stems above smaller plants. Planning how these flowering bulbs combine with their neighbors is key, though a large bank of Madonna lilies growing along a rustic fence or wall will make a memorable moment filled with fragrance and color. Slip them between flowering perennials throughout a planting bed to create a consistent theme or use just a few to strategically fill spots where spring flowers fade away.

Like annuals, bulbs can also be used as bedding plants, arranged tightly in large numbers. Tulips and hyacinths are popular choices for this kind of treatment, providing spring color unmatched any other way. A sequence of blooms can be planned, using early-, mid-, and late-season tulips, all planted together in a single bed, letting each emerge in its own time. As the flowers fade, however, plants like these typically need to be dug out and composted, as most are bred to perform best for just one season, and waiting for this mass of bulbs to recharge leaves an ugly patch in the garden. An alternative approach is to grow bulbs that naturalize in place. These are cultivars that propagate underground, year after year, and spread through garden beds, lawns, woodlands, or fields all on their own. Popular choices include daffodils and Siberian squill. The result is an ever-expanding carpet of blooms that come and go each spring, hallmarks of a new garden year (see the Recommended Plant Lists appendix for a list of great flowering bulbs).

ADDING TENDER PERENNIALS

Advanced gardeners and garden designers have one more layer they can add to the ground plants: tender perennials. These are plants that, with a little help and attention, come back year after year even though they are not hardy in that region. Most are tropical plants, native to climates close to the earth's equator where temperatures in spring, summer, fall, and winter are almost identical. In temperate climates, winter will kill these plants so they must be dug each fall, stored over winter, and planted again in spring. In warmer regions, we can sometimes leave them in place and devise a way to keep them insulated underground, such as covering them with evergreen boughs or planting them in winter-warm microclimates. The beauty of these plants is they act like annuals and bloom throughout the season beside winter-hardy perennial plants, or in dedicated beds all their own. It's one more way to add another layer of interest to the garden (see the Recommended Plant Lists appendix for a list of great tender perennials).

EDIBLE GARDENS

Edible gardens are designed to grow food. This food can be in many forms, from simple vegetables like beans, corn, lettuce, peppers, or tomatoes to fields of pumpkins and squash. It also includes herbs, like basil, oregano, and parsley, and fruits such as blueberries, currants, raspberries, and strawberries as well as orchard trees with apples, cherries, pears, and more. Edible gardens contain edible plants. Plain and simple. However, there is no rule that says an edible garden must consist of just edible plants, or that edible plants can't be grown elsewhere in the garden. Some edible plants, like borage, kale, or even blueberry bushes, have decorative attributes making them suitable for use in

Your home food garden plot does not have to look like a farm with monotonous crop rows.

the designed plant layer. Kale is a great sunny border foliage plant; borage sports beautiful flowers, and rows of blueberry shrubs make excellent hedging.

The concept of using edible plants in ornamental gardens is called "embedded edibles," and while not everyone chooses to do it, it's important because it breaks the typical construct of growing food separately from the rest of the garden, oftentimes fenced off and out of sight. The traditional vegetable garden has the reputation of being a place of toil, where we perform required chores to grow and harvest food, sapping the inherent interest, beauty, and fun from the process. Creative garden designers see the edibleness of a plant as just another attribute, like color, texture, or form, and as a result, our edible plants can jump the fence from the vegetable patch into other garden rooms. Even better, the entire concept of the segregated vegetable garden can be discarded and replaced with the idea of an edible garden as a setting to enjoy the fruits of our labor. Designed to grow food, but also beauty, scent, touch, and taste.

There are several ways to grow edible plants. We can lay out nice, neat crop rows, turn the soil to make garden beds, sow the seeds of what we want, then weed the beds and tend the plants until harvest time. All we need is full sun exposure, some decent dirt, and a fence to keep the critters out. Or we can design an edibles garden differently, still with long rows if we want them, but maybe we curve them just for fun, and add a small, squared plot at the intersection of two perpendicular paths. We can also mix our crops, basil with tomatoes, corn with squash and beans, or several lettuce types over lapping and interweaving in geometric patterns. In other words, no more boring rows that look like work. The edible garden becomes a place where, yes, there are chores to be done, but there's also a spot with some shade, a pergola, and a picnic table, where we can sit and sample the rewards. Maybe there's a firepit for late-night gatherings after the grape harvest, or a playful plot filled with strawberries for the kids. Let's not forget the flowers, not just those edible ones like calendula and squash blossoms, but as full-fledged swaths of bloom to attract the pollinators we need to make the fruits and vegetables we want. Consider including beds dedicated to cut flowers, like dahlias, delphiniums, snapdragons, and zinnias, for an artistic harvest. All of this can be the making of an edible garden.

Vegetables vs. Edibles

Let's clarify what a vegetable is. "Vegetable" is an imprecise term referring to the edible parts, whether roots, stems, leaves, fruits, seeds, or even flowers, of plants we grow. Traditional vegetables are herbaceous plants that provide edible roots (carrots), stems (rhubarb), leaves (lettuce), fruits (tomatoes), seeds (corn), and flowers (nasturtium). They are what we think of when we think "vegetable," and so plants like these will always play an important role whenever we choose to grow plants for food. There are, however, other edible plants, like berries (grapes), drupes (peach), and pomes (apples) as well as a treasury of herbs. Edible gardens, therefore, are more inclusive than vegetable gardens, hence the advent of the term.

Edible gardens should be located close to the house, easy to reach on a whim, allowing us to stroll out to casually gather some lettuce, tomatoes, and cucumbers for a fresh salad, some hot peppers for salsa, or a bunch of basil for pesto. Gardens that are close to the house are visited more frequently, and thus better tended, observed, and enjoyed. A good strategy is to place the edibles right off a terrace, alongside an outdoor kitchen, or design a path through the edible garden leading to another popular spot outside, like the driveway or garden shed. While full, all-day sun is best for growing edibles with large, fleshy fruits, such as zucchini, eggplant, or melons, patches of part sun can still produce leafy greens, onions, and herbs. So don't discount a slightly shady patch—include it in the plan and grow what will work. Edible crops also have different planting and harvest times, allowing us to design for these changes during the season, when, for example, the radishes come out and the peppers go in, or planning for crops that must be rotated to allow the soil to recover, such as for tomatoes (more on edible companion plants and crop sequencing in chapter 7; see the Recommended Plant Lists appendix for a list of great vegetables).

Culinary Herbs

Herbs like basil, cilantro, and parsley can be grown in and around other crops, but sometimes it's useful to give them their own dedicated plot. There is a long-standing tradition of designing herb gardens as separate rooms within the context of a larger garden, as a decorative space as well as a working herbary. The historical, cultural, and medicinal significance of herbs instills them with an irresistible magic that's easy to tap into when designing gardens for them. A patch of chamomile is not just beautiful, it's also a source for a unique tea as well as history. The name refers to ancient Greece and means "ground apple" because of the appley scent released when the stems are crushed. Chamomile also plays a role in a funny folklore among gamblers as having an uncanny ability to attract money. While almost all plants have some element of folklore attached to them, herbs seem especially suited to tales such as these.

A good idea is to plan an herb garden close to, or as part of, an outdoor kitchen. Most culinary herbs do well in pots or planters, providing an opportunity to grow them within this structural element and well within reach when they're wanted. There are perennial herbs as well as annual and biennial (two-season plants) herbs, which provide opportunities within an herb garden design for areas that can change from year to year, as well as places where plants can establish and mature. Combining herbs grown in the ground with potted herbs near a small table and chairs is a great way to grow what we want and design a garden room that is a pleasure to linger in (see the Recommended Plant Lists appendix for a list of great culinary herbs).

Fruits and Berries

While botanically a tomato is a fruit AND, technically, a berry, the discussion here relates to the common usage of these terms and the plants they represent. The fruits we are referring to here come from woody plants, trees, and shrubs, like apple and peach, or blackberry and boysenberry. As members of the canopy and understory layers, they may perform as edible plants in an ornamental setting or as decorative plants adding interest to an edible garden. There are cautionary tales of using fruit trees in ornamental gardens, mostly because of the mess they make with fallen fruits, especially near patio areas, decks, and swimming pools. In those places, it's better to plant the ornamental versions that don't produce fruit. However, a fruiting apple left to grow on its own, unpruned, with no intentions to harvest, can make a great addition out in a field where the profusion of apple blossoms will provide a spring show for our eyes and a bounty for pollinators. The resulting apples will not go to waste, but are bound to feed the local raccoons, woodchucks, and deer. Rambling wild berries can do the same, working well along woodland margins and ravines where adventurous adolescents and resident bears can gather a mid-morning snack. Nonetheless, these plants can be tamed for appearance and harvest within the garden as orchards and berry walks.

Orchards

An orchard can be a large open field planted with fruit trees, like apples, peaches, pears, and plums, spaced in grids to allow adequate space for each tree to grow to its full potential. An orchard can also be three dwarf trees planted

What About a Nuttery?

A nuttery is an orchard of trees that produces edible nuts, not fruits. These include almonds, butternuts, chestnuts, hazelnuts, hickories, pecans, and walnuts. The nut trees also make excellent canopy trees, as ornamentals or even shade trees once fully mature. Even as ornamentals, they will continue to make nuts to be gathered by humans and animals alike.

in a small backyard. What makes an orchard is the type of tree, and that there are at least three, either for cross pollination, or to achieve the geometry needed to graduate from a single specimen or a flanking pair. While three is all we need, the care required to grow orchard trees and harvest their fruit, no matter how many, turns any orchard into a working garden. They must be pruned to promote fruiting spurs, protected from pests and diseases, and the fruit diligently harvested on time. All this does not necessarily preclude the presence of beauty. First, orchard blossoms are some of the most beautiful, most fragrant to be found, especially in quantities from many trees growing close together and flowering at once. Next, choosing what to grow beneath these trees can create a spectacular setting when populated with spring daffodils, summer wildflowers, or a carpet of clover. Finally, though autumn colors of orchard trees aren't always the best, winter scenes of gnarled trunks and twisted limbs recount histories of seasons past. Horticulturally, an orchard requires all-day sun, but not a south-facing exposure. North slopes are preferred because they warm up slowly in spring, preventing the early emergence of new flowers that may be killed by a late frost, resulting in the loss of that year's crop (see the Recommended Plant Lists appendix for a list of great orchard trees).

Berry Walks

A berry walk is a fun strategy that keeps the rambling wild berries in bounds while providing easy access for harvesting. It's nothing more than a path lined on one or both sides with beds of berry shrubs. A good location for a berry walk could be leading to an edible garden or orchard, perhaps down to a pond, or before reaching the woods. The invasive and prickly nature of shrubs like blackberries and raspberries makes them less than desirable within the boundaries of a vegetable plot where they tend to run wild and encroach upon other plantings. They can, however, be planted safely outside the fence providing privacy within and their prickles making it that much more painful for deer or gophers to get in. As edible screens, they are unparalleled, planted as hedgerows between gardens or blocking views to utility areas (see the Recommended Plant Lists appendix for a list of great berry shrubs).

CHAPTER 7

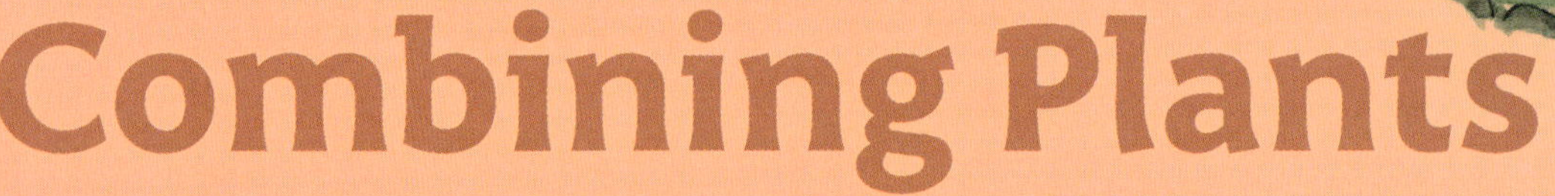

Combining Plants

Demonstration of how to combine plants based on attention to *form*, *texture*, and *color*; application of planting scheme techniques such as *massing* vs. *matrix*; and the best way to borrow ideas from other designers.

How you choose to combine the canopy, understory, and ground-layer plants in your plan will make or break your design.

The Art and Science of Combining Plants

There is an approach to gardening that focuses on the relationships between people, places, and plants. In the early 2000s, there was a magazine and television show called just that, *People, Places, and Plants*. While the publication and program came and went, the recognition of a working relationship between people, places, and plants when creating gardens holds true.

Successful garden designers combine plants to fulfill the needs and desires of the people meant to use and enjoy the garden while also matching the plants to the places they will grow. The concept is simple, but I believe the most important relationship is between plants and people. This is how garden designers use and choose plants for their gardens. Place is important, but it's simply where we do it, setting some limits on what can be accomplished dictated by sun, soil, and climate. The real potency and joy of garden

◂ Plants are the layer of many layers within a garden design, bringing your landforms to life as they soften the hard lines of structures.

design comes when we, as gardeners and garden designers, build relationships with the plants and begin to understand them intimately. Knowing more than just what they need to grow, but also how they will grow, how they will influence what grows around them, and ultimately how these combinations grow into a design.

This relationship between plants and people establishes the art of combining plants, but its foundation is science. There's a strange, magical connection that occurs between people and plants, and I have found that the bond grows stronger the better we understand how plants grow. It's why some of the best designed gardens I have ever visited were the work of botanists. There are gardeners who live to love plants; there are horticulturalists who learn to love plants; and there are botanists who understand and love plants. The best garden designers all practice on a deeper level, learning to unite the science of plants with the art of design.

PLANT THEMES

Designing with a theme may correspond to a specific garden style, like English or Asian, and while garden styles like these are formulated through landform and structure elements as well as plants, plants are the most influential elements within any garden style or theme. For example, an English-style garden could be formal or cottage, both of which suggest a particular look and feel of the plant layer. Formal suggests clipped hedges, stately trees, lawns, and hybrid tea roses. Cottage means perennial flowers, flowering shrubs and trees, field grasses, and rambling roses. A plant theme determines the plant palette, and the plant palette, in turn, guides how these plants are combined based on their growth habits, sun, and soil preferences and, most important, how the designer wants to see them in addition to how nature suggests they might grow on their own.

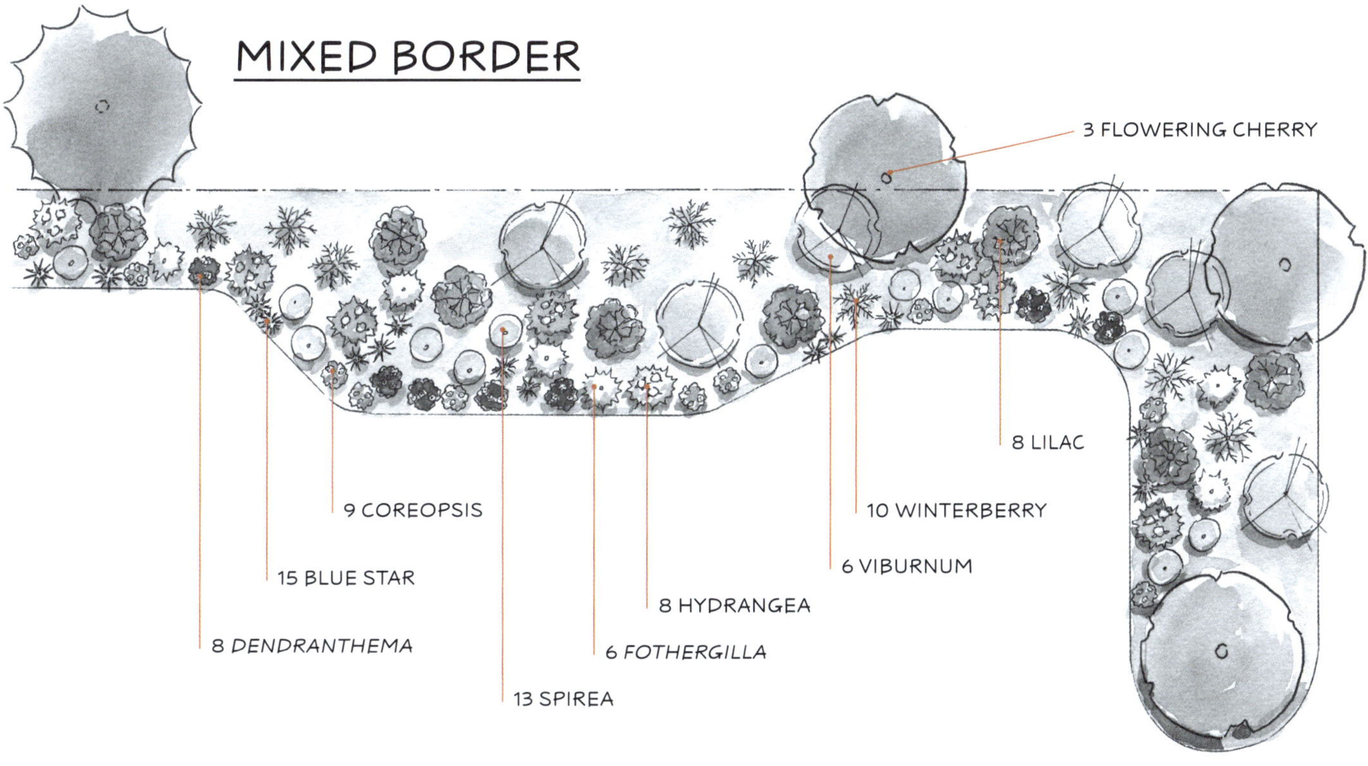

Mixed Border

A mixed border is exactly what the name implies. It is a garden border with a mixture of plants—trees, shrubs, and herbaceous perennials—set within the larger context of the garden. There is such a thing as a mixed shrub border, but the better version includes at least one tree and a layer of ground plants to knit things together. The concept allows for a diversity of plants to extend the interest of the mixed border planting through all seasons with overlapping bloom periods, distinct foliage, and diverse forms that evolve through the seasons, making sure there are enough woody plants to hold interest through winter.

The large shrubs in a mixed border will set the tone. Start with viburnum, winterberry, and lilac to anchor the composition, joined by smaller specimens of spirea, *Fothergilla*, and hydrangea mixed in and around the others, all as individuals, not in groups. In the open bays between these shrubs, and toward the front of the bed, a tapestry of well-behaved herbaceous perennials that form mounds or waves, like coreopsis, *Dendranthema*, and blue star, can be planted in groups to cover the shrub stems and blend the plantings to the ground. Finally, a single ornamental tree, such as a cherry or crabapple, can anchor one end of the bed and complete the scheme.

▲ Make your mixed borders diverse by including two or more species of shrubs and perennials in your planting plan.

Design your mixed shrub or perennial beds with an eye to the plant combinations viewed at an angle.

DESIGN BORDERS TO BE VIEWED AT AN ANGLE

One trick to designing any border, whether mixed shrub or perennial, is to combine the plants to be viewed at an angle. While the borders will be viewed perpendicularly, they are more frequently viewed at an angle as guests walk along their length, or from similar vantage points throughout the garden. For this reason, pay attention to how the plants will overlap in angled views and combine them so taller plants pop up from behind others, medium-size plants partially obscure those, and smaller plants weave in front of them all. Study the background, middle ground, and foreground and ensure that each layer blends together when looked at askew from front to back.

This blend can be achieved by never placing only tall plants in back, medium plants in the middle, and short plants in front. Bring some medium-size plants forward and push some back. Put a few tall plants here and there into the middle ground and push some short ones to the middle as well. Study how they overlap and view the border from all angles until it looks right from every vantage point. This isn't easy and takes practice, but patience gets us there. Also, in the front layer, come close and look straight down at the tops of the plants and study how they combine. These little vignettes make nice combinations on a small scale, while taller plants in back provide interest at eye level.

PERENNIAL BORDER

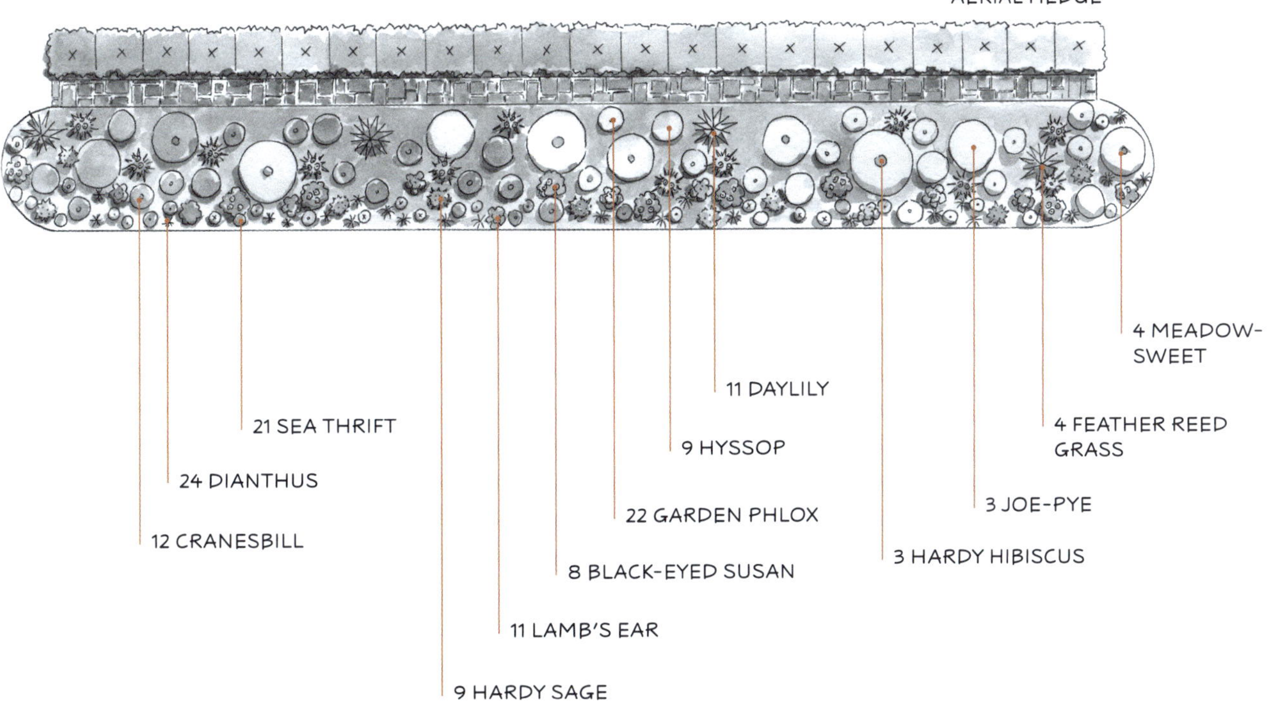

Think of the plants in your perennial border design as a scaled-down version of canopy, understory, and ground layer.

Perennial Border

Perennial beds are populated primarily with herbaceous perennial plants, though they can be supplemented with bulbs, annuals, and tender perennials, all chosen for their foliage, form, and flowers. The concept of an English long border is a common take on this theme, though island beds situated in a back lawn, or feature flower borders beside patios or along walls, are other popular iterations of this theme. The key is to use only herbaceous plants, most often meticulously tended, with timely pruning, staking, and transplanting, adding, and subtracting year to year and all season long.

Start with single specimens of large perennials, like Joe-Pye, meadowsweet, hardy hibiscus, and an ornamental grass, all placed in key locations along the border's length, then add middle-ground plants like hyssop and garden phlox with punctuations of daylily, followed by a collection of medium-height spreaders like black-eyed Susan, lamb's ear, hardy sage, and iris with low-growing scramblers like cranesbill, dianthus, and sea thrift. Drop in a few tall and medium annuals, like angelonia and coleus, and underplant with drifts of daffodils for a hit of spring bloom.

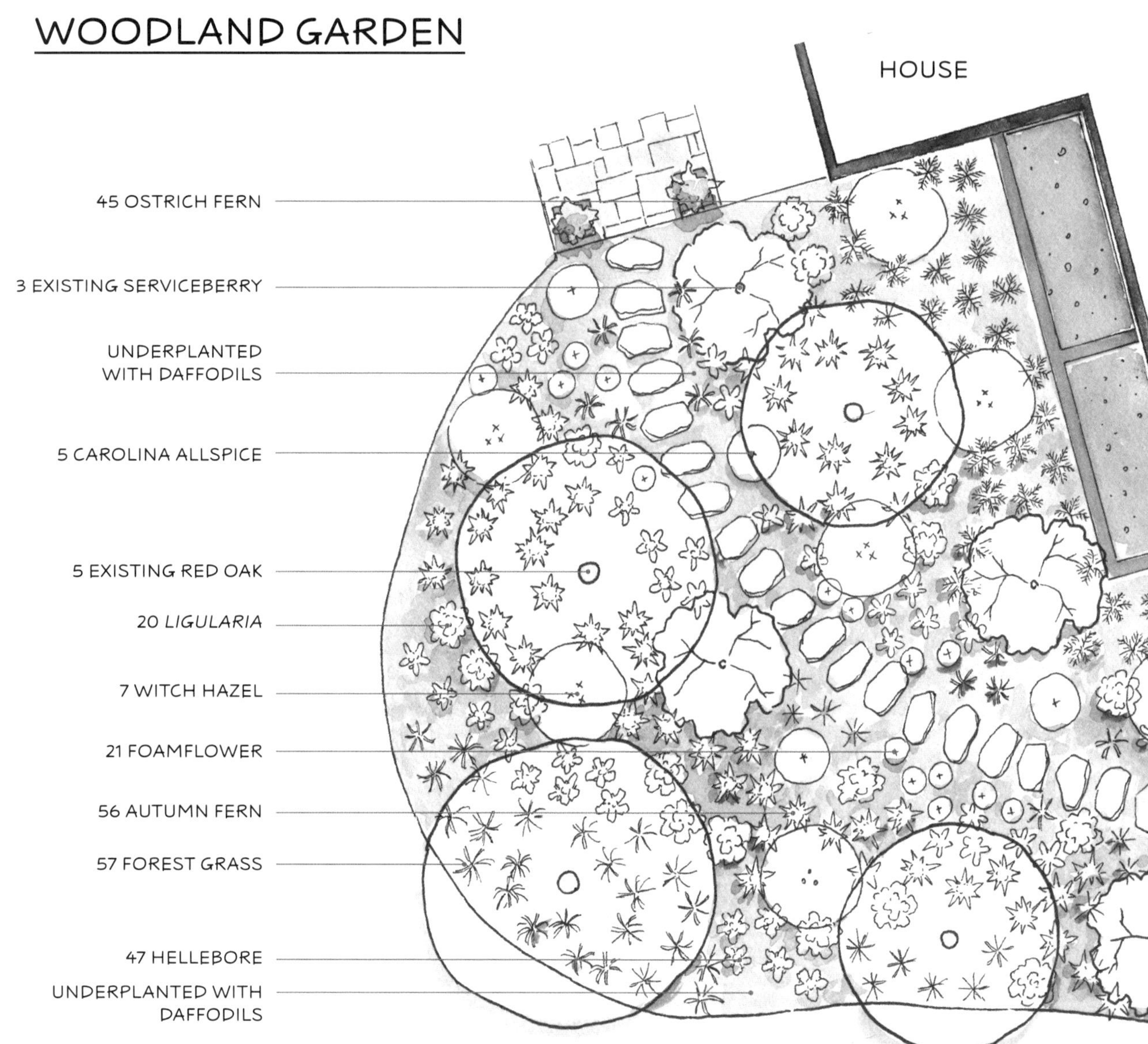
WOODLAND GARDEN
HOUSE
45 OSTRICH FERN
3 EXISTING SERVICEBERRY
UNDERPLANTED
WITH DAFFODILS
5 CAROLINA ALLSPICE
5 EXISTING RED OAK
20 *LIGULARIA*
7 WITCH HAZEL
21 FOAMFLOWER
56 AUTUMN FERN
57 FOREST GRASS
47 HELLEBORE
UNDERPLANTED WITH
DAFFODILS

Woodland/Shade Garden

Shade gardens are popular because many properties have pre-existing large canopy trees, or tall buildings that cast the garden in shadow. The best way to approach shade gardening is to look at it as an opportunity for a woodland garden. This means incorporating shade-tolerant shrubs as an understory layer, and shade-loving plants in the ground layer. Of course, you could limit or eliminate either. A canopy of trees with just a simple blanket of ground plants is an effective, elegant scene. But when punctuated with a few understory shrubs, a real woodland starts to emerge.

Foliage carries the day in a shade garden. Start the composition in and around the tree trunks with a few thoughtfully positioned understory trees like witch hazel or redbud combined with shade-loving shrubs like Carolina allspice, kerria, and *Diervilla* alongside some large perennials, like *Ligularia* or Rodger's flower. This will set the stage for a blanket of medium-size species like hosta, hellebore, and forest grasses combined with groundcover shrubs like *Skimmia* and dwarf deutzia. Within this mix, but close to the path, or wherever guests pass by, drop in low perennials, like barrenwort, lungwort, and foamflower, where they can be appreciated. Finish the planting with small bulbs like snowdrops or crocus scattered around in pockets where they will provide a pop of color in early spring.

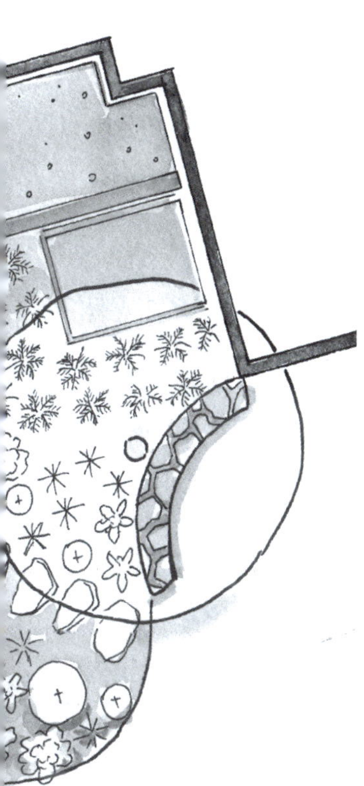

◀ Envision a flowing stream of foliage and flowers when arranging the ground-layer plants in your woodland garden.

Meadow Garden

Meadow gardens live in spaces without a canopy, though a woodland canopy may reside nearby. They are populated primarily with ground-layer plants, but these plants can, and should, have an extensive amount of diversity, from the use of grasses and sedges mixed with wildflowers and forbs of every shape and size. There are dry meadows, wet meadows, coastal meadows, alpine meadows, even desert meadows, all differentiated by regional climate and soil type in terms of fertility and pH. The beauty of meadow gardens is that they evolve over time as plants compete and combine.

Meadows are inherently diverse, even though the plants tend to grow and bloom in groups and masses, partially due to how they propagate from seed. A good mixture to get things started is a combination of annuals that can establish quickly and begin setting seed, with carefully chosen perennials mixed in and among the seedlings. The annuals will come and go and change over time, whereas the perennials become established and begin colonizing with underground roots and stems. A native shortgrass and flower meadow would consist of:

- Black-eyed Susan
- Butterfly milkweed
- Foxglove beardtongue
- Indian blanket
- Lance-leaf coreopsis
- Little bluestem
- Purple coneflower
- Sideoats grama
- Smooth aster
- Stiff goldenrod
- Wild bergamot

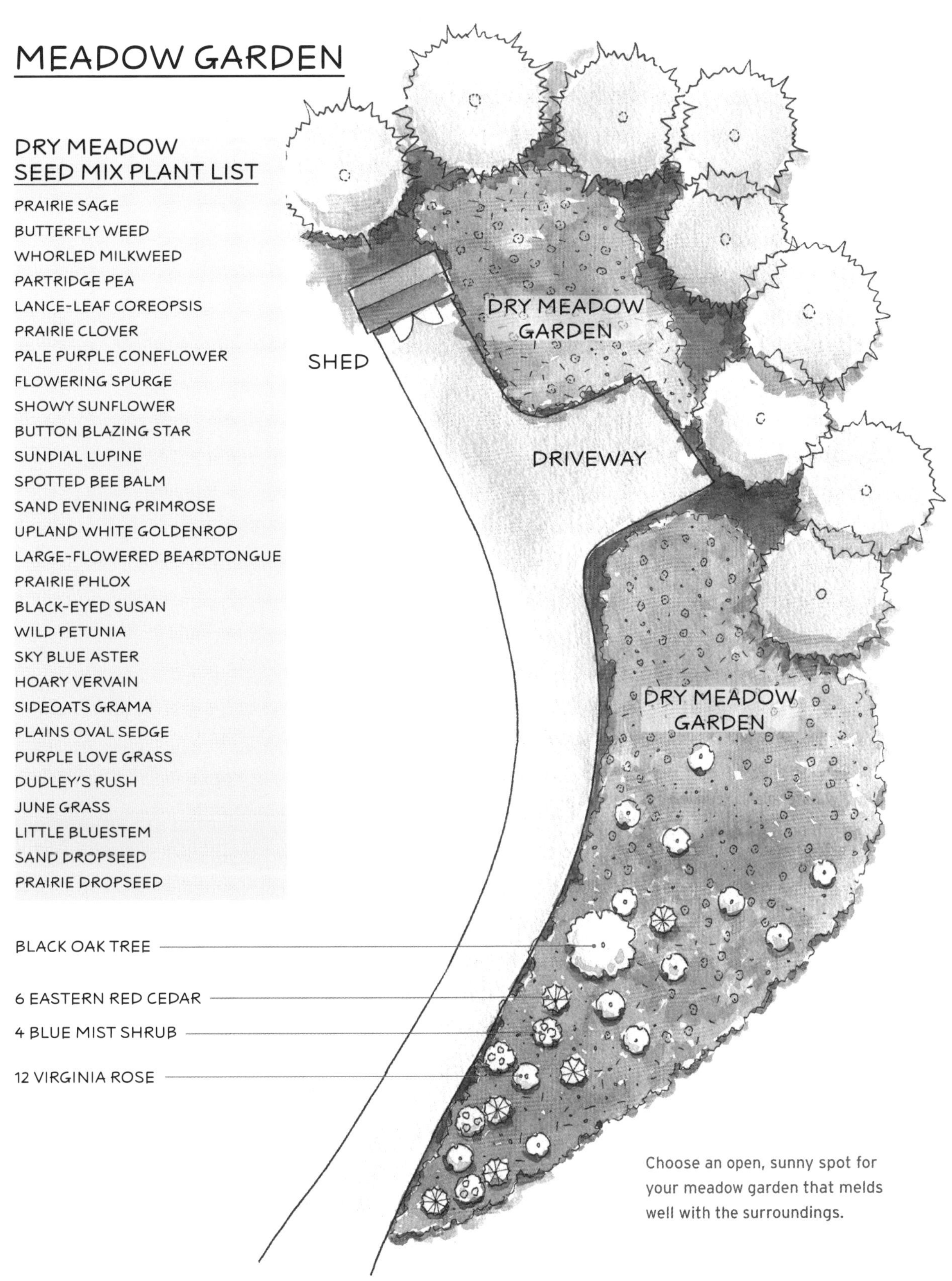

Choose an open, sunny spot for your meadow garden that melds well with the surroundings.

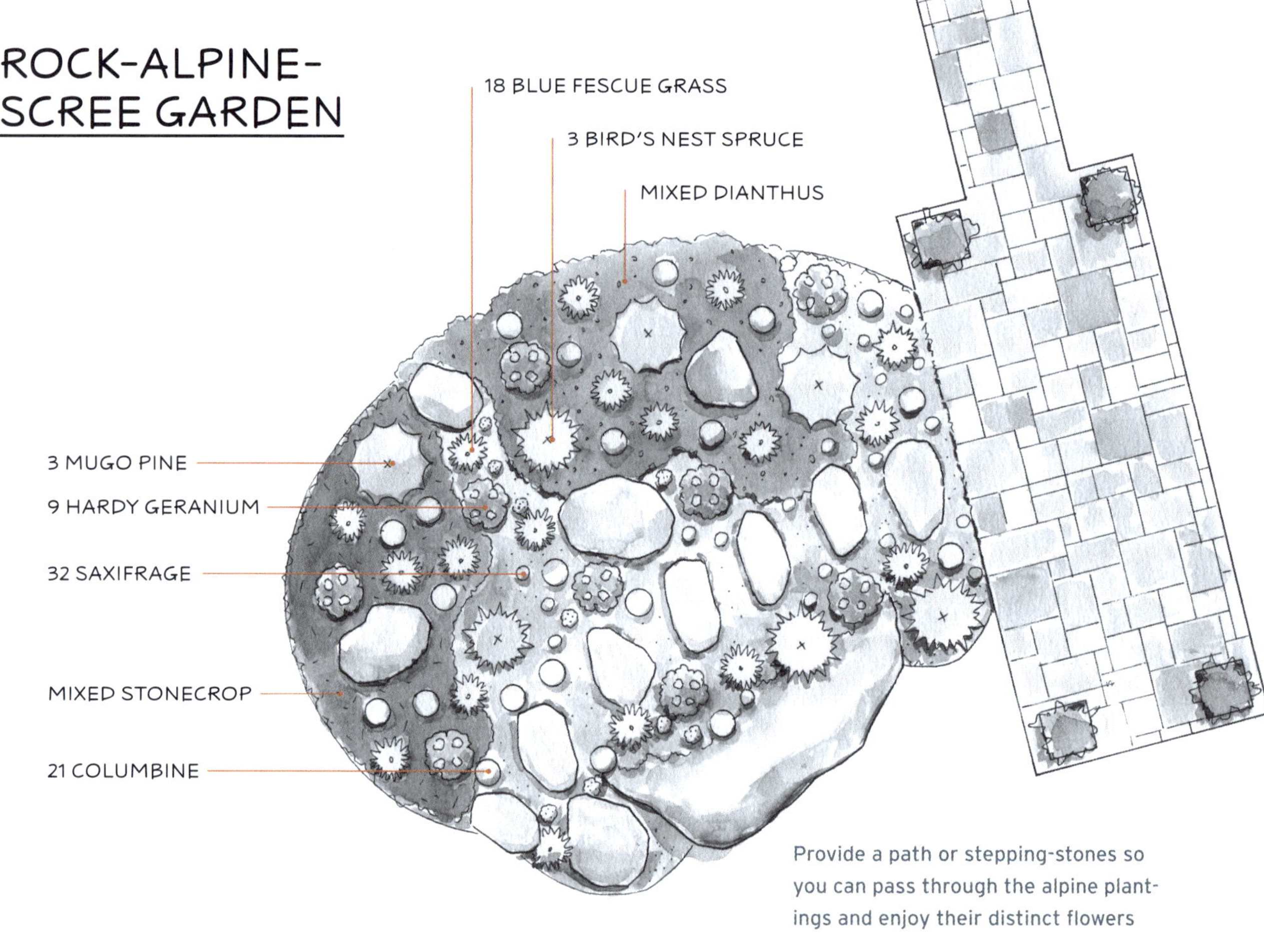

Provide a path or stepping-stones so you can pass through the alpine plantings and enjoy their distinct flowers and foliage up close.

Rock – Alpine – Scree Garden

A popular garden motif is that of the rock, alpine, or scree garden, which are somewhat interchangeable, but all possess a thin, less fertile soil topped with gravel or shingle stone. Gardens like these are often constructed from scratch, in the absence of any natural rock formations, though the better idea is to take a cue from some exposed ledge and make a garden that fits the conditions. A key to these designs is the way in which the plants combine with the stone, and how the plants often stand alone in the bed, segregated from their companions, but appearing to slowly creep toward one another.

Diminutive species are the mainstay plants for gardens with low fertility and sharp drainage. Low-growing saxifrage, sedum, dianthus, and fescue contribute foliage and flowers, while the addition of dwarf conifers, like mugo pine and dwarf spruce, serve as four-season anchors among the others. These can all be preceded by pockets of early bulbs, like snowdrops, *Chionodoxa*, and crocus, which will bloom and fade away. Self-seeders like wild violets, bellflowers, and columbine can also add a touch of serendipity to the design but may need to be weeded from time to time to keep them in check.

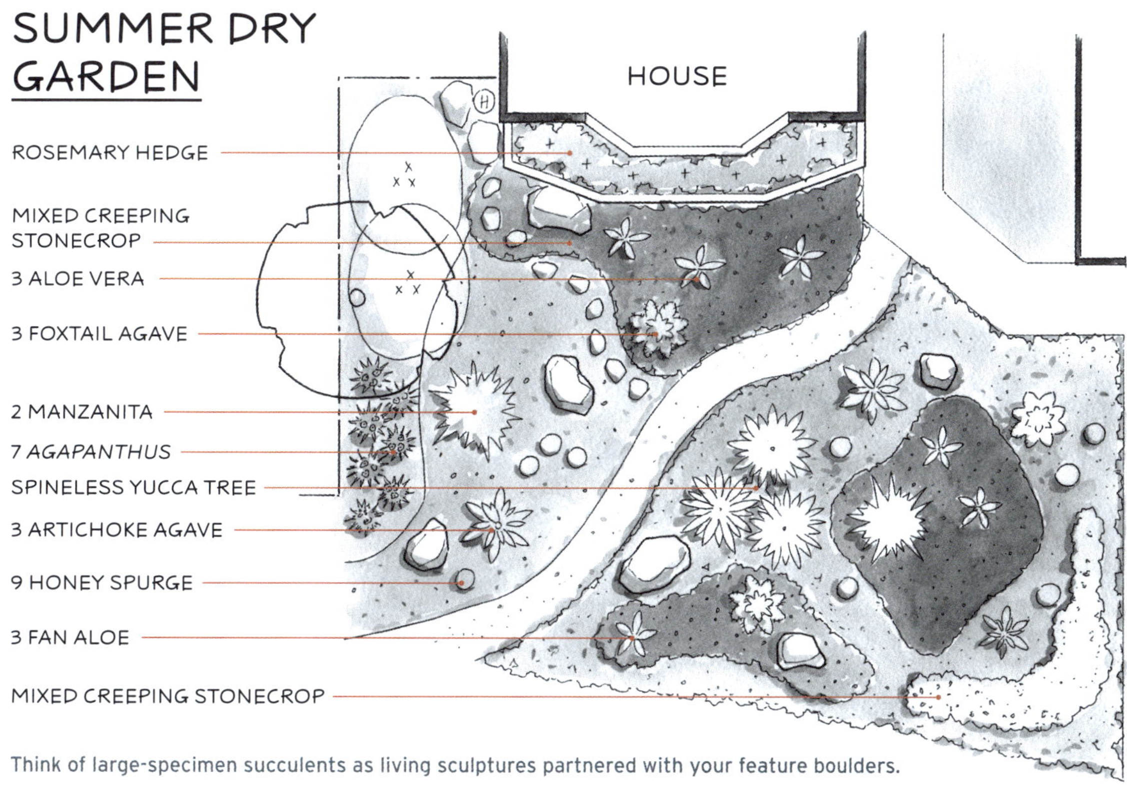

Think of large-specimen succulents as living sculptures partnered with your feature boulders.

Summer Dry Garden

"Xeriscape" is the scientific term for the plantings used in dry summer and desert gardens. This type of planting works in regions with climates that have little to no rain in summer, like parts of the American Intermountain West and much of California and Oregon. These plantings will survive where it basically does not rain from May through September but will also do well when winter rains arrive. Succulent plants are the mainstay because they can survive the months of drought, and then recover and grow during the wetter months. The soil, of course, is key. Lower fertility and excellent drainage are attributes of the soil profile these plants prefer, along with a mulch of pebbles and stones. The result is an easy-care garden built on a collection of specimen plants often treated like sculptures.

Turn to desert and Mediterranean plants when building a plant palette for a summer dry garden. Trees for these spots are limited, many of which won't grow especially tall, but jacaranda and pistache can get the job done, as well as date or fan palms once established. The shrub layer allows for more variety, with a manzanita, *Ceanothus*, and juniper leading the way. Many of these shrubs will grow slowly and stay small due to the limited resources of water and nutrients in a summer dry garden, but some start small and stay that way, like brittlebush and creosote. The ground layer can be quite diverse, with a focus on succulents like agaves, yucca, and euphorbia, all of which have many varieties to choose from, along with cacti, *Opuntia,* and even saguaro for the hottest, driest spots.

Rain Garden

Plants that don't mind growing in intermittently flooded or consistently wet soil are the staples of a rain garden. Locations for rain gardens often present themselves during the site survey when a low spot that fills with water and drains slowly is identified. The idea is to take advantage of the opportunity to grow plants that like it wet and turn a potential problem–standing water that becomes a hatching ground for mosquitoes–into a beautiful garden. Rain gardens can also be designed on purpose, by directing surface water runoff or drains where it can collect. Thirsty rain garden plants will absorb a lot of that water as they thrive in place.

Start with a willow, winterberry, or red osier dogwood shrub, but just one or two, as they will grow fast with all that water and can overwhelm the planting bed. Place the shrub toward the back and to one side to allow it to expand gracefully. If it's a very large planting bed, try a larch or bald cypress as an anchor tree and plant the shrubs nearby for a dramatic combination. The ground layer should be diverse to keep it interesting all season long. Try combinations of flag iris, great blue lobelia, marsh milkweed, *panicum* grass, and turtlehead.

▲ Choose rain garden plants wisely, as they will grow fast and knit together quickly.

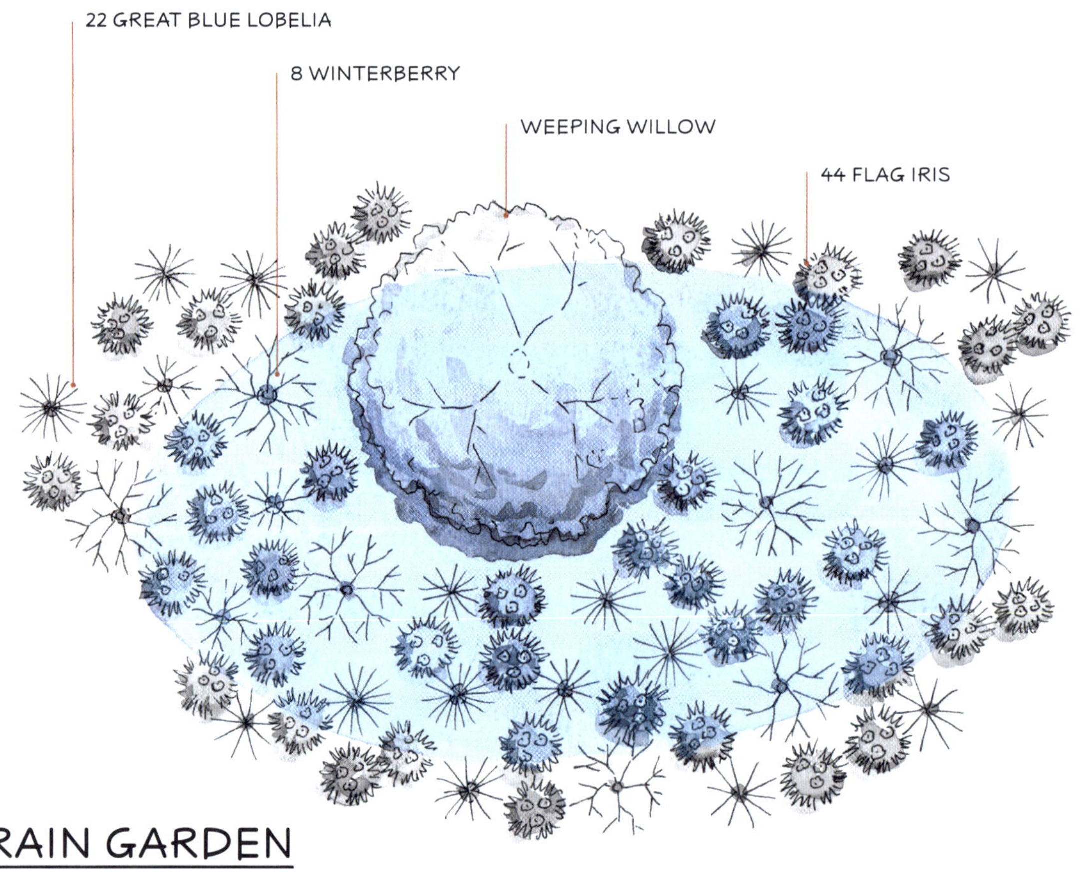

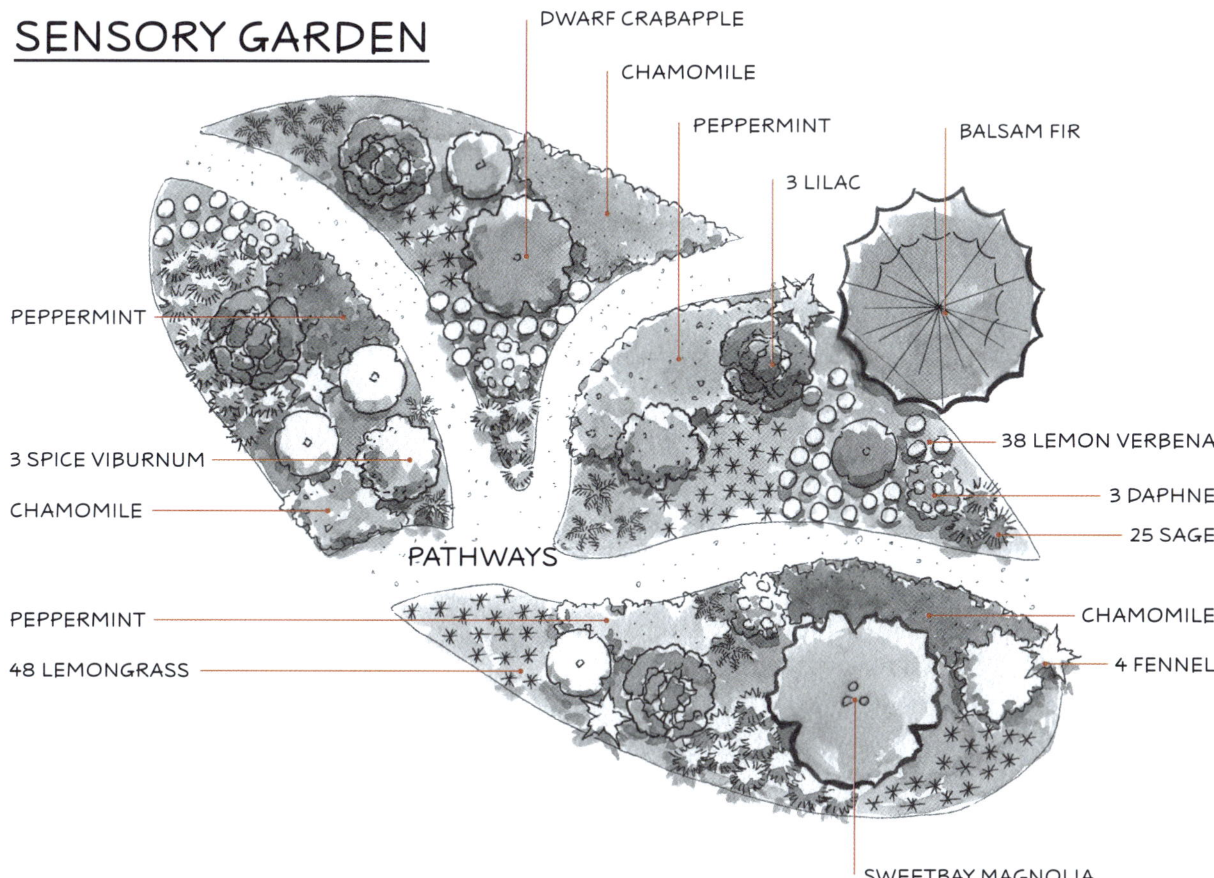

Sensory Garden

Sensory gardens are often designed for people with impaired vision, as they focus on the use of plants that excite our senses of smell, touch, and taste. The plantings are best if they are 1 to 4 feet (30.5 cm to 1.2 m) tall so they are close enough to interact with, though a fragrant tree or vine can also fit in. There are many herbs with foliage that, when touched, are quite fragrant and can also be fuzzy and safe to taste. Woody plants with unique bark, whether smooth and muscular, flaking or ridged, are also an excellent choice. The overall idea is to focus on the nonvisual aspects of the plants that make them special, and plant them so they are easily accessible to encourage close interactions.

Trees with powerful perfumes include crabapple, sweetbay magnolia, and balsam fir, while shrubs like lilac, spice viburnum, daphne, and, of course, roses, can't be missed. Use the woody plants with restraint because they bloom for only a week or two. In the ground layer, fragrance is easy. Include masses of chamomile, dill, fennel, lavender, lemongrass, lemon verbena, peppermint, sage, and scented geranium. The more of each plant the greater the impact, and with the scent coming from edible foliage, these herbs also provide an opportunity to engage our senses of touch and taste.

▲ Place plants as close to the paths as possible to ensure they can be experienced with all the senses.

Pollinator Garden

The idea behind a pollinator garden is to provide plants for beneficial pollinator insects, like moths, butterflies, and bees as well as birds, so they visit our gardens for our viewing enjoyment as well as to pollinate our plants, especially edible crops. For this reason, pollinator gardens are best placed near edible gardens, berry walks, or orchards. Some gardeners dedicate a raised bed or crop row to pollinator plants within the vegetable garden to ensure the pollinators find what they're looking for, including the crop flowers. Pollinator gardens also make excellent plantings in and around seating areas or other gathering spots in the garden where butterflies and hummingbirds can be observed. While pollinators will be attracted to many or most flowers in our gardens, a concentration of plants with flowers they really like is a great way to make a show while also supporting the surrounding neighborhood ecosystem that may not possess the diversity our insect friends need.

Focusing on native plants in a pollinator garden is the best first step because these are the species that local bees, butterflies, and hummingbirds like. The flowers, of course, are the key. There are some good tricks when it comes to finding the best flowers. For example, bees prefer blue, orange, purple, or yellow flowers that are easily accessible, like daisies. Butterflies favor pink, purple, red, white, or yellow flowers with a place to perch while they sip on nectar. And hummingbirds love flowers in vivid shades of purple, red, and yellow with a tubular shape they dip into with their long, narrow beaks. The list of pollinator plants is long, but a good group of perennials to start includes anise hyssop, bee balm, catmint, false indigo, lavender, milkweed, and yarrow. Some excellent annuals to choose from are borage, cosmos, lantana, and zinnia. We can also include shrubs like chokeberry, oakleaf hydrangea, and summersweet. Combine these any way at all and they will be sure to attract lots of pollinators to the garden.

▸ Pollinators are most active in spring and summer so populate your pollinator garden with plants that bloom mostly in those seasons.

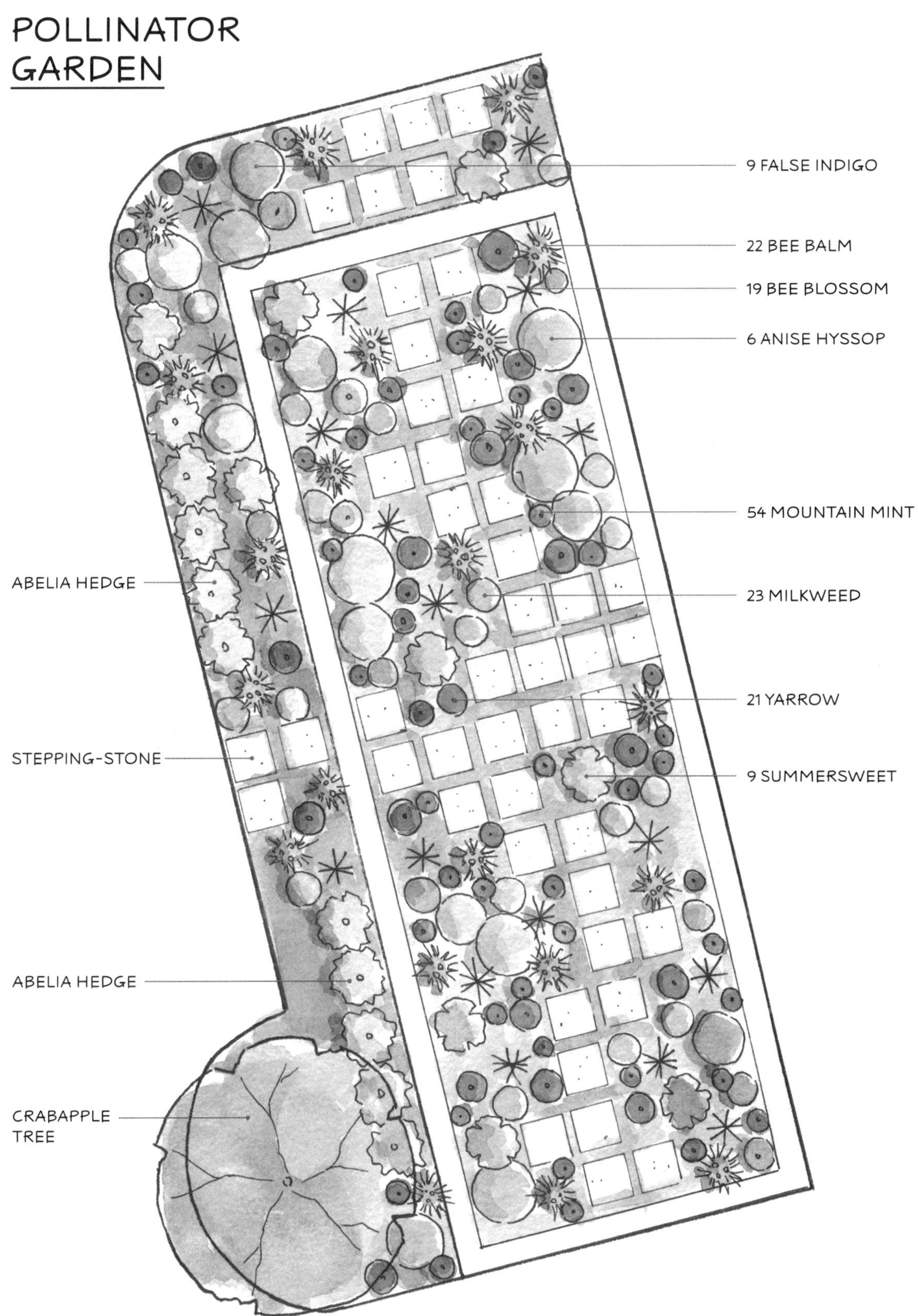

POLLINATOR GARDEN
9 FALSE INDIGO
22 BEE BALM
19 BEE BLOSSOM
6 ANISE HYSSOP
54 MOUNTAIN MINT
23 MILKWEED
21 YARROW
9 SUMMERSWEET
ABELIA HEDGE
STEPPING-STONE
ABELIA HEDGE
CRABAPPLE TREE

Bird Habitat

Borders designed for bird habitat rely on a diversity of understory plants and understory trees. Start with densely branched shrubs of different heights to provide cover for the birds and places where they can nest on the ground or in the scaffolding hidden by foliage. These shrubs should also provide food for the birds in the form of seasonal berries or the insects they attract, as well as nectar from flowers for hummingbirds. Plant them close enough to overlap so the birds can flit from one to the other without exposing themselves to predators. Add small trees with trunks that grow up through the shrubs or just beside them to give the birds a place to perch. Dense-growing perennials can also be added to the mix to provide more cover and places where insect food will be available, but keep the ground layer limited so the birds can forage on the detritus that falls below where a treasure trove of

Designing with Native Plant Communities

Working with a native plant community means building the plant layer, from canopy to understory on down to the ground, based on plant combinations found in the wild. For example, there is a type of forest called a maple-basswood forest, which has a canopy consisting primarily of these two species of trees. The substory consists of smaller trees like hornbeam, serviceberry, and witch hazel, and understory shrubs like leatherwood and snowberry. Growing beneath it all is a community of native woodland plants such as *Hepatica*, maidenhair fern, mayapple, meadow rue, and wild ginger. The concept is to take a recognized native plant community and create plant combinations for a garden design based on these species. The result is an ecosystem-based sustainable design. Native plant communities can also be used when selecting plants for more traditional gardens by focusing on cultivated varieties of these same native plants that grow together well in the wild.

Recognized Native Plant Communities of North America

- Dry prairie
- Maple-basswood forest
- Marsh-pothole prairie
- Mixed floodplain
- Oak-hickory forest
- Oak savannah
- Pine-fir-birch boreal forest
- River-lake margin
- Wet prairie

tasty insects like beetles and worms will abound. Use only species and cultivars indigenous to the region, often called native plant communities, as these are the plants local birds use.

Start with a framework of large shrubs like viburnum, holly, and elderberry as single specimens. Add smaller shrubs, like black chokeberry, cotoneaster, and juniper, in groups of two or three between the large shrubs. These all provide cover and food for a variety of birds. Bush honeysuckle is an excellent native for hummingbirds, but a nonnative bottlebrush can get the job done too. Don't be afraid to mix in nonnatives if you know the pollinators like them. Mix in a few perennial plants with good autumn seed production, like black-eyed Susan and coneflower, and some annual sunflowers. A perfect choice of tree would be a crabapple or serviceberry, both of which will provide some upper-level perching and nesting spots as well as a supply of edible berries.

BIRD HABITAT GARDEN

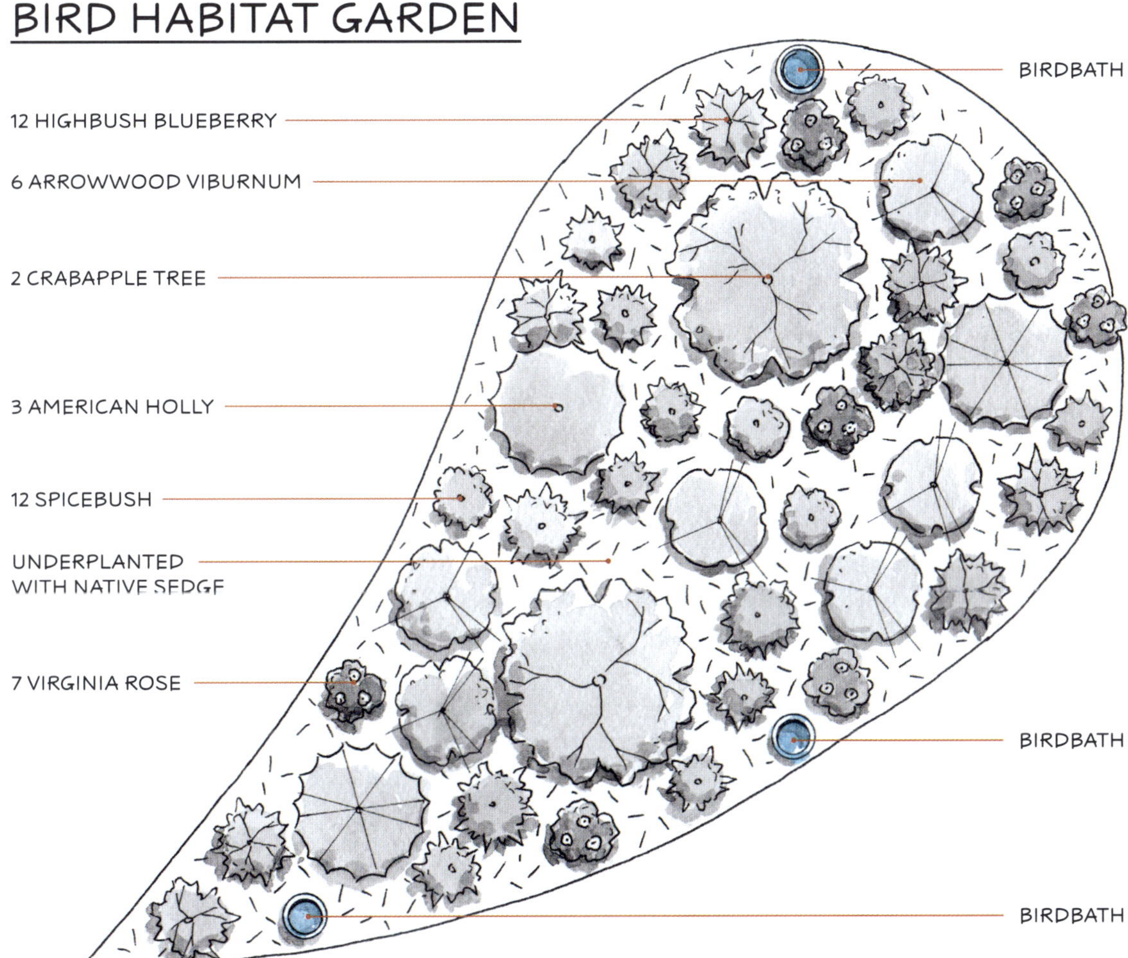

Make your garden a favorite for resident and migrating birds by combining plants that provide the food and shelter they need.

Design Is in the Details

There is a subtle distinction between combining plants and arranging plants that becomes clear if we distill it down to the details of how we use them in designs.

Arranging plants refers to their placement within the garden in relation to the other elements of structures and landforms, but also and especially in relation to other plants. For example, the spacing of trees as singular specimens or as groups. Quantity plays a role in this, such as how we position two trees in a setting differently from how we would arrange three, or five. Two are a set, or pair, connected by a single direct line. With more than two, that line changes. It can stay straight, or it can angle and diverge. As more trees are added, the number and geometry of the connecting lines between the trees will increase and complicate, or simply lengthen into a longer row. These basic arrangements appear relatively simple as we lay out plants, but they do ultimately affect the look and feel of a planting plan.

Combining plants means examining and understanding how plants grow and how they look next to one another. When we combine plants, we consider how they will grow together, not just how they grow on their own, though how a plant forms and grows on its own does matter. Plants with a bold form, a unique texture, or a stunning color can hold their own within a design and serve as singular specimens, but most plants we grow will work in conjunction with others. The leaf of one will set off the flowers of another. One form will reinforce another. One texture will stand out among others. One contrasting color will ignite them all. Combining plants means working with them intimately. Paying attention to the way they branch and stem, the size and shape of their leaves, as well as the form and color of their flowers. This is how we get down to the details of design.

DESIGNING WITH FORM, TEXTURE, AND COLOR

Anyone who has read a garden design article has almost certainly heard the mantra of how to design with plants by focusing on form, texture, and color. So, though it may seem cliché to say, thinking in terms of form, texture, and color is exactly how we must work out our planting plans. Each time we choose to use a plant in a garden design, whether as a single specimen or in combination with others, we must consider how the plant's form will stand out or meld into the scene, how its texture will contribute to what we see, and how its color will play a role in the overall scheme.

Plant Form

Form is the overall shape of the plant. It can be the natural result of how the plant grows, or it could be a shape maintained through pruning. There are many plant forms to choose from, such as balls, cones, mounds, and umbrellas. Trees and shrubs come in shapes determined by their branching patterns, for example, columnar, conical, irregular, open, oval, pyramidal, round, spreading, vase, and weeping. Herbaceous plants are even more diverse, with forms that spread across the ground, mound neatly, or stand tall with spikes, straps, or arching leaves and stems.

Step up your plant combinations by considering how their forms complement and contrast.

A FORM-BASED APPROACH TO PLANTING DESIGN

This technique, best used for the canopy and understory, reduces each plant to a simple shape. Defined in geometric terms, trees and shrubs can be classified as rectangular, triangular, or square, always working with the form of the mature plant. The approach helps us visualize the appearance and impact of various layers within a planting scheme, helping recognize depth as well as establish relationships between background, midground, and foreground features.

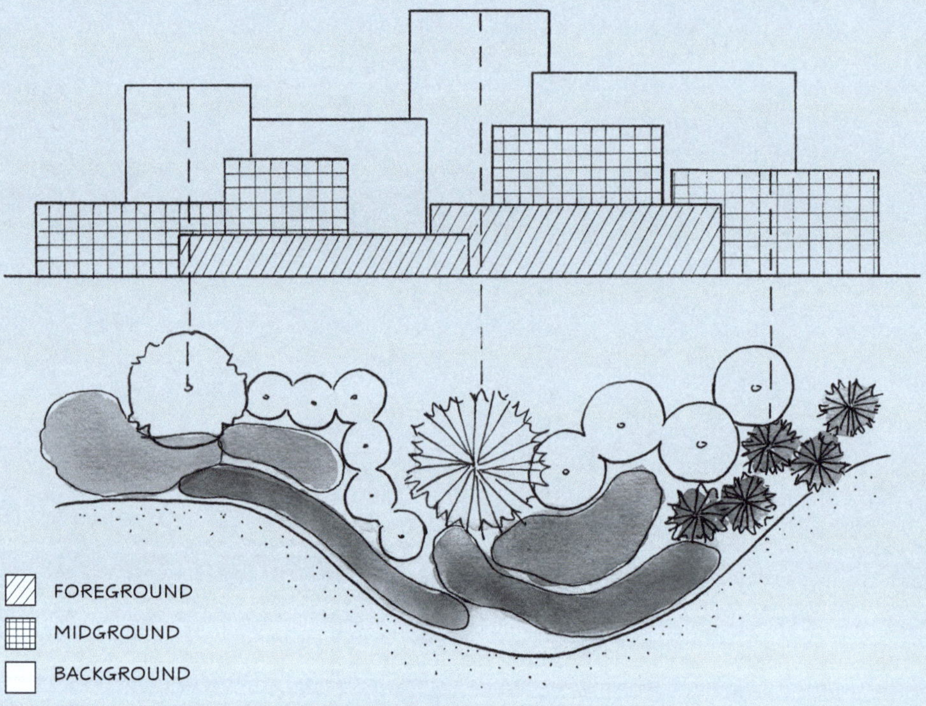

Transferring the abstracted elevation to a plan drawing allows us to visualize the various layers of plantings and the relationships between background, midground, and foreground features.

Strive for a diversity of foliage and flower shapes and sizes when building your plant palette.

Plant Texture

Texture is determined by the size of the plant's parts, primarily the leaves, but also the flowers, twigs, and stems. Foliage size varies widely from plant to plant, with leaves that can span a foot or more, to tiny needles less than an inch long. This provides opportunities to combine plants as a tapestry of textures. A familiar pitfall is to use plants that all have similar-size leaves, resulting in combinations that blur together and lack impact in the landscape. This is common in sunny gardens because sun-loving plants tend to have fine-textured foliage, like needles on conifers, or the linear and lanceolate leaves of drought-tolerant species. The trick is to find plants that thrive in sun but sport big leaves, such as hardy hibiscus and the tropical plants among our tender perennials, like canna lily.

The opposite is true for shade gardens. Most shade-loving plants have big leaves because they need more surface area to gather sun energy in shady spots. While a combination of large and medium-size foliage plants for shade are easy to find, fine-textured shade lovers are less common. Happily, ferns and forest grasses fit the bill.

Flower size and shape also contribute to plant texture. Some sport large blooms, like lilies, oleander, and roses, whereas others have tiny flowers that float above the plant, for example Russian sage, smoke bush, or sweet alyssum. While bloom time lasts for just a week or two for most woody plants and perennial flowers, they still have an impact on the texture of the plantings. Plants with lots of thin stems and twigs also create a fine texture, especially in winter months when the branches are bare. Designing planting plans for four seasons requires us to consider the textural appearance every plant presents in every season.

Plant Color

Working with color can pose a challenge if you have never studied color theory, but there are tricks of the trade that work well when designing with plants. First, work within the color wheel, which is a circular arrangement of colors organized by their chromatic relationship to one another. Colors opposite on the wheel are called complementary, and when placed side by side they make each other richer and brighter.

Turn to the color wheel to see the relationship between colors to create the perfect color scheme for your plant combinations.

Breathe vitality and positivity into your plant combinations with hot colors.

Evoke relaxation and calm by including cool colors in your planting schemes.

Purple with yellow is the easiest complementary color combination for garden designers because so many plants sport flowers and foliage in shades of purple and yellow. Next, try colors that are adjacent on the color wheel. They match because they are shades and tones of a primary or secondary hue. Finally, remember that green is going to play an outsize role in whatever color scheme you choose because most plants have green leaves, though often different shades of green, making the easiest color choice a green and white, a green and blue, or green and gold garden.

Foliage vs. Flowers

Back to the adage of "flowers are fleeting; foliage is forever." When it comes to designing with color, our first thoughts turn to flowers. All perennial plants, woody and herbaceous, have limited bloom periods, perhaps a week, maybe two or three. Their leaves, however, stay all season, and sometimes persist even through winter, making foliage a more reliable partner when selecting plants for color. Flowers, of course come in every shade possible, but hues of foliage represent well too. Green is a mainstay, with many shades to choose from, but there are also silvers, blues, golds, and burgundy-leaved plants that provide plenty of color options, especially when considering autumn leaves, which provide scarlet and orange as well. Variegated plants present combinations of colors on the same leaf, like green and white, gold and green, or silver and blue. Distinctive hues may cover the entire leaf, just the margins, or the veining. Altogether, it's possible to achieve almost any color scheme for a garden with thoughtful combinations of leaf and flower.

Hot vs. Cool

Color schemes can fall within categories of hot or cool. Picking one or the other for a planting plan is a great way to set a design theme while employing colors that look good together. Oranges, yellows, and reds are hot and explode in the garden like fireworks, creating lots of

Showcase some intensity through your flower selections with vivid displays of saturated hues.

Create a soothing scene with the soft look of pastels among your plantings.

visual excitement. Cool color schemes work with shades of silver, blue, green, and purple. They appear subdued and elegant and are often best suited for formal gardens or places where a sense of repose is desired.

Saturated Hues vs. Pastels

Like hot and cold color palettes, using saturated hues or pastels is another decision we make when selecting a color theme and picking the plants for a garden design. Saturated colors pop! Typical of sun lovers, when set amid a field of lush greenery, these hot hues will be noticed from a distance. Pastels are easiest to combine as they all seem to blend together nicely into subtly mixed masses, and there are many plants with pastel flowers to choose from that thrive in sun or shade.

COLOR PUNCTUATIONS VS. MASSES

Hits of color can be used effectively as punctuation within a sea of green. Green is a color that is always found in gardens so, although we can blend different shades of green, the best way to make a scene pop is to add color here and there. Flowers that rise on single stalks are perfect for punctuation. Another approach is to use splashes of color in swaths, grouping plants so there are enough to create the desired effect. Masses of color can come from foliage or flower, and a mix of both is best to keep the scheme alive as the seasons come and go.

BORROWED COLOR PALETTES

An excellent way to build a color palette is to base it on a work of art we like, especially a painting. The artist, who clearly knows a thing or two about color theory, has done the work for us. All we need to do is find plants that match the colors in the painting and plant them together. Pick one with three or more colors other than green and start building a plant palette. Landscape and garden scenes, especially by Impressionists, are perfect, but abstract art is also good, treating color in unique ways.

Even a modest reproduction inspired by Monet's water lily series can inspire the perfect color scheme for your garden.

WORKING WITH MASSES VS. CREATING A MATRIX

A commonly accepted way to arrange plants in gardens, especially herbaceous perennials in the ground layer, is to group them in masses. These same-plant groupings result in large swaths, as many become one. The technique is simple. Map out a section of a planting bed, choose a plant, and use enough of that single species to fill the space. For example, in 20 square feet (1.8 sq. m) of open ground with a desired plant that grows to 2 feet square (0.18 m) at maturity, we need at least ten plants to fill the space (20 / 2 = 10, or

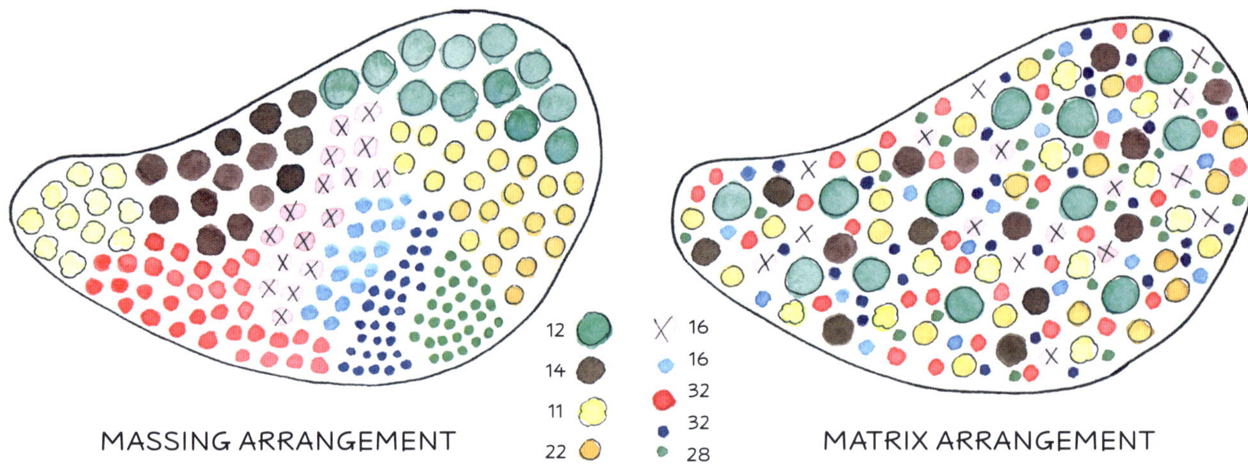

Choosing between masses or a matrix planting scheme will affect the evolution of your plant combinations over time.

18 / 1.8 = 10). Plants for adjacent mass planting are then chosen and the same thing is done until the planting bed is fully populated with several masses to complete the scheme. As a planting plan concept, it works best in large gardens with room to create masses with five or more plants. Fewer than that isn't enough to call it a massing.

The main drawback of designing with masses is that there will always be times during the season when a given species isn't in bloom or doesn't look its best. If a species blooms early in the season, it will leave a noticeable gap in a color scheme, and if it is a late-season bloomer it could appear inconsequential for months. For this reason, the best plants for masses are those that bloom for a long time, naturally repeat bloom, or present interesting foliage, stems, or seed heads to extend their season of interest. They should also have growth habits that allow them to knit together well.

A different, and often better, approach is to create a matrix planting scheme. Matrix planting is more akin to how plants grow in the wild, all mixed up and diverse. To set up a matrix, use that same list and quantity of plants as for the masses but scatter the plants throughout the bed as individuals to create a diverse matrix of plants instead of large swaths of plants. The main benefit of a matrix scheme is that, if we include species with different bloom periods, spring through fall, there will always be something of interest across the entire planting bed all season long. Matrix planting is great for small planting beds, where there isn't enough room to have sufficient masses to make it work. In a small bed, this might mean just three of one plant is enough, each one positioned near complementary neighbors to create combinations that highlight and contrast their attributes of form, texture, and color.

BLENDING GROUPS USING ARCS

There is a subtle trick to the placement of plants that will make the planting look more natural from the start no matter which technique is used. Instead of arranging plants in zigzag lines within a massing, drift, or weave, tie them together with arcs. The goal is to eliminate any obvious lines of plants within the arrangement. It's tricky, and subtle, and sometimes a plant just needs to be shifted an inch or two to achieve the desired effect, but the result is always a more natural look from the start that fills in better over time.

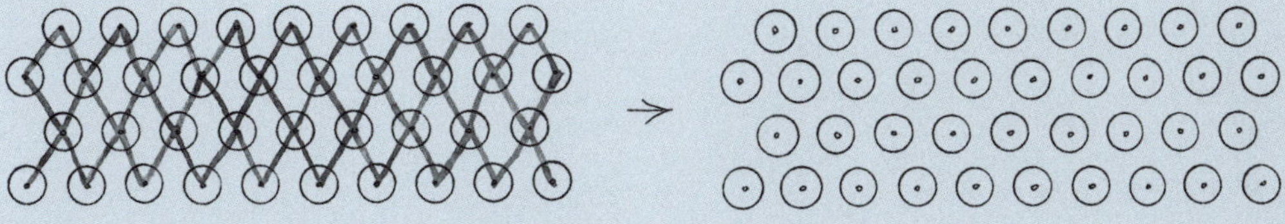

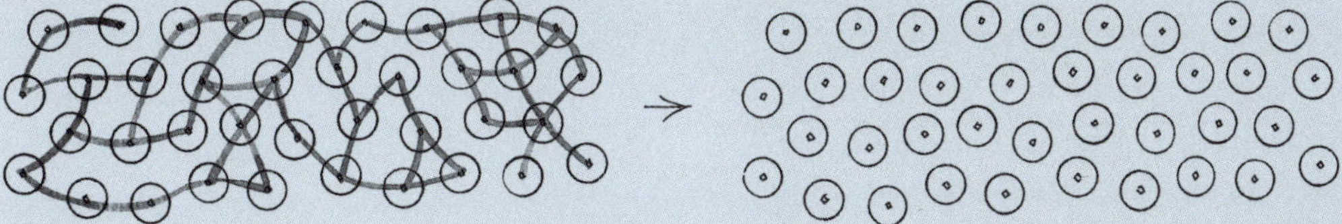

Plant arrangements look less contrived if you align them in arcs.

FOUR WAYS TO ARRANGE PLANTS

Inexperienced gardeners often have difficulty arranging plants so they look natural and combine well. A common rookie mistake is to plant two or three of the same plant in a row and repeat it with several species. The result is a static design that doesn't look good. Another way is to buy one of each plant and combine them. That results in what we call a "collector's garden," which can work, if that's the goal, but it looks contrived. What follows are four useful ways to arrange plants, all of which could be applied within the canopy, understory, or ground layer.

- **DRIFTS** are like masses in that they consist of multiples of the same species planted together. A drift, however, is smaller than a mass, and the spacing between the plants can be such that they do not knit together but hold their own individual form. In fact, uneven spacing helps create a relaxed, natural look.
- **FOCAL POINT** arrangements are created when a single specimen is surrounded by a grouping of another plant type so the focal point plant stands out. A good example is a small flowering shrub surrounded by a drift of low-growing perennials.
- **LINE UPS** should be reserved for formal planting schemes, or narrow beds where a linear design makes sense, for example along a path or in a tight spot in front of a fence. It's as easy as making two, three, or more straight rows consisting of the same species per row, and each new row lined up to fill the gaps between the plants in the row behind it.
- **WEAVES** are probably the best way to arrange plants not in a massing or matrix scheme. The idea is to use a combination of three or more species and arrange them so they overlap and weave together. A good approach is to use large, medium, and small plants, which could be trees, shrubs, perennials, or a combination. Arrange the largest first, in a drift, then sprinkle the others around them to form a larger drift of all the plants combined.

▶ Try any or all of these four familiar planting arrangements as you develop your design.

1. DRIFTS

SAME-PLANT GROUPINGS

2. FOCAL POINT

ARRANGE PLANTS AROUND A FOCAL POINT

3. LINE UP

MAKE THREE OR MORE STRAIGHT ROWS

4. WEAVE

WEAVE PLANTS IN AND OUT OF ROWS

Wolfgang Oehme and James van Sweden pioneered the New American Garden style with their thoughtful use of plant combinations.

Container Combinations

Combining plants in pots and planters is a great way to add moments of interesting form, texture, and color to the garden outside of planting beds. Combinations of summer-blooming annuals provide interest all season long but can also be combined with perennials and even small shrubs in large planters. The trick is to find plants that prefer the same sun and soil conditions. Container gardening is a great place to experiment with plant combinations because if the annuals we choose don't work, we simply don't use them again, and if the shrubs or perennials disappoint, we can remove them from the pot and replant them in the ground out in the garden.

Copying Combinations

Garden designers borrow good ideas for plant combinations wherever we find them, so when you see a plant combination you like in a book, magazine, online, or in a garden, feel free to copy it in a design. Public gardens are an excellent resource for great plant combination ideas. The famous Oehme, van Sweden 'Goldsturm' Black-eyed Susan, Russian sage, 'Karl Foerster' Feather Reed Grass combination they used at the Chicago Botanical Garden has been mimicked in countless planting plans because it works! The blooms peak together in mid- to late summer, last into early autumn, and transition well as winter approaches. Publications and public gardens make a point of labeling plants so it's easy to identify them and create a list to take to the garden center. If they grow together well in one garden, they should grow together well in another, assuming there is similar sun, soil, and a comparable hardiness zone.

Developing a Planting Style

All garden designers develop a planting style unique to their personal preferences and aesthetics. However, some properties call for a specific planting style based on architecture, geography, and climate. Other properties present opportunities for multiple gardens, all of which can be designed using a suitable style for the purpose of the space, for example a formal parterre garden close to the house, with a wild meadow garden farther afield. Designers typically start with whatever style best reflects the clients' preferences and the prevailing site aesthetics. As our practices grow and confidence increases, we develop a personal style and apply it to the properties at hand while remaining true to the character of the site. Nonetheless, most garden designs fit within one of three planting style categories: traditional, naturalistic, or sustainable. These styles can be melded together to create unique results, but more often there are areas of a property where each approach works best, such as for an entry garden, a seating area, or a stroll garden (more on designing garden spaces like these in chapter 9).

TRADITIONAL/FORMAL GARDENS

The hallmark of a traditional planting style is a formal application within several key garden types: perennial flower borders; mixed shrub borders; and trees within a greensward lawn. These plantings can be arranged and combined to create an accepted style best suited to temperate climates with adequate summer rain and relatively mild, winter dormancy periods. The approach hinges on the use of mixed masses within the planting scheme in both the understory and ground layers, and a restrained use of canopy, in the form of specimen trees set within an open lawn area or adjacent to the mixed borders and perennial beds. Plants are arranged in set groups, as focal points, in even numbers for a symmetrical look, or drifts of odd numbers of plants. They are also controlled through cultivar selection and maintenance techniques, like pruning and staking, to ensure they perform as desired. Greenery is the main backdrop to these plantings, with low or tall uniform hedging to create a framework within which the plant groupings are displayed. Seasonal highlights are accentuated through plant sequencing so there is something interesting on display throughout the year, or by dedicating different garden areas as seasonal highlights. For example, a spring ephemerals walk, a summer border, or an autumn grove. The traditional planting style is what we see, though often in a less refined form, as typical home landscaping, and is best suited to homes with Georgian, Tudor, and colonial-style architectures.

NATURALISTIC/ COTTAGE GARDENS

The naturalistic planting style is a form of controlled chaos that allows the plants to obscure the geometry of the design with a casually arranged and maintained plant layer limiting the use of clipped hedges or neat-growing trees and shrubs. Structures, like fences and walls, shape the garden. Plants soften these structures and fill things out. Plants are presented as they would grow on their own, taking care to arrange them based on their complementary and contrasting forms, textures, and colors, to create interesting combinations in every season. Winter is down time for naturalistic planting schemes because they rely heavily upon herbaceous plants, but the canopy and understory as well as elements within the structure layer, like pergolas, walls, and patios, can hold the design together, forming the bones of the garden during fallow months. Garden areas where a naturalistic style makes sense are typically farther away from the house, such as a property perimeter border, an island bed set in a lawn, or the entire backyard garden, though the loose style also works perfectly in conjunction with more causal architectures like Cape Cod, Craftsman, and farmhouse.

SUSTAINABLE/NATIVE GARDENS

The planting style most dependent upon the unique character of the plants is the sustainable garden style. Site informs plant choice when building planting schemes with sustainability in mind. In other words, the plants in the design are the plants that grow best on that site with the least amount of continued care once established. This differs from the casual chaos found in the naturalistic/cottage style where plants are carefully curated. A sustainable planting style entails putting the plants in the ground and letting them grow wild allowing them to compete for resources like nutrients, water, and even sun, then wait and see which ones thrive. All the work is done upfront, choosing what to grow based on what's native to the region or endemic to the site. A matrix-style arrangement works best, but masses can be employed by broadcasting seed or planting small plugs or pots of herbaceous plants. Trees and shrubs are chosen carefully, based upon a pre-existing or regional-specific native plant community, then positioned strategically in groups or groves. Meadows, forests, and fields are the domain of this planting style, though it can be applied in and around multiple architectural styles, especially contemporary, mid-century modern, and prairie-style homes.

Edible Companion Plantings

Combining edible plants is an entirely different affair compared to ornamentals. With edibles, it is all about production, though there are aesthetics involved because there is no reason an edible garden can't also be attractive. However, form really does follow function when it comes to edible plants because we grow them so we can eat them. There are two techniques for successful edible companion planting. The first is crop sequencing, based upon the seasonal growing requirements of each crop. The other is crop rotation, which is a crucial aspect of organic gardening essential to keeping the soil fertile so we can grow healthy, delicious crops year after year.

CROP SEQUENCING

Edible plants are like other plants in that each species has a prime season for growth. For example, some trees break dormancy before others in spring and they all have slightly different bloom periods. Edible crops also have seasons, but it's a simpler dichotomy: cool vs. warm. To get the most out of an edible garden, we can grow two

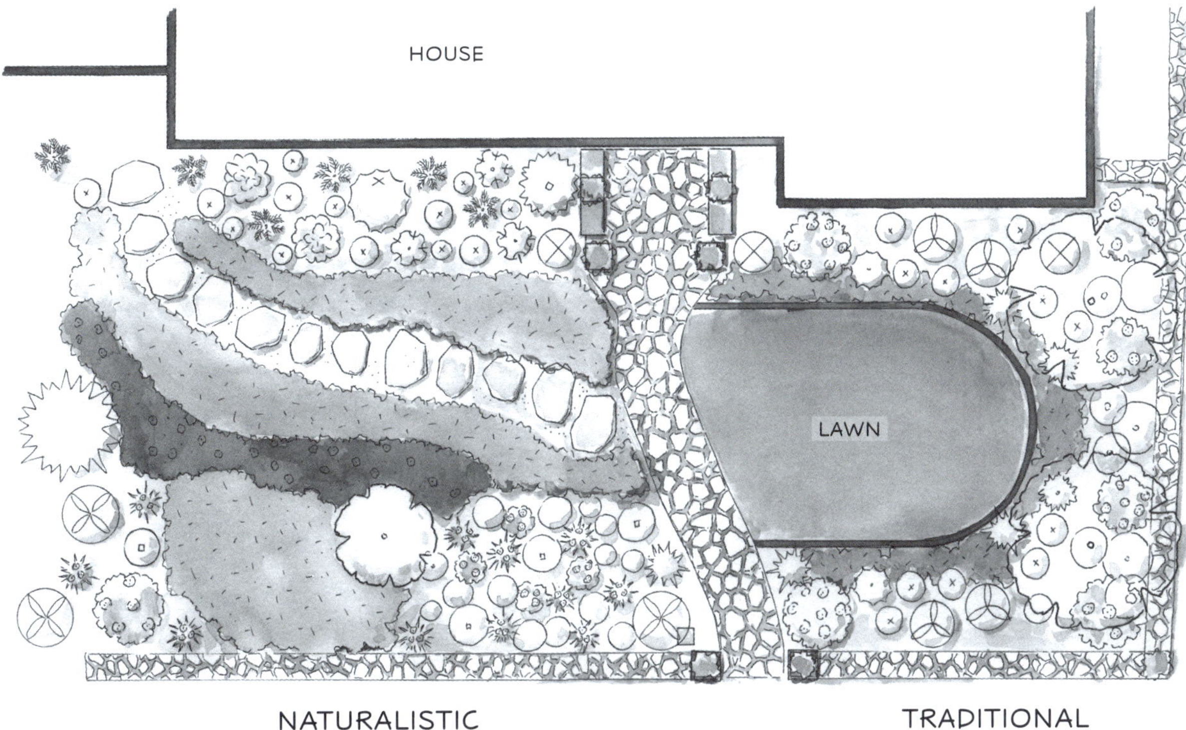

Planting style should be informed by your personal preference, the design's purpose, and the character of the site.

or more crops in sequence in the same plot, starting with a cool-season crop, like spinach, in early spring, harvesting it, then planting another, like peppers, to carry through summer. Then another cool-season crop can be planted after the warm crop is harvested before winter sets in. The result is a garden with nonstop crops and a steady supply of seasonal food. It is absolutely the best way to eat seasonally, and it all can come from our own backyards.

Cool-Season Edibles

Cool-season crops are the first ones to plant, from several weeks to a couple of months before the last frost date, assuming the soil is workable. These edibles need cold temperatures to germinate, grow, set fruit, and mature. Some are even winter-hardy, like kale and Brussels sprouts, and benefit from a light frost, which converts their starches into sugar, improving taste. The key is to plant them early enough in spring so they can finish and be harvested before it gets too warm, which will cause lettuces to bolt (set seed) and become bitter, or radishes to turn hard and pungent. We can sow cool-season edibles in early spring and again in late summer and into fall, but it must be early enough so they reach maturity before the onset of summer, or winter (see the Recommended Plant Lists appendix for a list of great cool-season edibles).

Frost Dates

When planning a crop sequence, the most important dates are the approximate final frost date in spring and the first frost date in autumn in that region. The final frost date determines when cool-season crops can be planted outside (typically a few weeks before that), and the first frost date determines how long the growing season will go on, allowing for late-season crops to finish. The numbers of days between these two dates is the climatological growing season, which can range from 51 to 100 days in mountain zones, 151 to 200 days in temperate zones, and up to 300 days in very warm regions. Coordinate the number of days to maturity for each crop and determine the best time to plant and sequence them.

Warm-Season Edibles

Warm-season crops require higher soil and air temperatures and must be planted after the final frost date. In cool climates, we start these plants from seed indoors and transplant them into the garden once the soil and air heat up. In warm climates with longer growing seasons, they can be sown directly into the garden. Planting or sowing warm-season edibles coordinates perfectly with harvesting the cool-season plants. This makes it easy to plan for a bed with leafy greens or peas to be converted to a pepper or melon patch. Warm-season crops have one growing cycle per year, from late spring to late summer, after which nighttime temperatures are too cold, even though daytime temperatures may still be warm. Autumn is the time to harvest these summer crops and get a second batch of cool-season edibles started (see the Recommended Plant Lists appendix for a list of warm-season edibles).

CROP ROTATION

As stated by the Royal Horticultural Society of the United Kingdom: "The principle of crop rotation is to grow specific groups of vegetables on a different part of the vegetable plot each year. This helps reduce a buildup of crop-specific pest and disease problems and it organizes groups of crops according to their cultivation needs." So, when it comes to combining plants in the edible garden, a basic understanding of the importance and application of crop rotation can help inform our choices for what to grow when and where. In fact, it is an excellent way to guide a formal plan, or design. Crop rotation becomes one of several criteria, including sun exposure, water needs, as well as form, texture, color, and flavor profile, for choosing what to grow and where to grow it. Plan the rotations beforehand and keep a garden journal to track what is planted and where each year.

A Simple Four-Year Crop Rotation

Crop rotation focuses on annual crops. Perennial vegetables such as asparagus and rhubarb aren't included. There are four categories of plants: fruit, root, leaf, and legume. Each must be rotated and grown in a different bed each year so a good edible garden design should divide the garden into at least four sections, or beds, to accommodate the rotating crops. Follow the sequence of fruit, root, leaf and legume, using one or more plants from each category that follows:

- **FRUIT** Corn, cucumbers, eggplant, melons, peppers, potatoes, summer squash, tomatoes, winter squash
- **ROOT** Beets, carrots, celery, fennel, leeks, onions, parsnips, radishes, sweet potatoes, turnip
- **LEAF** Arugula, broccoli, bok choy, Brussels sprouts, cabbage, cauliflower, kale, lettuce, spinach, Swiss chard
- **LEGUME** Chickpeas, cowpeas, dried beans, green beans, edamame, fava beans, lentils, soybeans

Perennial Crops

Perennial vegetables don't fit within the crop sequencing or rotation schemes. They need dedicated beds where they will regrow year after year so be sure to set aside space for them in addition to beds for sequencing or rotating crops. Some vegetables, like asparagus, take many years to establish and provide a decent harvest so savvy gardeners prepare perennial crop beds where they won't be disturbed and plant them first. A list of great perennial edibles includes:

- Artichoke
- Asparagus
- Chives
- Garlic
- Horseradish
- Ramps (wild leeks)
- Rhubarb
- Strawberries

CHAPTER 8

Rules of Design: Principles, Informants, Keys, and Elements

Lesson on the general and specific *application of design principles* of unity, function, simplicity, and repose; *design informants and keys*; and how to work with the *visual design elements* of contrast, harmony, scale, balance, and mass.

Garden design, like any other design practice, follows some basic rules. Many students in my garden design classes arrive with some design experience, such as graphic design, fashion design, interior design, even architecture. They understand design principles such as unity, function, and simplicity, know how to find ideas or metaphors to inform their designs, and understand how to apply basic visual elements like scale, harmony, and balance to a design, but they lack a thorough understanding of the plants and materials used in gardens. Although much design vocabulary is transferable from one type to another, precisely how it is applied differs among disciplines. How we achieve a sense of unity in a garden is different from how it is done when creating a new business logo. In gardens, we are working with land, built structures and, most important, plants, which means how we apply the rules of design is unique. There are many opinions among professionals about what the core principles, informants, keys, or elements of design are. What follows is my personal take on how to apply these shared rules of design when creating gardens.

Design Principles

There are three design principles at the core of any garden design: *unity*, *function*, and *simplicity*. If we stay true to each, there is a good chance the design will succeed. In some ways, all the other design elements, informants, and keys that follow are meant to support the application of these three principles, and by keeping these three principles in mind as we work through a design, many decisions will be made for us, simply by sticking to the rules we've made.

Rules and restrictions are good for a designer's creativity. It is easier to stay on target with an idea or a plan if there are limitations to what can be done. Choosing between an infinite number of options as compared to two or three is harder than we think. By keeping our eye on the prize and letting the principles of unity, function, and simplicity guide our decisions, the best version of the garden we want to create will emerge.

◀ The Vitruvian Man is a drawing by Leonardo da Vinci and the sunflower seeds are a spiral arrangement that follow the Fibonacci sequence derived from the golden ratio.

UNITY

Unity is everything. A unified garden design looks right and, more important, feels right when we see and experience it. It will exhibit aspects of harmony and balance, two of our most important visual elements, but there is more to it than that. Unity in garden design is reflected as a sense of belonging. The garden belongs where it is, the garden structures belong where they are, crucially, the plants belong, and ultimately those who use or visit the garden know they belong too. The best way to make this happen is to work within the plant layer and use plants suited to the region. This means native plants, or if not true indigenous species, then plants that have become endemic or representative of the region through their continued use over time. For example, if we're looking to introduce a large canopy tree in a Connecticut garden, the tree that best represents the regional aesthetic, and, of course, will thrive in that climate, is a sugar maple. Indeed, a sugar maple tree, a key contributor to New England's fall foliage show, in a backyard with a rope swing is pure Connecticut charm. In Iowa, we'd choose a bur oak. In Georgia, it would be *Magnolia grandiflora*, the Southern magnolia. This sense of belonging within the plant layer can be extended from the canopy, through the understory, and down to the ground-layer plants.

Another way to find unity in a garden design is to match the garden to the architecture. This is especially useful in residential garden design because the house is the most important structure on the site. Gardens are meant to surround and complement the house so it makes sense that the garden style matches the house. If it's a small Cape Cod, design a cottage garden. If it's a center hall colonial, make the garden symmetrical, just like the house. Of course, some design rules can be broken to create a sense of tension and perhaps pull off a new idea, but we must know the rules before we start bending or breaking them. We can try to design a casual cottage garden with naturalistic plantings outside a sleek contemporary-style home, but the safer bet is to match the architecture and do something with masses and a limited plant palette.

Ultimately, unity is achieved when the design ties together landform, structure, and plants into a cohesive whole, each element working to serve the greater purpose of the design. Instead of a house with a garden surrounding it, we have a house and garden. Together, they feel like one. This is not easy to achieve, but it is easy to recognize. The house no longer stands separate from its surroundings but sits nestled comfortably within the landform while the garden structures tie the house to the outdoor spaces, and the plantings enliven it all.

FUNCTION

Every discrete garden space, like the front, side, and backyards, serves a function within a garden plan. The front yard may be designed as an entry garden, the side yard as a utility area, and the backyard a play space (more about designing these outdoor spaces in chapter 9). Garden designers must determine the level of usefulness of each garden space, which then influences all the design decisions that follow. While the uses of a garden are established during the scope of design phase, as these needs and wants are refined the level of usefulness, or function, will continue to drive decisions. Purely functional designs aren't necessarily best. The best designs strike a balance between function and form, for example easy access between the herb garden and the kitchen, or adequate seating space on the patio that is also somehow interesting and beautiful. In fact, sometimes playing with the form of a design can help us find new ways to make the garden spaces work. For example, a curved path that shortens the walk from the kitchen to the compost pile, making composting easier. These functions set limits on our designs but, once again, limits lead to new ideas, especially when striving for beauty and a sense of place.

SIMPLICITY

The "KISS" method of design is something that has been taught for decades. The acronym, reportedly coined in 1960 by an aeronautical engineer at Lockheed, stands for "keep it simple stupid," which, in recent years, has been softened to "keep it simple silly" or "keep it super simple." Whichever way, the idea is the same: The best designs avoid unnecessary complexity. Design, whether for a garden, a house, or a city plan, is always better if the solutions to the problems presented are simple and uncluttered. Garden design is problem solving, for example finding the best location for a vegetable plot, or the best plants to use for hedging. While any decent design can solve problems, the best designs find the most elegant solution by answering the needs of the design as well as fulfilling our aesthetic goals. The danger for new garden designers is that they let their love of plants get the better of them. They can't help themselves and are compelled to fit every plant they have ever heard of or loved into the plan. This is a mistake because the result is bound to be a cluttered collector's garden that they alone will appreciate. Although there is nothing wrong with a collector's garden if that is the goal of the design, it doesn't make sense everywhere all the time. Anyone inclined to fall prey to this type of overabundance, which can also come in the form of excessive landform or overengineered structures, must recognize when it is happening and rein it in. A good technique is to start a design with a simple, limited plant palette. Perhaps just two or three trees, maybe five shrubs, and ten herbaceous ground-layer plants. This forces simplicity into the plant layer, which is the most likely element where unnecessary complexity can crop up.

A simple design is much easier to read and understand. What we're looking for during the design process are "aha" moments when a great idea suddenly appears. Solving design problems with results that look good and work well is a little like solving a riddle. Once we know the answer it seems obvious, as if there wasn't any other choice. That's when we know the design is working, and our ideas are on track. Design is basically a game of creativity. Finding ideas is fun, but until we land on the best ones it can be frustrating. Try to embrace the challenge by striking an appropriate balance between function and form that stays true to the goals of the design.

SIX STEPS TO MASTERING THE RULES OF DESIGN

1. **LEARN THE RULES.** To play a game we must read the rules to understand how the game works. How many dice do we roll, or cards to deal or draw. The same is true for design. What is meant by "unity"? How do we ensure for function? When is simplicity helpful? We can't play the game until we know the rules.
2. **PLAY BY THE RULES.** When confronted with a design problem, apply the rules—the principles, informants, and keys—to find a solution for that problem. We are practicing the rules.
3. **MAKE THE RULES ROUTINE.** Through repeated use we become so familiar with how the rules work we almost forget that we need them. We are applying the rules without thinking.
4. **REFER TO THE RULES WHEN CHALLENGED.** When a difficult design problem presents itself, we can fall back on our knowledge of the design rules to help us find a new solution. We are reviewing the rules.
5. **BEND THE RULES.** When the rules we've always used suddenly fail to solve a design challenge, we must take our knowledge of a rule and find a way to make it fit. We begin changing the rules.
6. **MAKE THE RULES.** After confronting enough design challenges over time and finding ways to solve them, we may discover a new way of doing things, which we can then follow for ourselves and share with others. We are now writing new rules.

Design Informants

Design informants are the launching points of garden design, helping us find the best ideas to transform a simple outdoor space into a memorable garden. Design concepts can arise from almost anywhere, but there are great ways to jump-start the process. These include tapping into our most inspiring experiences and personal values, recognizing unique visions for how we want to use the garden, staying true to a specific garden style, or accentuating distinct attributes of the existing site. A design informant can be as simple as a line from a poem or as comprehensive as a social land ethic. The goal of any informant is to generate ideas, and though not every idea will become part of the design, they push us forward and guide us along the way.

INSPIRATIONS

One potent informant available to every garden designer is a passion for plants. A single species can easily kick things off, for example a love of roses becomes a rose garden. The same could work for hydrangeas, or Japanese maple trees. If the dream is to grow these plants, then finding ways to use them throughout the garden can become a guiding light. Plant types, like medicinal herbs or pollinator plants, can also lead the way, and as soon as the theme is convoked, the design process begins. Natural landscapes, like forests, grasslands, and seashores, are also powerful informants. After a walk in the woods, we may be inspired to create a woodland garden, envisioning a carpet of ephemeral spring flowers beneath a succession of native trees growing alongside a stream. By taking cues from natural scenes, like rock outcroppings covered with mosses and ferns, or undulating meadows receding toward the horizon, ideas pop—ideas we then translate into our designs.

The same is true when we visit great gardens, either public or private. Observing a successful garden is a great way to find inspiration or, even better, borrow ideas, like a plant combination, hardscape application, or landform pattern. We can do this through magazines, books, or websites, but the best way to experience a garden is in person, making public gardens an excellent source for inspiration. Even better are private gardens occasionally open to the public. Many towns, communities, and garden clubs sponsor tours of private gardens anyone can join. Visits to friends with great gardens are also excellent sources for design ideas, as is simply driving through neighborhoods and checking out the front yards.

VALUES

Our personal and professional values should always inform our designs, and there are three main value categories to consider: ecology, sustainability, and connecting with nature.

Garden design works with nature so it is easy to link it with ecology. Designing a garden is a lot like planning or building an ecosystem. We don't take cues just from nature, we build it, but in such a way that we can enjoy it comfortably while appreciating how it works. Inspired to create ecosystems in our backyards, with all the flora and fauna that entails, our approach to design will reflect those values. Plant choices will hinge on how each species contributes ecologically, not just aesthetically. This goes hand-in-hand with a sustainable approach, since both entail working with nature, but when we hold sustainability as a value, we take things a step further. Sustainable designs require fewer upfront inputs so we find ways to work with existing landforms, utilize low-impact hardscape like permeable patios and dry-stacked walls, and focus on plants that establish easily and survive on their own without irrigation, fertilizer, or pruning.

Finally, something as simple as a desire to connect with nature can guide a design. Connecting to nature means different things to different people. It may be a screened-in raised porch with a view to a bird-friendly habitat garden, a mown path through a meadow where we can hear the insects hum in the sun and watch fireflies flit and float on summer nights, or a place to touch the soil and grow food from our own patch of ground. The idea is simple, but it can take many forms, and inspire design ideas for discrete garden spaces within a master plan or inform an all-encompassing approach.

VISIONS

All designers are visionaries. Garden designers must envision what their gardens will become by looking into the future to see how the garden will be experienced by their owners and keepers, visitors, and passersby. Our visions guide us as we think through the problems of design as a form of ideation, from conceiving how a garden will be experienced to making those experiences real. What will it be like to sit on that terrace in spring when the cherry trees are in bloom? Or on a summer afternoon after a thunderstorm? Or in autumn when the fallen leaves blow across the stones? This is what garden designers do as they design. They think, "What will it be like when?" As an informant, it may be one of the most durable design moves because it transcends the elements of landform, structure, and plants and taps into the human experience.

Another important informant touches upon the joy of being inspired by pure experimentation. Garden designers should be adventurous, try new things, grow new plants, and shape the land in ways that make it interesting, fresh, and exciting. While this isn't always what is wanted, some aspect of experimentation should be present in every design. It could be a surface water control system using tightly knit, rooted plants that slow and absorb runoff from strong storms, or perhaps an out-of-the-way place to try new plant combinations before they are introduced to the main borders. Maybe an artistic approach to building a fence with recycled rebar and driftwood. As an inspirational informant, experimentation can take our garden designs places we have yet to imagine.

STYLE

At a basic level, garden styles can be divided between formal and informal, though there is some specificity involved when considering garden style as a design informant. Formal versus informal is much more a measure of the geometry and patterns of the design elements, like formal square parterres bordered with boxwood versus curvilinear beds filled with wildflowers. A strict formal garden reflects a preference for simpler shapes and a regimented use of plants. Some people prefer that; others prefer loose arrangements for a naturalistic, informal style. Naturalistic, however, does not mean wild. It is a suggestion, or mimicry, of natural forms within a controlled pattern. There is also something of a hybrid between the two that has developed over time, notably a contemporary-style garden. Like the architectural style of the same name, contemporary-style gardens blend a formal geometry of clean lines with an informal arrangement of plants within those lines. The result is a garden that looks and feels timeless yet timely. A nifty trick. The scheme is well suited to several architectural styles, like mid-century modern, prairie style, Art Deco, Bauhaus, and the contemporary farmhouse style. While it makes sense to pick a garden style to match the architecture of the house, the gardens themselves can establish a style of their own, especially as the driving force of a design, as any good informant will be.

There are national garden styles to choose from too, like English, French, Italian, Asian, and Islamic, however all these styles land somewhere on the formal-to-informal spectrum.

- English gardens can be quite formal, yet the gardenesque trend popularized in England during the end of the eighteenth century accentuated a "nature improved" aesthetic, slightly less formal and more naturalistic.
- French gardens somehow always seem to look and feel modern, with a focus on strict geometry and rational lines.
- The beauty of an Italian garden resides in how the structures shape the garden spaces, and how the plantings are controlled with a traditional touch.
- Asian gardens almost always exhibit a level of control above and beyond any other garden styles, for example Zen or temple gardens, but there is always an acknowledgment of nature, though strictly controlled.
- Islamic gardens take the use of pattern to new heights, with a required sense of enclosure mandated by the desert climates where the style originated.

Using any of these national styles as an inspirational informant for a design is an excellent way to adopt a set of rules or find a place to start.

SITE

The final informant is site. The best gardens always belong, and there is no better way to achieve a sense of belonging than with a design heavily informed by the site. Although some designers may choose to work in opposition to what the site suggests, taking what the site offers is a much more productive approach. In fact, there is something we call the "genius" of the site—that special something that makes it unique. It can be a thing, like a landform, a structure, or a plant, but more often it is more intangible. There is always something about a site that makes us feel a certain way when we are there or think a certain way when we are designing its gardens. It's a sixth sense of sorts, but to find it we must believe landscapes can be magical, and that places can possess powers sensed but not seen.

Of course, there are more rational ways to understand a site, such as urban, suburban, or rural, and find inspiration from any corresponding positive or negative attributes based upon geography.

- Urban sites can be completely enclosed, yet still feel exposed, like a small backyard in a city surrounded by multistory structures.
- Suburban sites are the most diverse, ranging from orderly, planned developments that are too new to possess any real character to established neighborhoods built up organically over many years.
- Rural communities, or the hinterlands, are different altogether, often possessed of natural landscapes on the site itself, or within view from the garden.

Whatever the case, surrounded by open fields with views of distant mountain peaks or hidden deep in the woods, the site will always serve as a design informant, but how we choose to use it, as inspiration of paramount importance or simply working within its constructs, is up to us.

Design Keys

Organization, enclosure, and access are three keys to unlocking the potential of an outdoor space. Together, they guide the design by establishing the geometry of the gardens, set physical boundaries within the plan, and provide interconnections between outdoor rooms. Each key is foundational to the plan, and these next steps of the design process mark the moment the design drawing begins. This also marks the moment when aspects of design like ratio, negative space, frame, and focal points enter our work vocabulary. How we handle these keys will affect the design's development over time so it is crucial to understand from the start how we intend to organize, enclose, and provide access to, from, and within our gardens.

ORGANIZATION

Organizing gardens is more than just a matter of deciding what goes where, though that is a part of the process. Organization means how we shape and define a garden on every scale, from a single plant to the entire site. An organizational scheme is directly tied to the geometry used when laying out planting beds, lawn areas, patios, decks, walkways, or anything else on the ground. This geometry is either rectilinear or curvilinear, determined by the lines we draw: straight lines, curved lines, or a combination. Straight lines and rectilinear shapes make a garden look and feel solid, structured, formal. Curved lines and the curvilinear shapes they create are loose and free, naturalistic. Therefore, when designing a formal-style garden, use straight lines and rectilinear shapes. If we want to design a naturalistic-style garden, use curved lines, or arcs, to create curvilinear shapes.

Rectilinear is easier than curvilinear. With a rectilinear organization, we simply lay down a straightedge and draw the lines. Curves, on the other hand, take practice and time to get just right. It can take several tries to find the perfect curve, whether we're drawing them freehand, with a drafting tool, or in a CAD program. The best way to do it is to not think about the curve and just keep drawing versions until it finally looks right or pick the best version among all attempts. There are also drafting techniques for curvilinear plans using overlapping circles, tangent or transecting lines, and their resulting arcs. Whatever the method, straight lines are always easier to draw, but not always the best organizational lines for a design.

▶ The lines you draw, whether curved or straight, will have a lasting effect on the look and feel of the final design.

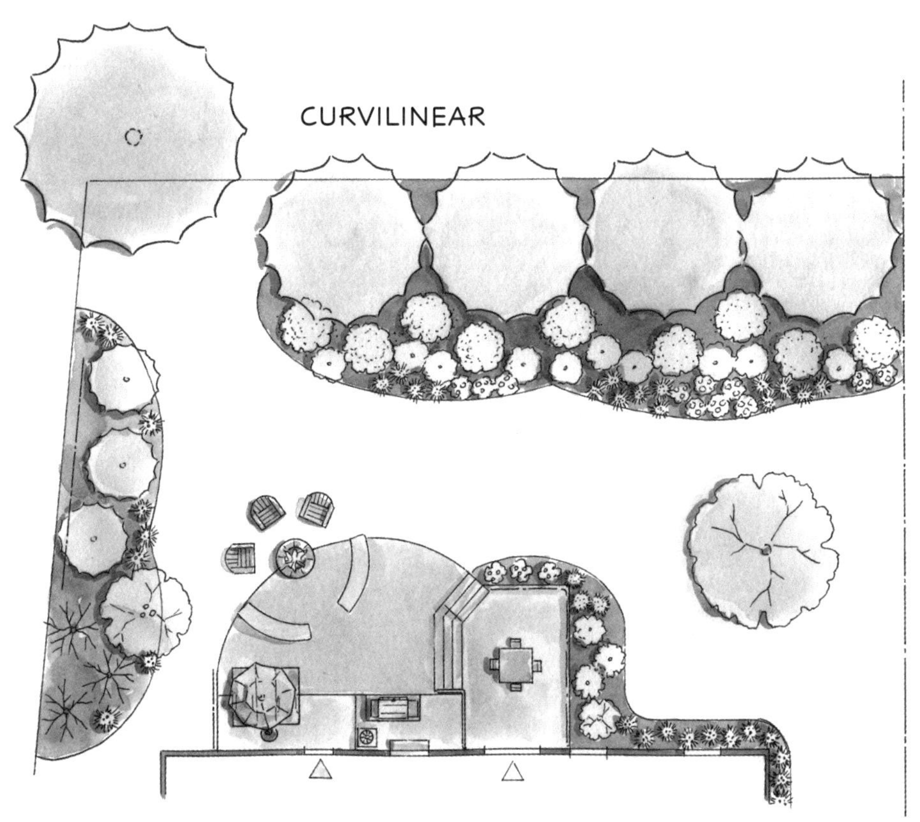
CURVILINEAR

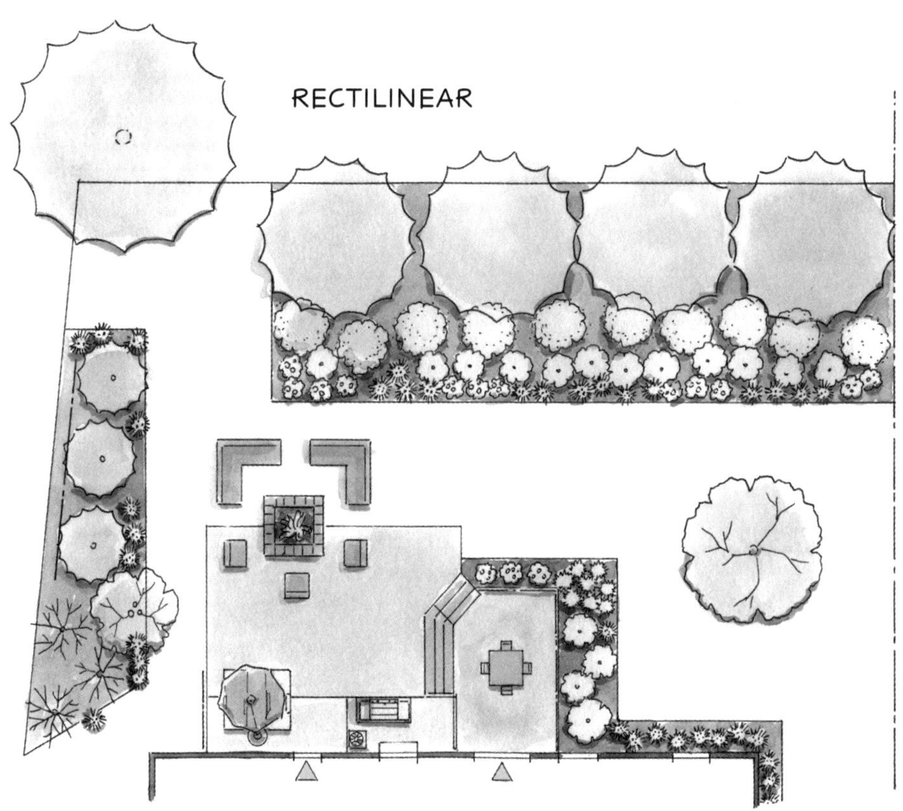
RECTILINEAR

THE GOLDEN RECTANGLE / RATIO

A golden rectangle, or ratio, is a rectangle that can be cut up into a square and another rectangle just like the original, but smaller. That rectangle can also be cut into a square and another rectangle just like the original, but smaller again. This can be repeated over and over to produce a sequence of squares and rectangles that can be combined into a well-proportioned rectilinear organizational scheme. From this geometry, it is also possible to form curves (a Fibonacci curve) or proportioned circles inside the resulting squares and use them as the basis of a curvilinear scheme when laying out the basic geometry of a plan.

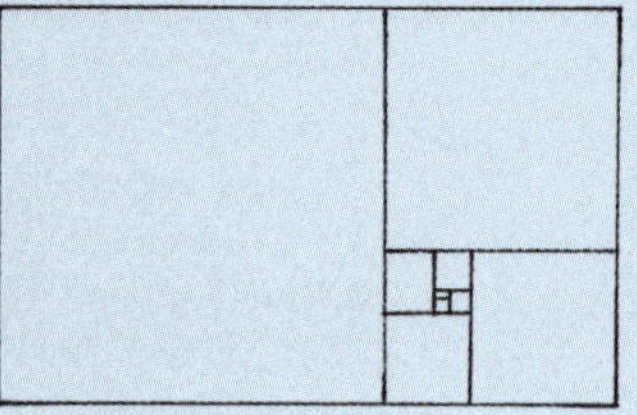
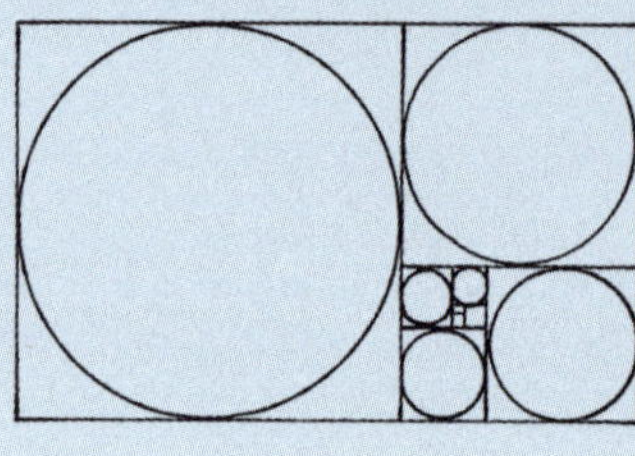
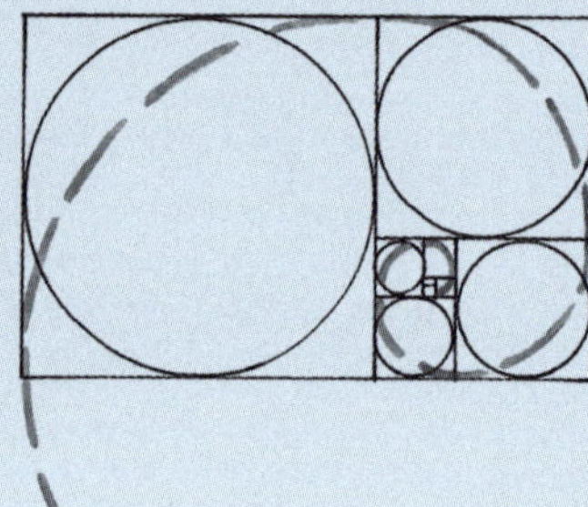

A trick for finding the most pleasing proportions is to base your design on what is known as the golden ratio.

ENCLOSURE

Creating a sense of enclosure is an important key when designing gardens. The word "garden" comes from the Old English "geard," meaning "fence, enclosure, or courtyard," and the Old Saxon "gyrdan," meaning "to enclose" or "gird." While not all garden spaces are fully enclosed, some sense of enclosure is necessary for the garden to feel like a place of its own, unique within the world that surrounds it. Gardens are discrete outdoor spaces so it's easy to imagine them as outdoor rooms, or garden rooms. Designing garden rooms has been a long-established conceit employed by garden designers for a reason. It works. Seeing outdoor rooms as equivalents to their indoor counterparts—such as a front entry garden as an outdoor, semipublic foyer; the backyard as a family room; and the outdoor kitchen on a patio as, of course, the kitchen—allows us to section a site into rooms and establish a solid sense of enclosure.

The garden rooms become extensions of the house, and those directly adjacent to the house, like a patio or deck, tend to be more formal, with structures to make them comfortable. As we move farther from the house, the rooms tend to relax and become a little wilder, influenced as they are by the increasingly natural setting. Finally, at the farthest points from the house, especially on a large property with multiple acres, we may cross the frame of the garden, and find ourselves no longer within a garden room, but outside of the design altogether.

When designing garden rooms, we make them the same way an architect constructs an interior room, with floors, walls, and ceilings. A garden floor can be a lawn, a wooden deck, a stone patio, a walkway, or even a covering of plants we don't walk on. Walls can consist of actual walls built of stone or wood (fences), or possibly a hedge, anything vertical that encloses the space. Garden walls can also be see-through, just like a window in a house, with openings in the outdoor wall, or by using what are called veil plants with weeping branches or loose forms. Garden screens or lattice also works well as walls. Finally, every room has a ceiling. In the garden, this is the sky, the underside of a tree canopy, or a structure like a pergola or arbor. The designer must choose the types of floors, walls, and ceilings that will define their garden rooms.

ACCESS

A crucial key to any garden design is something called "access," or how we move into, about, and through a garden. For example, getting from the sidewalk to the front door, the back door to the compost pile, or from garden room to garden room. Whatever the number of entry points and garden areas there are, we must find comfortable and interesting ways to get from place to place. This requires paths and walks, whether well-defined or simply suggested. When dealing with slopes, we need steps and stairways, which are basically walks or paths going up or down a hill. Or we can eschew steps and work with ramps. Frequently used passages are best designed to be straightforward and comfortable, like a solid paver walk, whereas paths that lead us deeper into the garden can develop over time as a footpath, or be purposely designed as difficult to find, adding intrigue to the destination beyond. Access can also be infinite, such as when a path ends at an open lawn, allowing us to choose any direction instead of being guided.

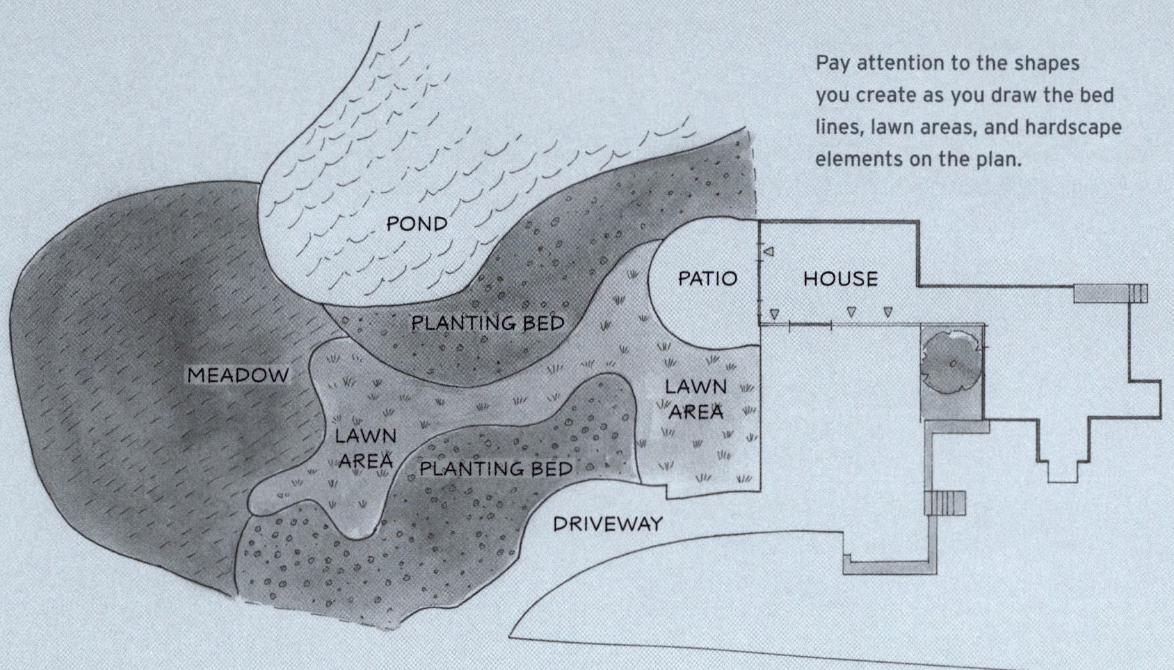

Pay attention to the shapes you create as you draw the bed lines, lawn areas, and hardscape elements on the plan.

CONSIDERING NEGATIVE SPACE

Anyone who has taken an art drawing class learned what negative space is when they were instructed to draw a still life without drawing the subjects (a vase, a flower, an apple) but, instead, draw the space around them. While at first this sounds confusing, the exercise forces students to study the shape of the space around each thing and by drawing it, the vase, the flower, the apple emerge. The concept of negative space also applies when we draw a garden plan because every line we draw, whether it is straight or curved, also creates the edge of a shape on the other side of the line. The best examples are bed lines adjacent to lawn. The bed line defines the shape of the bed, but it also defines the shape of the lawn. While we consider the size and shape of our planting beds carefully, we must not forget that those same lines also shape the adjacent spaces, such as lawn. Negative space also extends into the third dimension, as the shape and size of plants and other garden objects rise above the ground plane.

It takes practice to envision the three-dimensional negative space that emerges as you develop a planting plan.

Frame

The frame of a garden design defines the limits where the gardener's influence ends. On smaller suburban sites, this is usually at the property line, often marked by a fence in back and maybe some perimeter shrubs in front. Most frames are easy to establish because gardens rarely extend onto neighboring lots. However, a design on a small lot can try to appropriate views into and through neighboring properties, for example, via a conjoined front lawn or an open view to a lake or pond. If there are no pleasing views to appropriate, or if the views are ugly, the frame of the design should signal the end of the designed space with a wall, fence, or hedging plants.

On sites with multiple acres, the frame is where the garden ends and the land outside the frame, though still part of the site, is purposely not designed. There may be a land use restriction for such areas, like a dedicated wetland or forest preserve, or it may be left out of the design on purpose, since turning a full 5-, 10-, or 20-acre (2, 4, or 8 ha) property into gardens requires a lot of effort and resources. In cases like these, we treat areas outside the garden frame with a light hand, allowing nature to dictate how to include them in larger concepts for the site or for future development.

Most important, accessways need to be interesting, especially when they connect garden areas or take people to a special spot, like a view or secluded bench. Start by setting up focal points, like a tree, a large urn, or a gate, to attract the eye. A single focal point at the end works for straight paths whereas a sequence of focal points is required for a curved path, since the sight line changes as we move along. Once we capture the visitor's eye with the focal point, we've captured their feet and can now lead them down the path. That's when we deliver an experience, by choosing the width of the path, its material, and sensory elements like fragrant plants or water fountains. If it's a purely functional path, it will be straight and uncluttered. If it's a pleasure path it may meander with interesting moments along the way.

When designing the access into and within a garden, it is important to think about transitions, from into and out of the garden, from the house or other buildings, as well as transitions between individual garden rooms. It's best if these connections are seamless, allowing for a comfortable sense of flow. However, we also want to signal transitions. An excellent way to do this is to simply change the floor of the garden room. Passing from a patio to a lawn instantly signals a transition, but we can work more subtly. The pattern or material of a path can change from irregular flagstones to crushed gravel to signal a room change. Transitions can also be marked by flanking plants, like sentinels at the gate, or the subtle shade cast by a subcanopy tree.

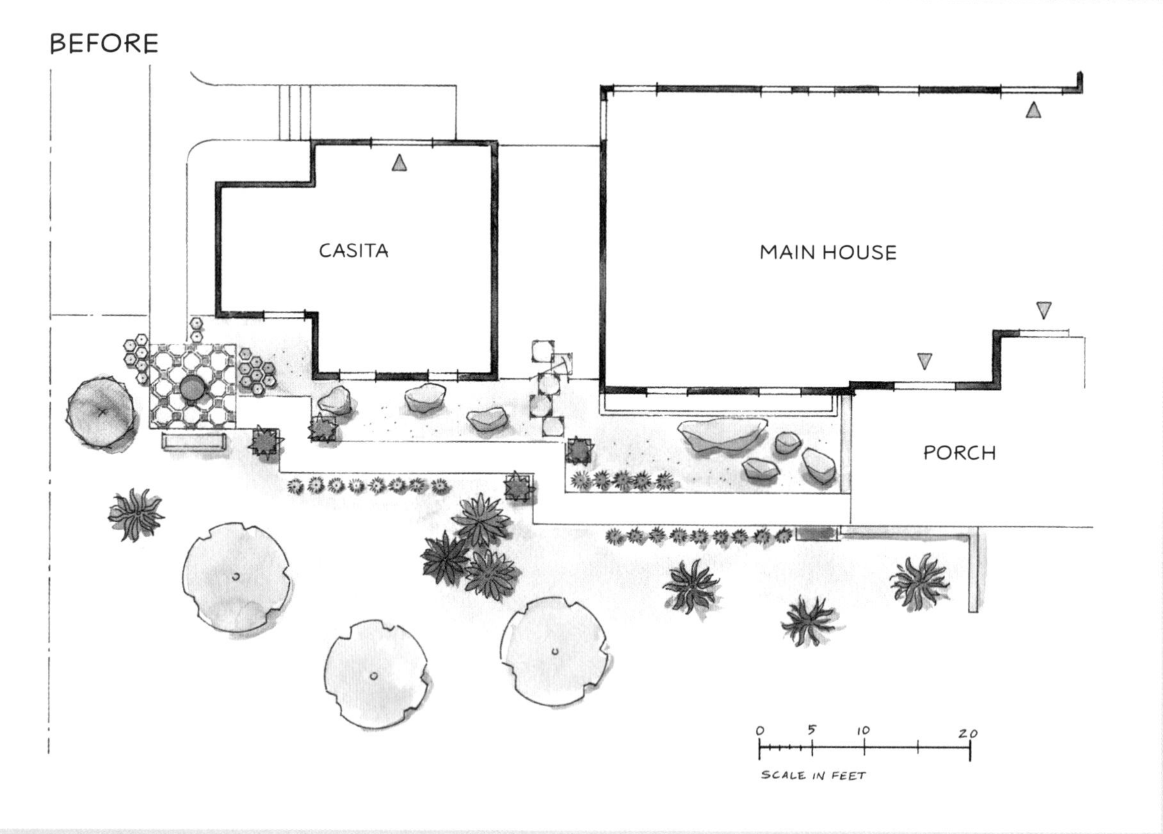

FOCAL POINTS AND THE REGULATING LINE

The keys to using focal points effectively in a garden design are placement and restraint. Too many focal points become confusing and diminish their impact. A focal point should attract attention for a reason, to guide guests along the path or pull them into an interesting space. From a distance, they can anchor a cluttered planting, giving the eye a place to rest among a tangle of flowers and foliage. Their placement will shape how a garden is viewed so putting focal points in the right place matters. At or along paths, in the center of a garden, at the top of a hill, anywhere they can attract attention and then transfer that attention to their surroundings. That's a successful focal point. They aren't the reason for the garden, but they are an invitation to check it out. Focal points come in many shapes and sizes, from rare plant specimens, plants in pots, garden art objects, and unique geological features to breathtaking views.

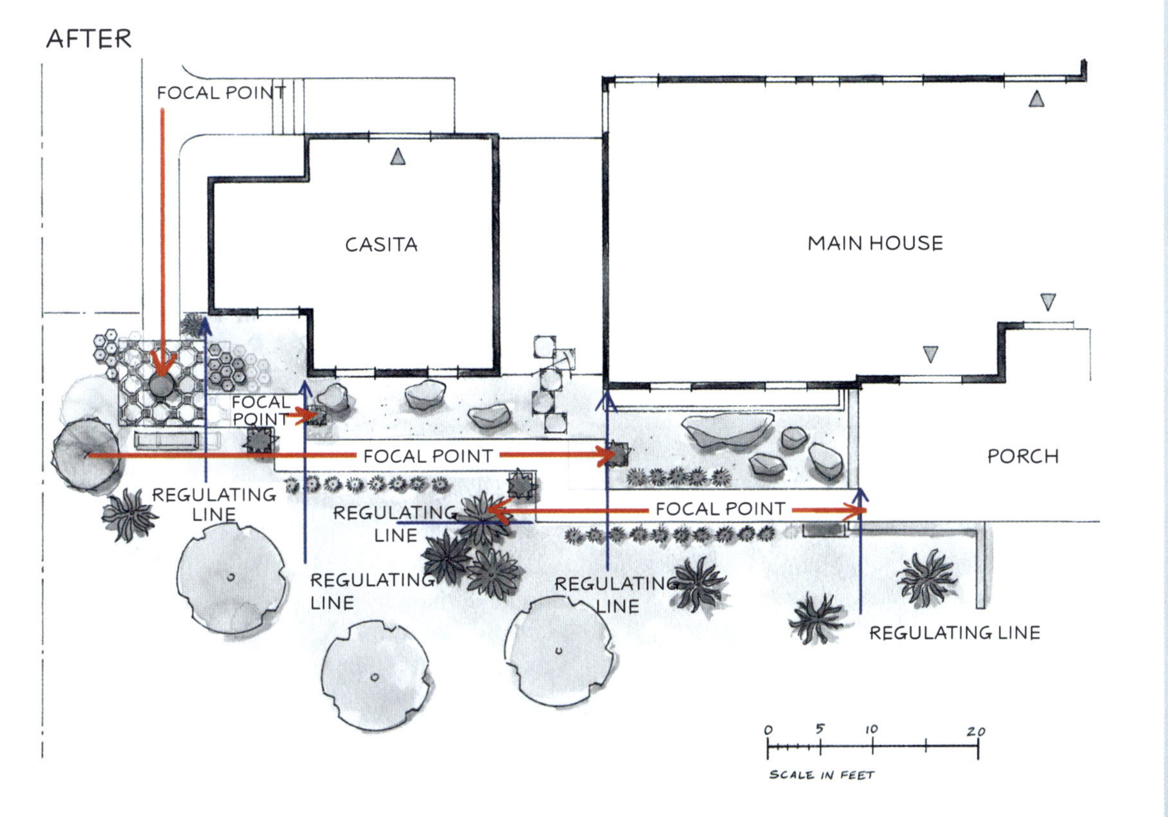

This leads to a discussion on the regulating line. The idea here is that key locations, such as a doorway, the corner of the house, a prominent tree, or terrace edge, can generate an imaginary line to connect and organize the design, resulting in a plan that looks and feels cohesive. A regulating line helps us fix the fundamental geometry of a design, in a sense providing a framework for the plan that will underpin whatever naturalness of the plant layer is introduced afterward. Some say it is the use of the regulating line that separates professional from amateur design.

◀▲ Work with focal points and regulating lines to find the subtle shifts that will improve your design.

The Six Visual Elements of Design

While most designers would agree that the principles and keys described previously are fundamental to the practice of design, some may consider the visual design elements that follow to be just more principles or keys. This is fair; however, visual elements are a different category of design rule. They are simple tricks of the trade that assist with the design details once the larger character of the project has been established through the application of principles, informants, and keys. These visual rules relate to how a garden is seen, which, of course, translates into how it is experienced. They can be applied discreetly throughout a design or broadly across every garden element. The six visual elements of design are:

1. Contrast
2. Harmony
3. Scale
4. Balance
5. Mass
6. Pattern

CONTRAST

Contrast, as some designers with a penchant for cookery like to say, is "the spice in the dish." The comparison is apt. Too much salt can spoil a soup, but just the right amount will bring out all the other flavors. The same is true when we add contrast to a garden design. It can come in many ways but, visually, it arrives with the introduction of a contrasting form, texture, or color and, most effectively, within the plant layer. If the plan is for a formal garden of boxwoods clipped into perfect orbs of varying sizes and arranged with space between for ground-layer plants, then we need to set off these prevalent forms with something different. By interplanting among these strong forms with something loose and amorphous, like wisps of feather grass or sedge, the bold forms of the boxwoods suddenly appear stronger.

The same can be done with texture, most notably leaf sizes when working within the plant layer. Imagine a sunny cottage mixed border filled with shrubs, perennials, and annual flowers, all growing together in a jumble. It would be difficult to discern any difference among the plants with their crisscrossed stems, foliage, and flowers, unless we add something unlike all of them, something large and smooth, like an urn. Suddenly the blur of plant textures comes into focus now that there is a contrasting texture to compare them to. We could also have chosen plants with exaggeratedly sized foliage or flowers, like a banana tree or dinnerplate dahlias, for the same effect.

Finally, color contrast. Take a garden filled with lots of purple and blue flowers and drop in a yellow-orange bloomer to make them all pop. Even better, work with light and dark. There are many shade-loving plants that have deep, dark foliage, like hellebore, *Ligularia*, and painted ferns, so mix in something light and bright, like golden sedge, and suddenly all those dark plants stand out beside their glowing neighbor. Using light-colored plants in shady spots is always a good move, as they help brighten areas and lessen the strain of seeing through the shadows. Place a brightly colored pot in a shady spot filled with ferns to achieve all three elements of contrast at once: a bold form, a smooth texture, and a bright color.

HARMONY

Whether it is the planting scheme, the choice of garden structures, or the shaping of the landform, harmony in garden design is a little like unity in that it is the quality of achieving a pleasing and consistent whole. Harmony occurs when everything that makes a garden makes it better. In the plant layer, the best way to do this is with color, specifically the use of color echoes, or different shades and tones of the same hue echoing across a plant combination. The colors can come from any part of the plant, in fact it works better if the echoing shades and tones are from a combination of flowers, foliage, and stems. Take, for example, a simple spring container planting of purple violets (flowers), young purple-leaved cabbage (foliage), and red-stem Swiss chard (stems). Each plant sports a shade of purplish red but on a different plant part. The next step for this combo could be to bring in some complementary color echoes, with a few yellow violets and a yellow-leaf lettuce all planted in a yellow glazed pot. The complementary colors make it pop but keep the echoes alive.

Another way to bring harmony into a garden design through color is with all the different shades of green. Plants do come in many colors, like yellow, blue, purple, and silver, but because chlorophyll, that magical photosynthetic substance all plants need to fuel their growth, is green, most plants we use in our designs will have green leaves. This shared trait is perfect for using different shades of green to visually harmonize the plantings. A preponderance of green in the garden also allows us to harmonize with other design elements, especially the structures–garden structures painted verdigris, a dark, gray-green that blends well with the plants, serve as perfect foils for viridescent foliage. Garden green is also why cobalt blue containers look great in gardens. That hint of aquamarine harmonizes perfectly with nearly every shade of green. There are also wonderful, earthy browns and rustic grays that look good with green. Color choices are made every time we add an object into the design and should harmonize with what is already there.

SCALE

A proper scale means making things fit. The best way to decide if the objects and elements of a design are on the same scale is to examine them and ask if they look right. It's a "you know it when you see it" aspect of design. When the scale is off, it should seem obvious. For example, an 80-foot (24.3 m) spruce tree looming over a single-story house is a scale mistake. It may not have appeared so from the start, but it grew to become that way. When it comes to plants, especially large plants, we must consider their future growth. That friendly Joe-Pye plant with monster blossoms atop 12-foot (3.6 m)-tall stems growing out by the pond's edge is perfect. Planted up against the backyard deck, it quickly overwhelms the scale of the space. Too small a scale can also pose problems. An 8-inch (20.3 cm) flowerpot set along a walkway is a tripping hazard, not a focal point or fun feature. Step it up instead to something significant, like a 28-inch (71.1 cm) container filled with annual flowers.

It's not just plants that need to be set to the proper scale. Hardscape features like walls and walkways should also look and feel as though they fit the garden. Overengineered walls and pergolas in small gardens are a common mistake. While we don't want these structures to be flimsy or weak, no one needs a 5-foot (1.5 m)-thick, crenelated wall with turrets surrounding their modest suburban split-level home. That said, when it comes to structures like decks and patios, as well as garden beds, garden designers must think bigger. We are working outdoors so the base scale we start with is "the world"! Quite simply, a 12 × 12-foot (3.6 × 3.6 m) room feels different when it is an outdoor space, like a patio. Outside, it seems small, so, we increase the dimensions, let's say 25 percent, to find the right scale, making the 12-foot (3.6 m) patio 15 feet (4.5 m) square. If that doesn't feel right, try another size.

Of course, all of this can change, depending upon the location of the structure. If it's in the middle of a wide-open field, we'll need to go even larger. If it's nestled in a small, quiet corner of the garden, smaller might be fine. The size of the house also matters, since a small garden outside a tiny cottage is just right, but larger gardens are required if the house, or any other buildings on or adjacent to the property, is setting the scale. It's not just the elements in the garden that need to match a certain scale. The entire garden itself needs to fit the site so large properties call for larger gardens and, correspondingly, large garden rooms. In addition, the scale can change as we move through the garden, enlarging in one area, then diminishing in another. Changes like this make the overall garden more eventful as each discrete space assumes a unique character based on scale.

▶ The scale of the plantings in the top drawing is too large for the house. The scale of the plants in the middle drawing is too small, but the scale in the bottom drawing is just right!

TOO LARGE

TOO SMALL

JUST RIGHT

THE TWO-THIRDS RULE

One practical rule to follow when setting the scale of a garden bed or other outside space is the two-thirds rule. Basically, the depth of beds and borders should be at least two-thirds the height of whatever structure or garden element backs them. This will create a three-dimensional space that fits the scale of the structure. Front foundation plantings, a type of landscape bed popular only in America, too often fail this test. They are typically much too shallow and appear tacked on to the front of the house. To get it right, measure the height of the house up to the roof peak. If that measurement is 30 feet (9.1 m), then some garden element needs to extend at least 20 feet (6 m)—20/30 = ⅔ (6/9 = ⅔)—away from the foundation of the house. The bed doesn't have to run the entire length of the structure, but some of it, or some garden element, like an island bed on the other side of the front walk, or even a lamppost, can satisfy the rule. If there is room to extend more than two-thirds, do it. If there isn't enough space to reach two-thirds, take it all and add vertical elements like fastigiate trees to mitigate the height of the house. The two-thirds rule also applies to beds along garden fences, hedges, and tall perimeter plantings.

Transform your boring foundation plantings into a front entry garden by applying the two-thirds rule.

BALANCE

Another excellent way to achieve harmony is through balance. Balance is a hallmark of good design. We want our designs to look balanced as a whole, yet also reflect a quality of visual equanimity down to the smallest structure or plant combination. The level of detailed attention given to any space within a design must be balanced with how much attention is paid to every other area of the property. Poor balance is obvious when we study a design plan and notice a lot of interesting things happening on one side of the drawing, but limited action on the opposite side. Similar evaluations must be made about the balance within each garden room, as well as individual planting schemes in garden beds.

There are two types of balance: symmetrical and asymmetrical. Symmetrical balance is when the two halves of a planting scheme, or the organization of a space, are mirror images of each other, either side of a dividing line. For example, if there is an ornamental cherry tree planted at one corner of the house, then there must be the same-size ornamental cherry tree planted at the opposite corner of the house. Twin evergreen trees flanking the front door represent another instance of pure symmetry; symmetry that provides a static balance, best suited for formal schemes. Symmetry is the simplest way to achieve balance and can be used effectively, but it should never be forced. It tends to come to us naturally, likely because human bodies are symmetrical, with two eyes, ears, arms, and legs, one on either side of a center line.

There is, however, a more dynamic way to achieve balance, through asymmetry. Asymmetrical balance means there are enough objects or elements on either side of a dividing line, for example the front door of the house, so the front garden plantings appear visually balanced. There could be a flowering crabapple tree at one corner, but two or three large viburnum shrubs on the other corner to balance it. A single holly tree flanking the door could be balanced by a hydrangea and some ornamental grasses. The trick is to include an equal amount of visual mass on each side so it all looks balanced. This approach works best in front of an asymmetrical façade or within an irregular garden space. While it would be wrong to impose symmetrical balance on an irregularly shaped space, asymmetrical balance, due to its dynamic nature, can be applied to a symmetrical space to relax its overriding static quality.

MASS

We mentioned visual weight in our discussion about balance, and it refers directly to how we apply mass in a design. Mass in this context is not how heavy something is but rather how heavy something looks. For example, an arborvitae as opposed to a redbud tree. The arborvitae looks heavier than the open-canopied redbud because the dense foliage of the arborvitae stops the eye. However, the clean green of arborvitae is visually lighter than the dark green foliage of a yew tree. The yew's darker hue absorbs more sunlight than the arborvitae, making it the visually heavier of the two. Color and density determine an object's visual mass, even with deciduous trees. Compare an open-branched,

▶ Strike the right balance in your designs with a symmetrical or asymmetrical arrangement of elements.

UNBALANCED

SYMMETRICAL BALANCE

ASYMMETRICAL BALANCE

Include anchor plants or objects, like a boulder or urn, to give your eye a place to land within the composition.

USING EVERGREENS AS "ANCHORS"

Evergreen plants are excellent visual anchors within any planting scheme. Oftentimes, the ground-layer plants, or even the understory shrubs, can possess a light, airy character, especially when combined in masses of similar texture and form. To provide gravitas to a loose planting, like a perennial bed or wildflower garden, you need anchor plants to keep things moored to the ground. Most evergreens, like boxwood, holly, yew, and spruce, have strong visual weight, making them perfect anchors in a planting scheme. The fact that they retain their foliage through winter means they will function as anchors when the deciduous shrubs are just sticks and herbaceous perennials have died down to the ground. Evergreen anchors carry the garden through winter, but to do so they must be carefully arranged into a pleasing pattern, or rhythmic sequence.

light green-leaved witch hazel to the intricate twiggy structure and deep purple foliage of a copper beech tree. The beech tree has more visual mass. While mass works best when building balance in a design, it can also be an element of contrast, such as a cement urn nestled among the flowers, an element of great visual mass anchoring lighter plants.

Structures also have mass, determined by their form, texture, and color. Compare a picket fence to a stone wall, or a brick walkway to a mulched path. The visually heavier structures have more visual weight and thus more impact within the design. They stand out and hold things together. Structures with less mass blend into their surroundings, which could be what we want for certain objects, like an arbor or trellis. The materials we choose for our structures will determine how massive they look, and thus shape the garden. The colors of stone or wood also define the mass of many garden structures. Light and bright hues feel light and bright. Dark browns, blues, and grays hold things in place.

PATTERN

The visual design elements just discussed are all tools to create patterns within the design. Humans respond to patterns. We also impose patterns on what we think we see without even

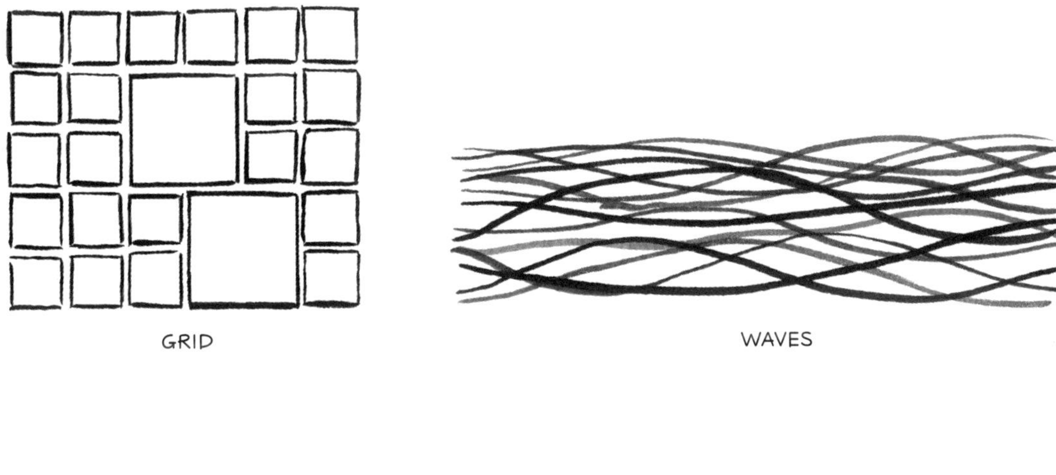

Pay attention to the lines of your design and observe the patterns that develop over time.

trying. It's a natural response that helps us understand what we are seeing, turning our focused gaze into an open view that allows us to see past individual objects and recognize the whole of the moment. Visually, we use mass, contrast, balance, harmony, and scale as contributors to the pattern. However, there are three key ingredients we must also apply when establishing patterns: line, shape, and rhythm.

The lines of a design, such as those that form objects within garden rooms, like planting beds, patios, walls, or walks, are elemental pieces of the pattern. Straight or curved, crossed or tangential, lines are the foundation of every pattern. From the interaction of these lines, shapes emerge, which are the building blocks of the pattern. Then finally, a rhythm is set and the pattern takes hold. All this can be done at every level of the design, from the overlapping elements of landforms, structures, and plants, within each elemental layer itself, and finally down to the granular level of individual slopes, stonework, or plant combinations. Patterns emerge no matter what, and it is up to the designer to apply them wherever they can to improve the design.

A basic pattern, such as a grid, is easy to read and thus simply experienced. A more elegant pattern, like parallel waves, provides a sense of movement and relaxation, like being rocked to sleep. Something complex, like an intricate weave of arabesques, poses a challenge that may be appreciated by some and misunderstood by others. The best way to work is to watch the patterns emerge on the drawing and follow their lead before trying to force an idea where it might not work.

While the youthful garden is filled with new plants, many are years, even decades, away from exhibiting the fullness of their mature selves. As a result, garden designers plan for time on every scale, from how each day changes through the hours, how every month changes with the passing days, how years are shaped by the changing seasons, and finally how the garden evolves through the years. Time plays a role, as new garden structures and plantings are built and developed, new design ideas are adopted, abandoned, and revisited, and the garden assumes a life of its own. Before long, the garden designer is responding to new influences and impulses. A second site survey, conducted ten years in, reveals a new set of needs, wants, and desires, new pros and cons, all of which continue to inform the garden into maturity, and finally old age, but on a timescale unlike ours, when forty or fifty years is just the beginning.

Imagine today what your garden will become and design it that way.

REPOSE AND TIME

A less visual, but more visceral, design element is that of repose. Repose is a sensation, a calming effect that is somewhat unique to gardens. There is an instinctual response to any space we enter and interact with, and gardens are especially adept at provoking emotions, like excitement, comfort, and relaxation, among many more. Plants have the strongest effects on our emotions, so how we use them in a design is paramount. One such emotion is a sense of repose, where peace and calm settle over us. Gardens are renowned for exhibiting a sense of repose, so much so that it is often expected that the garden will provide it. However, interactions like these take time to develop and are usually found only in mature gardens.

CHAPTER 9

Designing Useful and Beautiful Garden Spaces

Illustrations of *designed discrete garden areas for specific functions*, such as an entry garden, terrace, pool area, edible garden, or herb garden, as part of a larger master plan or as individual garden spaces.

Starting with a Design Concept Plan

The first version of a garden design plan is a design concept plan. Concept plans present ideas for the arrangement of the spaces within the property, such as public, semipublic, and private spaces, along with the transitions between these areas. In a home garden plan, public spaces are sidewalks or public areas adjacent to the property. Semipublic spaces are driveways, front walks, and porches—any area that would be reasonable for someone to enter the property without permission. Private spaces are areas like side yards and backyards, where it would be considered trespassing for a stranger to enter without permission. Concept plans also provide the design details, like proposed structures and plants. A concept plan is a guide to the creation of the garden, not a construction plan or step-by-step set of instructions. Most garden makers work off a concept plan, allowing them to adjust along the way as the garden is created.

This chapter presents eight design concept plans. The first five designs are discrete areas within the larger master plan design of the Valley View property that was the subject of the site survey and analysis in chapter 2. The final three designs are concept plans of discrete spaces in three different properties located in other regions of the country. Together, these eight designs represent a typical spectrum of garden spaces and demonstrate how to approach the design of each for optimal use and beauty.

The hallmark of a good design concept plan is that it shows how specific spaces on the property will be shaped and used. A good way to go about this is to name each area based on location, use, or theme, such as an Entry Garden, Poolside Garden, or Stroll Garden.

Ultimately, garden design is the shaping of outdoor spaces using landform, structure, and plants so it makes sense to designate a proposed garden by use or location.

◂ Picture yourself in the garden of your dreams and create a design that includes everything you see.

CHOOSING AN AESTHETIC

Every designer must choose a design aesthetic for a given design project, or in the case of more experienced designers, develop their personal design aesthetic. This can happen naturally, or with forethought. The following list represents some common considerations when forming an aesthetic for an individual garden or for a career of garden making.

- **COPYING TRENDS** While there are benefits to copying popular trends in gardening within a design, it is more important to use a trend as a launching point and expand it into something special.
- **CLIENT-PARTNER REQUESTS** When designing a garden for others, it makes sense to listen to what they like and then provide it, but a good designer will do more and find ways to provide something new and exciting.
- **PERSONAL PREFERENCE** The best gardens result from a talented designer left unfettered to explore options and ideas for a garden, creating what they feel is best while working within the rules of design.
- **TRADITIONAL DESIGN** Typically, the result of a clear structure geometry and basic-care plantings, traditional garden design fits most suburban properties with traditional architecture. A good example is the entry garden (see page 234).
- **RUSTIC DESIGN** Loose structure geometry with casual plantings is the hallmark of a rustic design aesthetic, best suited to rural spaces or large-acreage properties. A good example is the backyard garden (see page 238).
- **FORMAL DESIGN** The result of a strong structure geometry with highly controlled plantings, formal designs are suited to estate properties and public gardens where order is valued. A good example is the herb garden (see page 248).
- **PERFECTED NATURE OR NATURALISTIC DESIGN** Employs extensive use of all three plant layers but with complimentary use of structures, like paths or furniture, with focal points that guide visitors through spaces. A good example is the poolside garden (see page 240).
- **SUSTAINABLE OR NATIVE DESIGN** Relies on curvilinear geometry married to the landform with thoughtfully integrated structures and a plant layer featuring indigenous species designed to evolve over time. A good example is the stroll garden (see page 242).

DEVELOPING A GARDEN STYLE BASED ON TREATMENT OF MAIN ELEMENTS

A personal design style can be developed over time or adopted using established motifs and elements within a garden plan. Here are a few examples to choose from:

- **CONTEMPORARY** Overwhelming use of rectilinear geometry regardless of landform with a crisp application of materials for structural elements and high simplicity within the plant palette.
- **EUROPEAN COUNTRY** Features invitations to explore the surrounding landscape while furnishings provide immediate transitions from indoor to outdoor rooms with a significant use of plants to soften and decorate the outdoor spaces.
- **ASIAN** Always includes actual water or some representation of "flowing forms," and a primary structure such as a teahouse, pavilion, or torii gate surrounded by curated plantings cared for meticulously with labor-intensive maintenance practices.
- **URBAN** Functionally efficient use of limited space that requires imaginative approaches to how the central role of structures interact with the lush plantings, yet minimal influence from landform features.
- **MEDITERRANEAN** Highlights of gravel pathways, patterned tiles, meticulously clipped hedges or topiary, underplanted with succulents and fragrant herbs, set on a terraced hillside, and featuring a focal water fountain or pool.
- **ECO-FRIENDLY** Incorporates principles of environmental sustainability using native plants that support birds and pollinators, the application of local materials for garden structures, and the preservation of existing landforms.

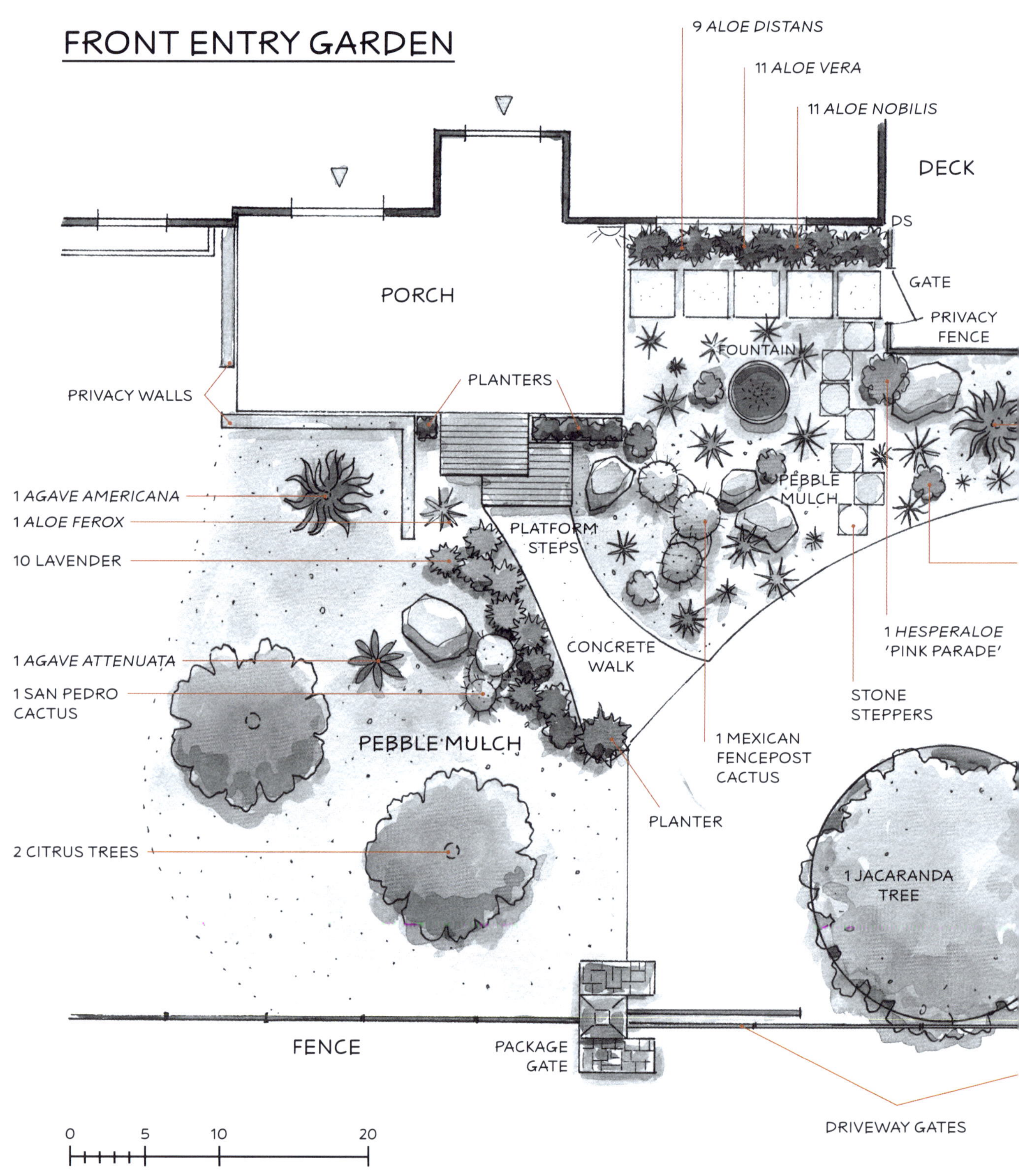

FRONT ENTRY GARDEN
9 ALOE DISTANS
11 ALOE VERA
11 ALOE NOBILIS
DECK
DS
GATE
PRIVACY FENCE
PORCH
FOUNTAIN
PRIVACY WALLS
PLANTERS
1 AGAVE AMERICANA
1 ALOE FEROX
10 LAVENDER
PLATFORM STEPS
PEBBLE MULCH
1 HESPERALOE 'PINK PARADE'
CONCRETE WALK
1 AGAVE ATTENUATA
1 SAN PEDRO CACTUS
STONE STEPPERS
PEBBLE MULCH
1 MEXICAN FENCEPOST CACTUS
PLANTER
2 CITRUS TREES
1 JACARANDA TREE
FENCE
PACKAGE GATE
DRIVEWAY GATES
0
5
10
20
SCALE IN FEET

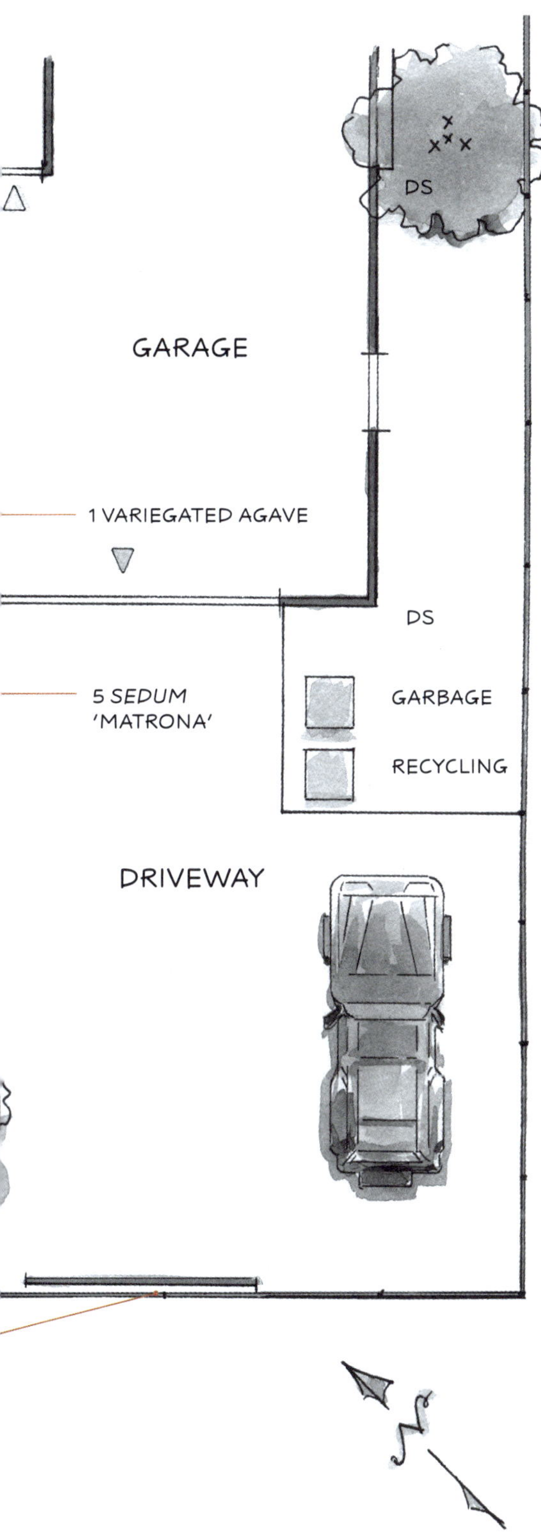

Entry Garden

LOCATION: Northern California

HARDINESS ZONE: 9a

SUN EXPOSURE: Morning Shade / Midday Sun / Late-Day Sun

SOIL: Sandy Loam

This front entry garden design was developed based on an architectural remodel of the house that included a relocation of the front door and the addition of a new front porch. The driveway was also reconfigured, and the front walk widened to allow for a more comfortable approach to the house. Two secondary walkways of stepping-stones allow for access to the property's private side entrance from the driveway or front porch through a privacy fence and gate. A small fountain/birdbath is included for a cooling sensory effect and to provide a water source for the many birds that live on and around the property. A new jacaranda tree is featured in the reconfigured driveway circle, and a desert garden planting scheme with drought-tolerant plants such as agave, yucca, aloe, and lavender combined with decorative boulders set in a rock-and-pebble mulch provide an easy-care garden plan suited to the region's hot, dry summers. Also proposed are two automated security gates located at the entrance to the driveway, coupled with a package delivery kiosk building on the privacy fence along the front property line.

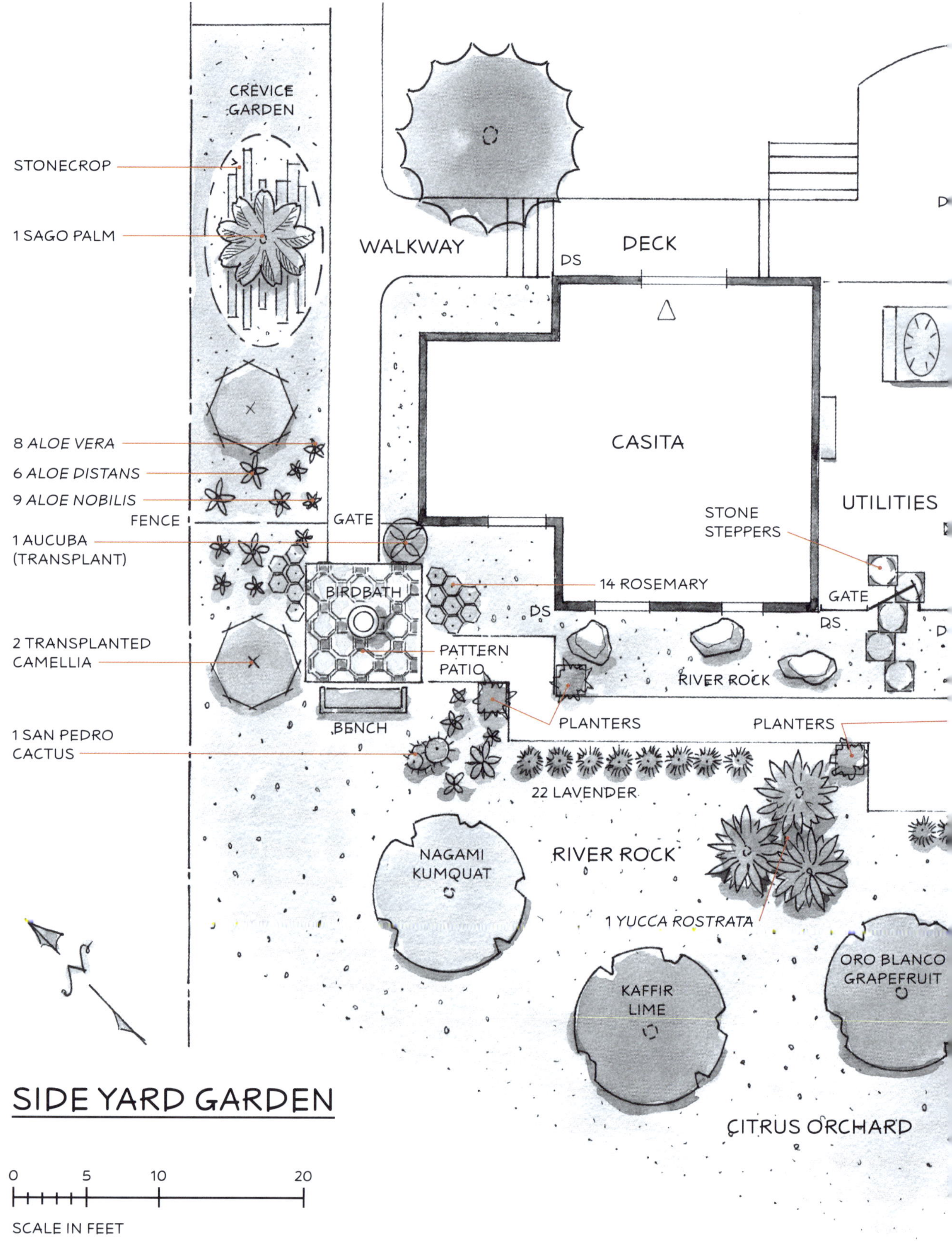

SIDE YARD GARDEN

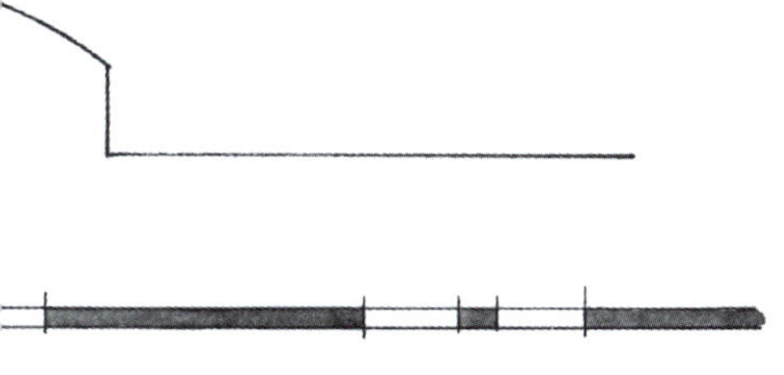

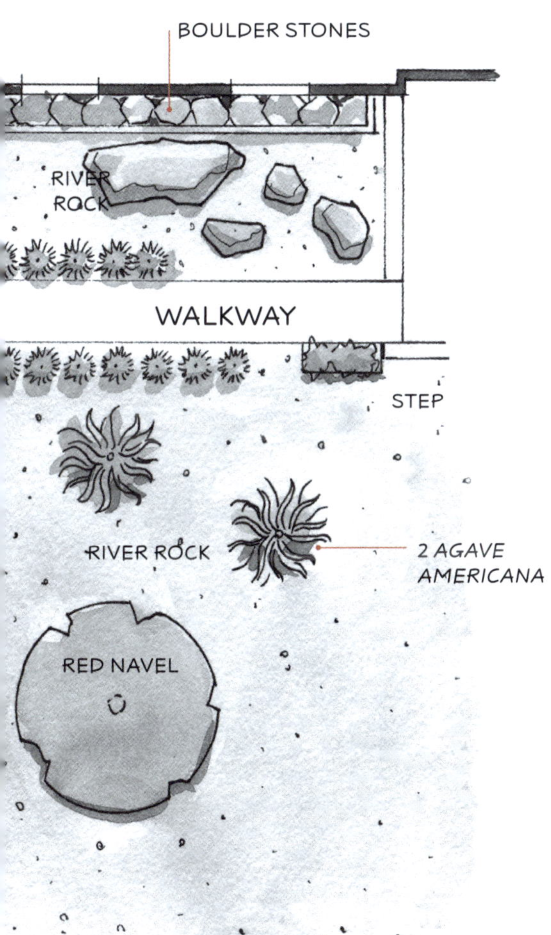

Side Yard Garden

LOCATION: Northern California

HARDINESS ZONE: 9a

SUN EXPOSURE: Morning Shade / Midday Sun Transitioning to Part Sun / Late-Day Sun Transitioning to Shade

SOIL: Sandy Loam

This side yard garden extends along the front face of the house and connects to a second detached casita used as an office/art studio. The concrete walkway originates at a gap in the porch enclosure wall and leads to a fenced-off utility equipment space behind a gate and between the two buildings accessed via stepping-stones. The walk continues to a seating area at the corner of the casita, then around the corner to a fence gate leading into the backyard. Focal points play a key role in the design, leading guests along the walkway softened with rows of lavender and highlighted by an orchard of citrus trees in the front yard area. Planters signal turns in the walk as does a large specimen yucca tree. The seating area nook is a patterned patio floor with a bench and a birdbath, planted with rosemary and aloe, backed by a mature transplanted camellia harvested from the backyard. Passing through the gate is a matching camellia and then a crevice garden with a specimen sago palm underplanted with stonecrop. The crevice garden functions as a focal point when viewed from the deck entrance to the casita. The beds along the walkway are decorated with large boulders nestled in variable-size river rock. The citrus trees are mulched in peastone gravel.

Backyard Garden

LOCATION: Northern California
HARDINESS ZONE: 9a
SUN EXPOSURE: All-Day Full Sun
SOIL: Sandy Loam

The backyard garden is a combination of a summer dry garden and a bird habitat garden and features a site for a greenhouse as well as an edible garden. A concrete walkway originates at the newly configured back deck, leads to the greenhouse and edible garden, then cuts through the bird habitat garden and winds past the summer dry garden.

The summer dry garden consists of drought-tolerant agave, aloe, and yucca featuring a queen palm set amid decorative boulders and large river rock.

The bird habitat is an expansion of existing bird-friendly shrubs located on the property, with some transplants and multiple new species of natives, like coyote bush and ceanothus, plus three mulberry trees to provide canopy and lots of fruit for foragers. The bird habitat jumps the pool fence into the back acre, to provide a sight and sound buffer of the neighboring property to the deck seating area. A small lawn is located just off the deck adjacent to the bird habitat and is the only patch of lawn proposed for the property. A utility area with a potting shed, woodshed, compost bins, and a rainwater collection tank is conveniently located to service the greenhouse and the edibles garden.

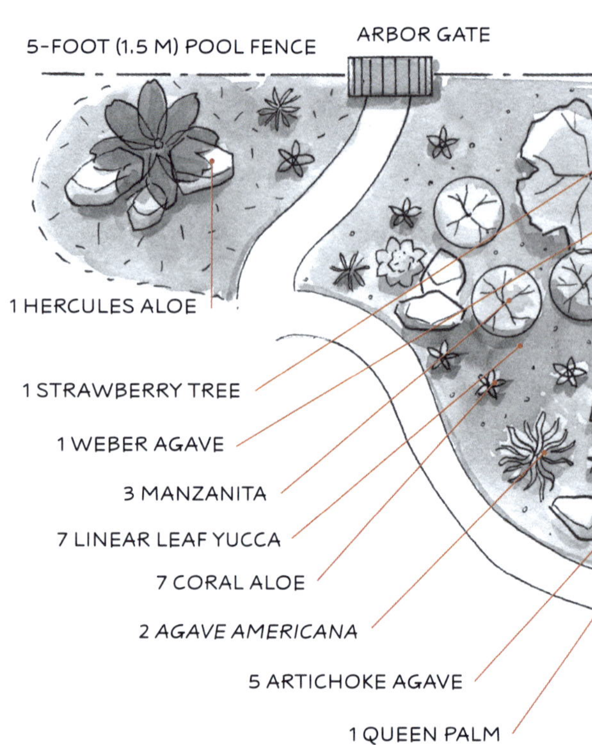

MIXED GROUNDCOVERS
SUNDROPS
FLEABANE
FOOTHILL SEDGE
CARPET MANZANITA

BACKYARD GARDEN

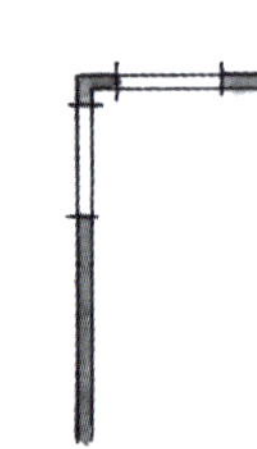

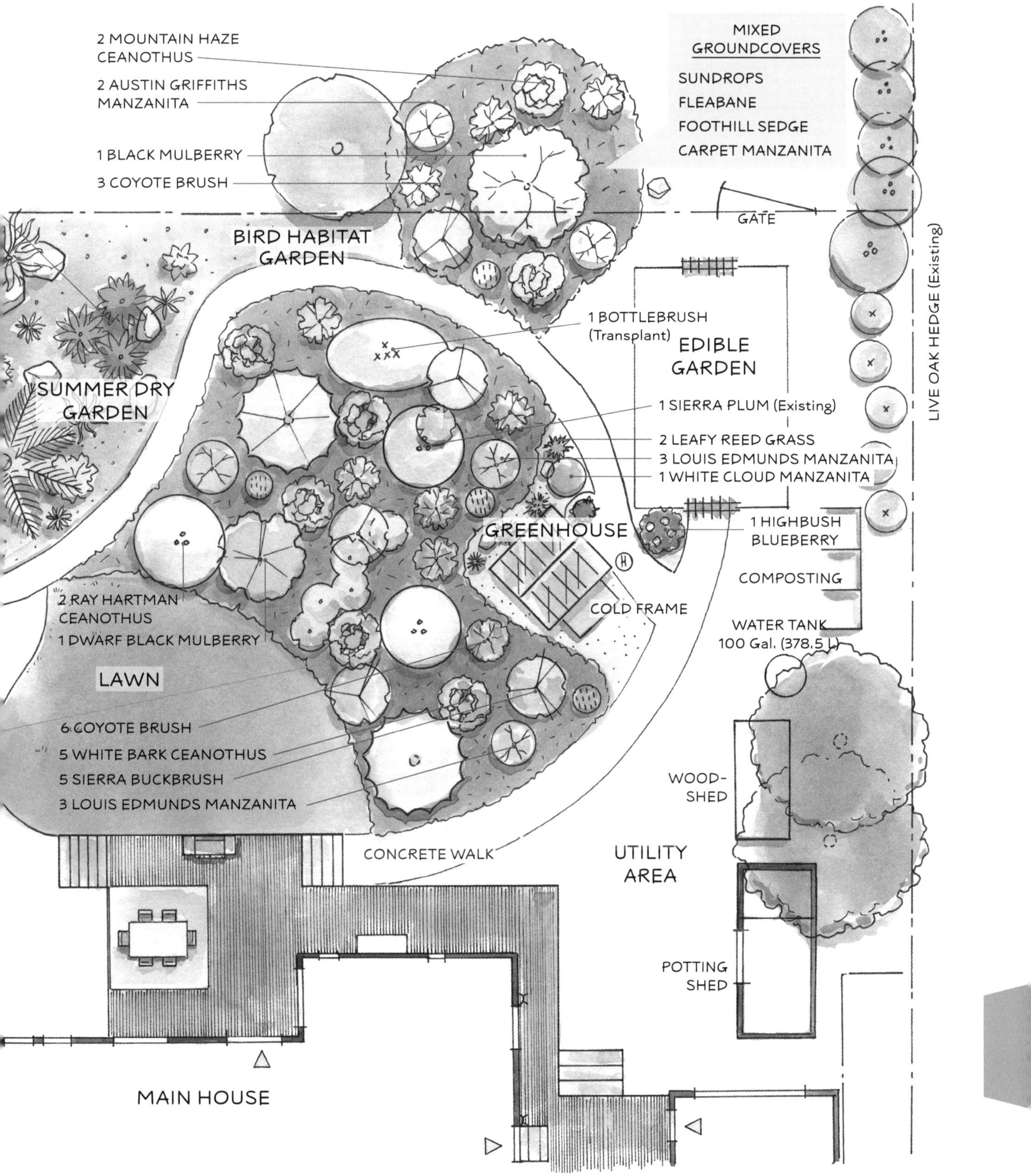

2 MOUNTAIN HAZE CEANOTHUS

2 AUSTIN GRIFFITHS MANZANITA

1 BLACK MULBERRY

3 COYOTE BRUSH

MIXED GROUNDCOVERS

SUNDROPS

FLEABANE

FOOTHILL SEDGE

CARPET MANZANITA

GATE

LIVE OAK HEDGE (Existing)

BIRD HABITAT GARDEN

SUMMER DRY GARDEN

1 BOTTLEBRUSH (Transplant)

EDIBLE GARDEN

1 SIERRA PLUM (Existing)

2 LEAFY REED GRASS

3 LOUIS EDMUNDS MANZANITA

1 WHITE CLOUD MANZANITA

GREENHOUSE

1 HIGHBUSH BLUEBERRY

COMPOSTING

COLD FRAME

WATER TANK 100 Gal. (378.5 L)

2 RAY HARTMAN CEANOTHUS

1 DWARF BLACK MULBERRY

LAWN

6 COYOTE BRUSH

5 WHITE BARK CEANOTHUS

5 SIERRA BUCKBRUSH

3 LOUIS EDMUNDS MANZANITA

WOOD-SHED

CONCRETE WALK

UTILITY AREA

POTTING SHED

MAIN HOUSE

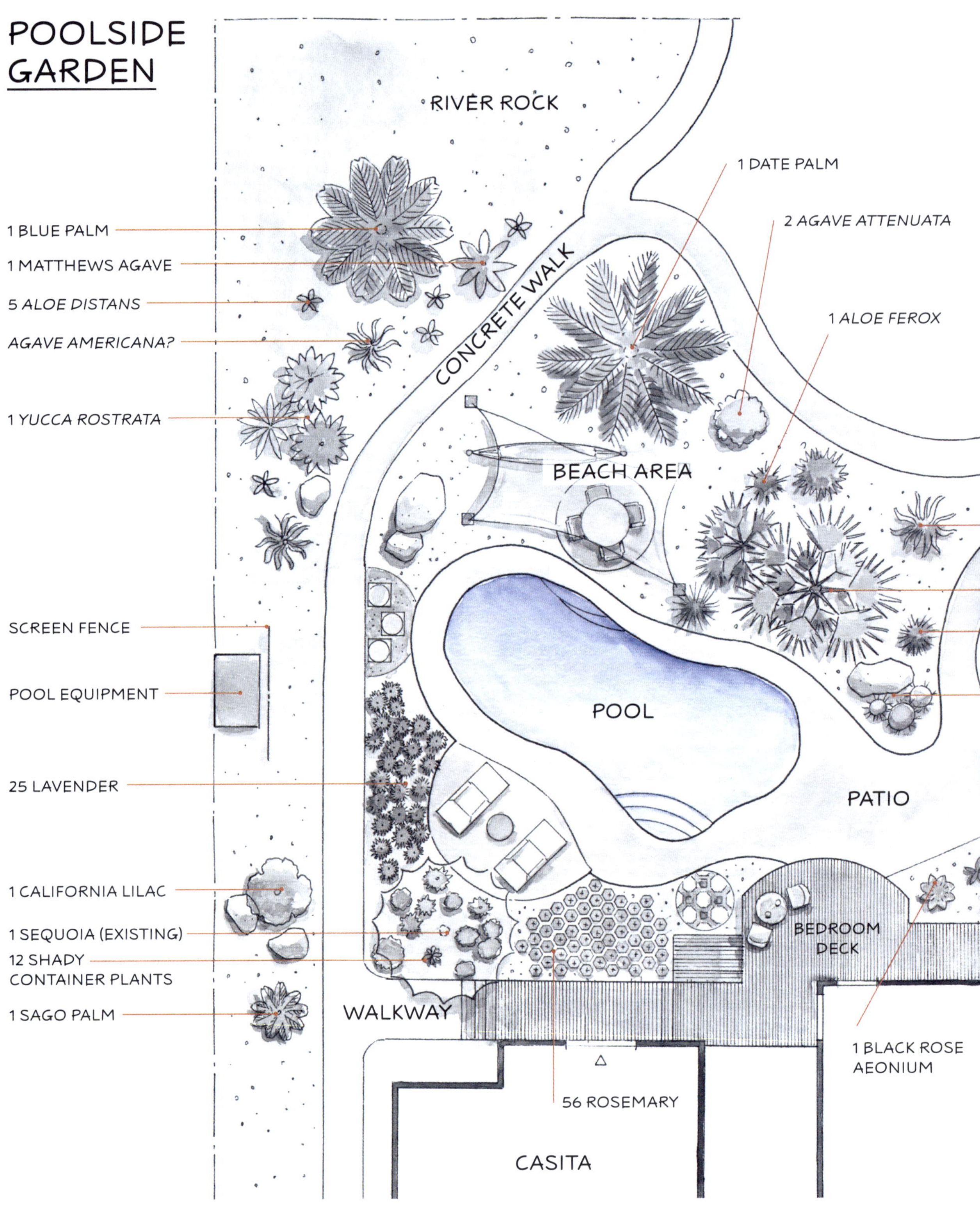

POOLSIDE GARDEN
RIVER ROCK
1 DATE PALM
2 AGAVE ATTENUATA
1 BLUE PALM
1 MATTHEWS AGAVE
5 ALOE DISTANS
AGAVE AMERICANA?
CONCRETE WALK
1 ALOE FEROX
1 YUCCA ROSTRATA
BEACH AREA
SCREEN FENCE
POOL EQUIPMENT
POOL
25 LAVENDER
PATIO
1 CALIFORNIA LILAC
1 SEQUOIA (EXISTING)
12 SHADY CONTAINER PLANTS
BEDROOM DECK
1 SAGO PALM
WALKWAY
1 BLACK ROSE AEONIUM
56 ROSEMARY
CASITA

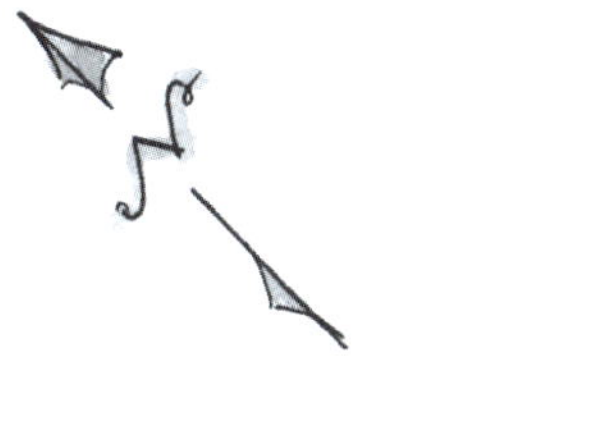

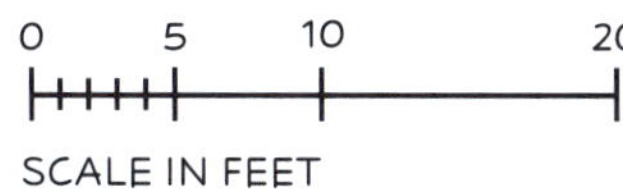

1 VARIEGATED AGAVE

2 CALIFORNIA FAN PALM

3 *ALOE DISTANS*

1 MEXICAN FENCEPOST CACTUS

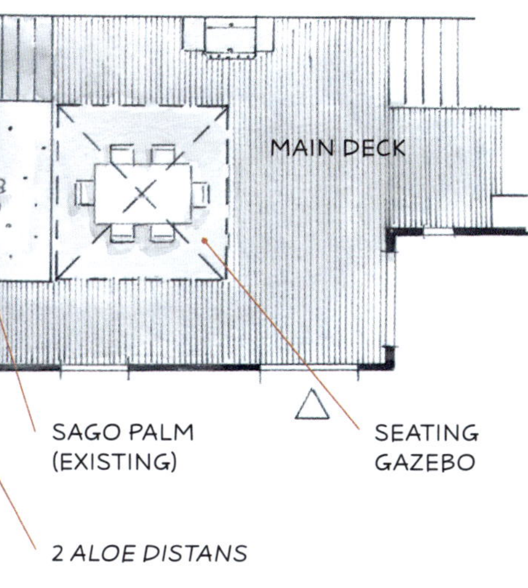

MAIN HOUSE

Poolside Garden

LOCATION: Northern California
HARDINESS ZONE: 9a
SUN EXPOSURE: Full Sun
SOIL: Sandy Loam

The poolside garden ties into the reconfigured back deck connecting the main house to the casita. A planting bed for the existing sago palm extends along the length of a bridge linking the main deck to a bedroom deck and the casita entrance. The expanded poolside patio connects to a concrete walkway leading to the summer dry garden as well as around the poolside garden beach area and a patio furnished with table seating and a hammock located under a sun sail. Another seating area with two lounge chairs is positioned in the late-day shade of the existing sequoia tree surrounded by masses of lavender and rosemary for fragrance and mosquito repellence during spring. There is shared access from the bedroom deck and the casita entrance down to the pool via a wide set of stairs. The beach area features the existing fan palms, a new date palm, agaves and aloes, with a blue palm, yucca, agaves, and aloes filling out the beds across the walkway near the 6-foot (1.8 m) privacy fence along the property line. The planting beds feature decorative boulders, river rock in assorted sizes, and actual beach sand in the beach area.

Stroll Garden

LOCATION: Northern California
HARDINESS ZONE: 9a
SUN EXPOSURE: Part Sun / Shade
SOIL: Sandy Loam

The stroll garden covers the back-acre woodland populated with valley oak, live oak, and gray pine trees. The interconnected pathways are shaped by the subtle sloping landform, providing easy transitions from one garden area to another through a variety of trail loops. Unique stops along the way include a council ring with a totem pole carved from an existing gray pine, cut down but leaving a 30-foot (9.1 m) trunk intact; a clearing for a bell tent for spring and fall camping; and a secluded picnic area. Along each winding trail are strategically placed benches with signal trees at key intersections and flanking the arbor gate entry from the backyard garden. Individual garden areas are defined by the ground plantings in, around, and beneath the existing canopy trees of oak and pine. The ground layers consists of patches of native wildflowers, savannah grasses, and sunny and shady meadow plants, resulting in a tapestry of plants that adds diversity to the 1-acre (0.4 ha) plot. The bird habitat garden extends into this space from the backyard garden and two new California sycamore trees will be planted to replace some canopy lost by the removal of several poorly performing or problem trees. A proposed solar-panel array located in the sunny meadow will power pumps for the rain collection tanks, pool equipment, and greenhouse utilities.

WILDFLOWERS

ARUGULA
PHACELIA
BUCKWHEAT
COSMOS
CALENDULA
SUNFLOWER
SAFFLOWER
MARIGOLD
CILANTRO
COREOPSIS
TITHONIA
ZINNIA

SHADY MEADOW

ANGELICA
MEADOW RUE
STRAWFLOWER
LEYMUS WILD RYE

SUNNY MEADOW

CORNCOCKLE
CALIFORNIA FESCUE
PRAIRIE SUN RUDBECKIA
DWARF SUNFLOWER

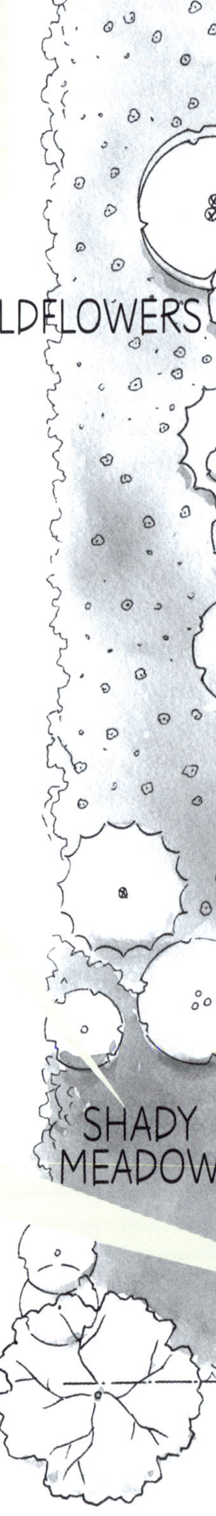

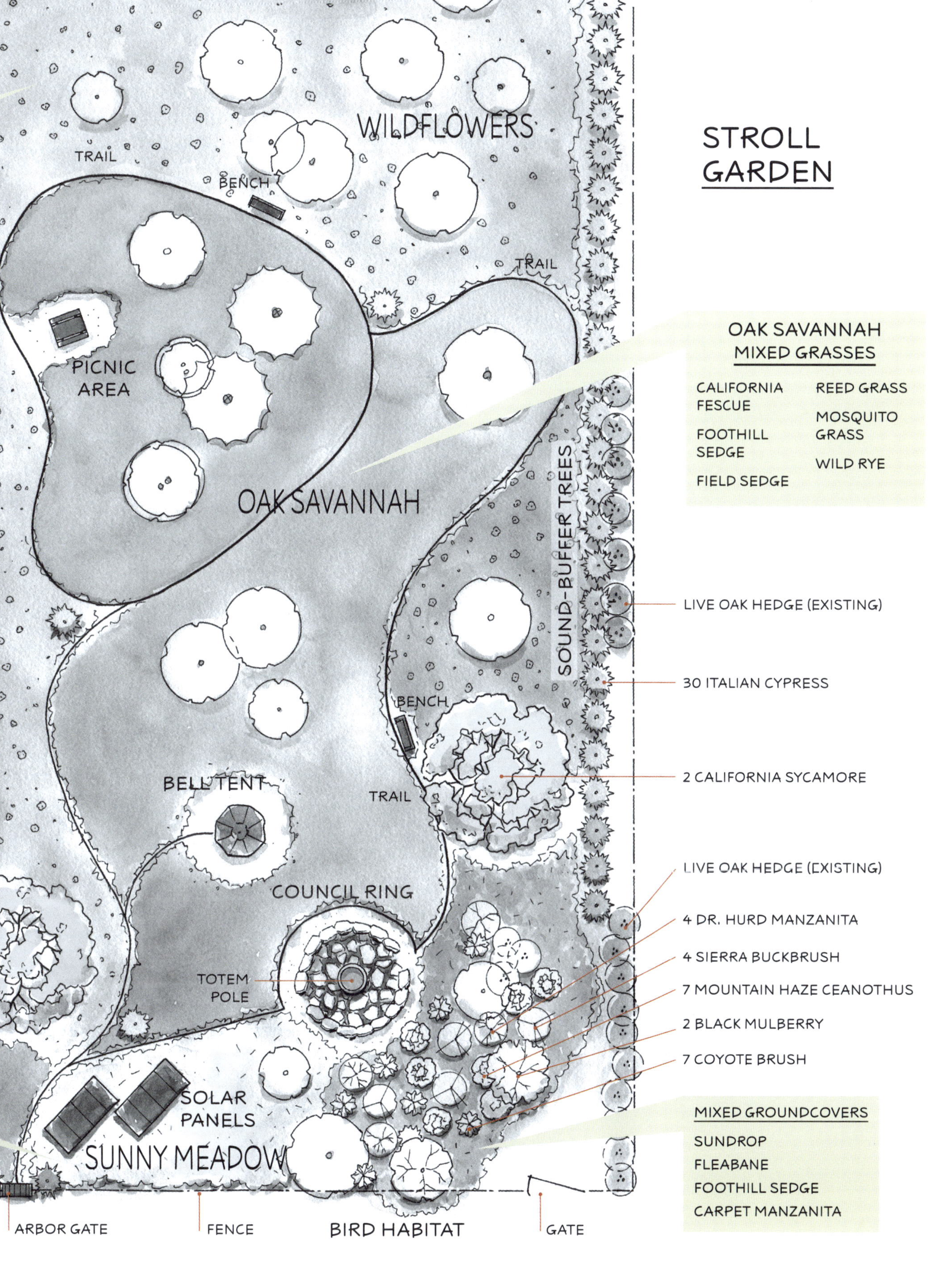

STROLL GARDEN
WILDFLOWERS
TRAIL
BENCH
TRAIL
PICNIC AREA
OAK SAVANNAH
SOUND-BUFFER TREES
BENCH
BELL TENT
TRAIL
COUNCIL RING
TOTEM POLE
SOLAR PANELS
SUNNY MEADOW
ARBOR GATE
FENCE
BIRD HABITAT
GATE
OAK SAVANNAH MIXED GRASSES
CALIFORNIA FESCUE
FOOTHILL SEDGE
FIELD SEDGE
REED GRASS
MOSQUITO GRASS
WILD RYE
LIVE OAK HEDGE (EXISTING)
30 ITALIAN CYPRESS
2 CALIFORNIA SYCAMORE
LIVE OAK HEDGE (EXISTING)
4 DR. HURD MANZANITA
4 SIERRA BUCKBRUSH
7 MOUNTAIN HAZE CEANOTHUS
2 BLACK MULBERRY
7 COYOTE BRUSH
MIXED GROUNDCOVERS
SUNDROP
FLEABANE
FOOTHILL SEDGE
CARPET MANZANITA

Terrace Garden with Outdoor Kitchen

LOCATION: Southwest Connecticut

HARDINESS ZONE: 7a

SUN EXPOSURE: Full Sun

SOIL: Loam

This bluestone terrace garden is the perfect setting for an outdoor kitchen, dining, and seating areas. A pergola covers an ample dining table adjacent to the grill and other kitchen appliances with a casual seating area nestled in the corner of the terrace near a shade tree backed by deep beds filled with shade-loving perennial plants. A row of holly separates the terrace from the rest of the backyard to the south, but some stepping-stones allow easy access to an open lawn area complete with a playset, central sundial, and Adirondack chairs. Fragrant plantings of lilac, daylily, and phlox define the edges of both spaces and help soften the transition from stone terrace to lawn. Another discrete seating area with a bistro table and chairs is tucked into the corner near the house. Tropical planters flank the main seating area and are also placed in corners where the house and terrace meet. A wall fountain serves as a focal point aligned with the passage between the lawn and the terrace, and a trellis attached to the house supports a kiwi vine to help soften the expanse of façade. A smaller entry terrace transitions from the main space to doorways into the house, featuring another tropical planter and low-growing, well-behaved perennials.

8 PINK ASTILBE
TROPICAL PLANTER
5 WINDFLOWER
20 BACHELOR'S BUTTONS
16 SNOW-IN-SUMMER
TROPICAL PLANTER
1 KIWI VINE
TRELLIS
HOUSE
6 FOAMFLOWER
WALL FOUNTAIN
5 LENTEN ROSE
6 TIDE HILL BOXWOOD
6 FOAMFLOWER
6 TIDE HILL BOXWOOD
5 LENTEN ROSE

0 5 10 20
SCALE IN FEET

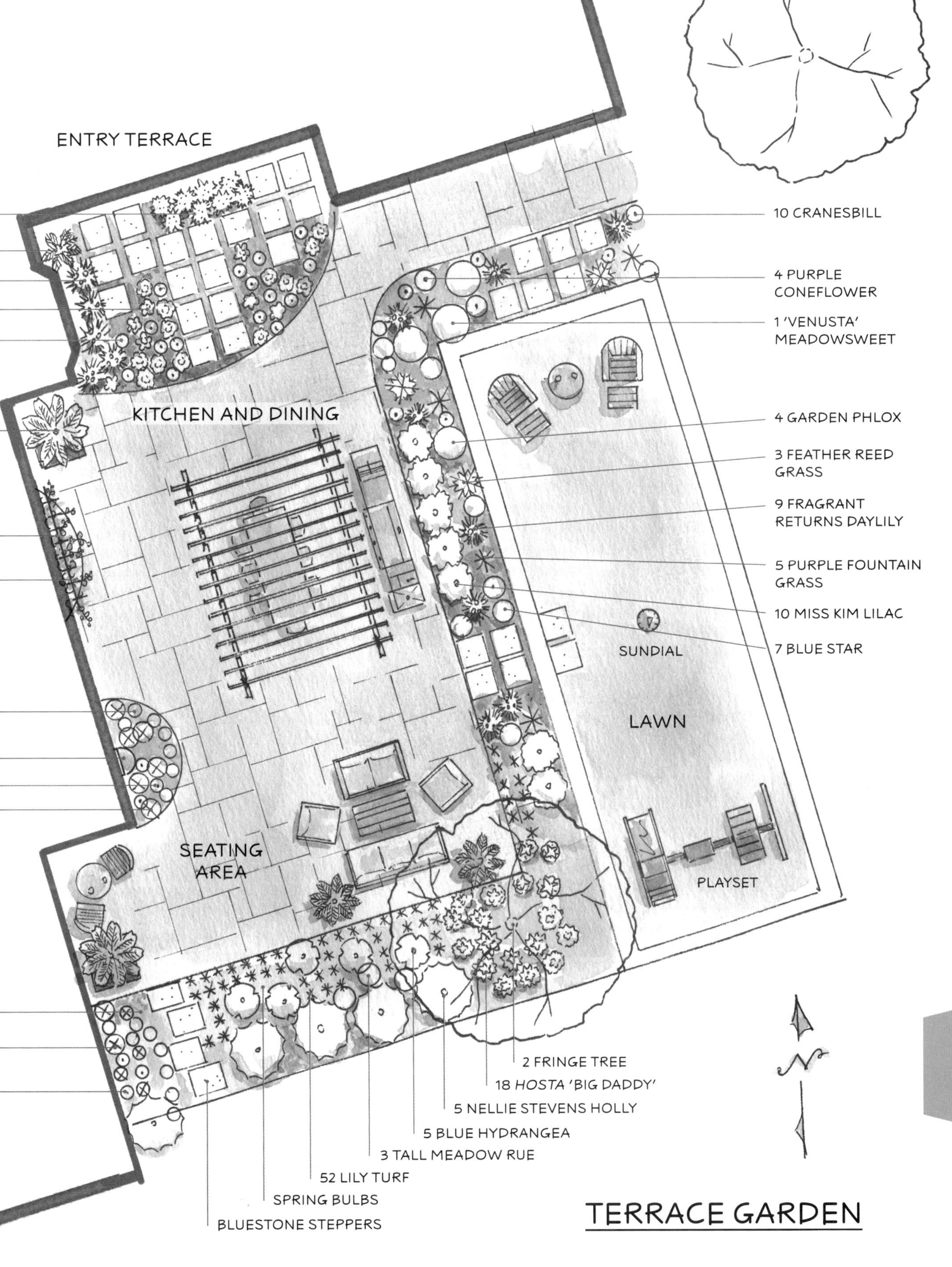
ENTRY TERRACE
KITCHEN AND DINING
SEATING AREA
LAWN
SUNDIAL
PLAYSET
10 CRANESBILL
4 PURPLE CONEFLOWER
1 'VENUSTA' MEADOWSWEET
4 GARDEN PHLOX
3 FEATHER REED GRASS
9 FRAGRANT RETURNS DAYLILY
5 PURPLE FOUNTAIN GRASS
10 MISS KIM LILAC
7 BLUE STAR
2 FRINGE TREE
18 HOSTA 'BIG DADDY'
5 NELLIE STEVENS HOLLY
5 BLUE HYDRANGEA
3 TALL MEADOW RUE
52 LILY TURF
SPRING BULBS
BLUESTONE STEPPERS
TERRACE GARDEN

Edibles Garden with Greenhouse

LOCATION: Northern Minnesota
HARDINESS ZONE: 4a
SUN EXPOSURE: Full Sun
SOIL: Silt Loam

Practical geometry predominates in this garden space sufficient for six large crop beds in cedar planters and a casual seating area with a chimenea and a pergola-covered table with chairs. The result is an edibles garden that provides a place to spend time relaxing as well as tending crops. Compost bins are conveniently placed just outside the fence with a large double-gate entrance and a single gate leading to four orchard trees: self-fruiting peach and plum, plus two types of apple trees to provide cross-pollination. Also outside the fence are a mixed berry patch with currant, blackberry, and raspberry and a long blueberry hedge that frames the yard. Proximity to the house is achieved with a flagstone patio and walk leading from the nearby greenhouse. Outside the greenhouse is a dedicated pollinator patch to attract bees and butterflies to the nearby crops. Specified crops in the beds consist of leafy greens, root crops, tomatoes with basil, perennial plantings of asparagus and rhubarb, pole beans grown over self-supporting trellises, and a dedicated cut flower bed. Two raised planters are available for chives, mint, and dill, with climbing sweet peas scrambling up the fence to hide the compost bins and a grapevine to drape over the pergola. The ground around the planter beds is covered with landscape fabric and woodchips, the chimenea oval is edged and filled with pea gravel, and the central space is lawn.

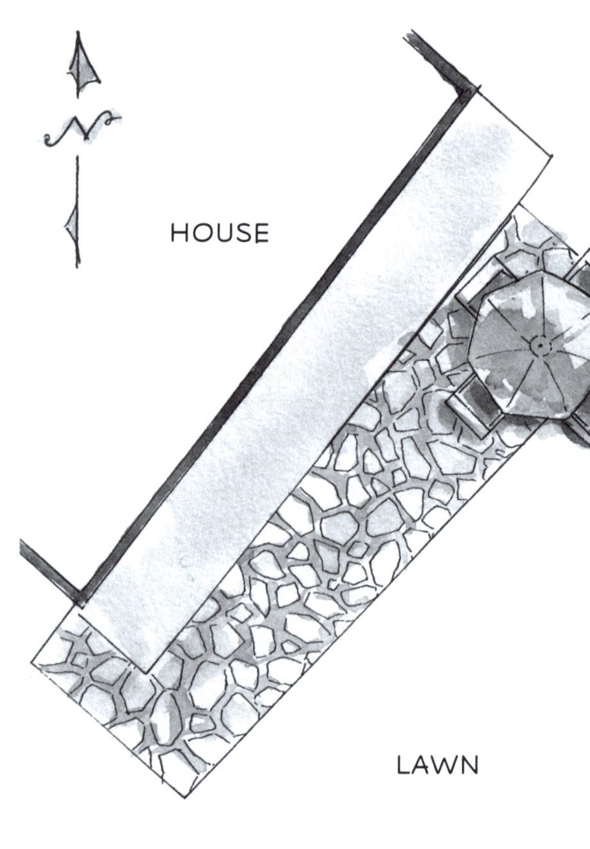

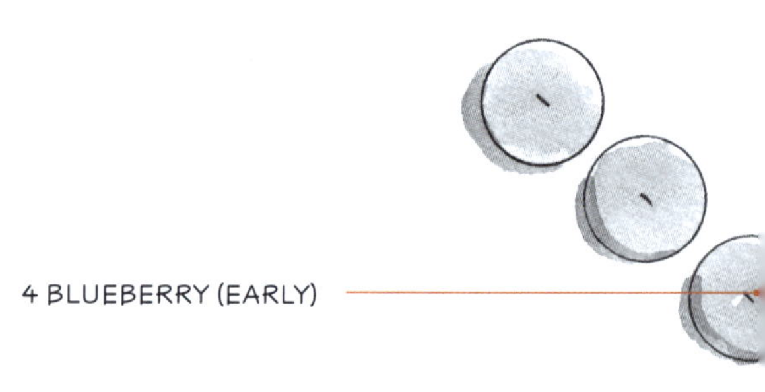

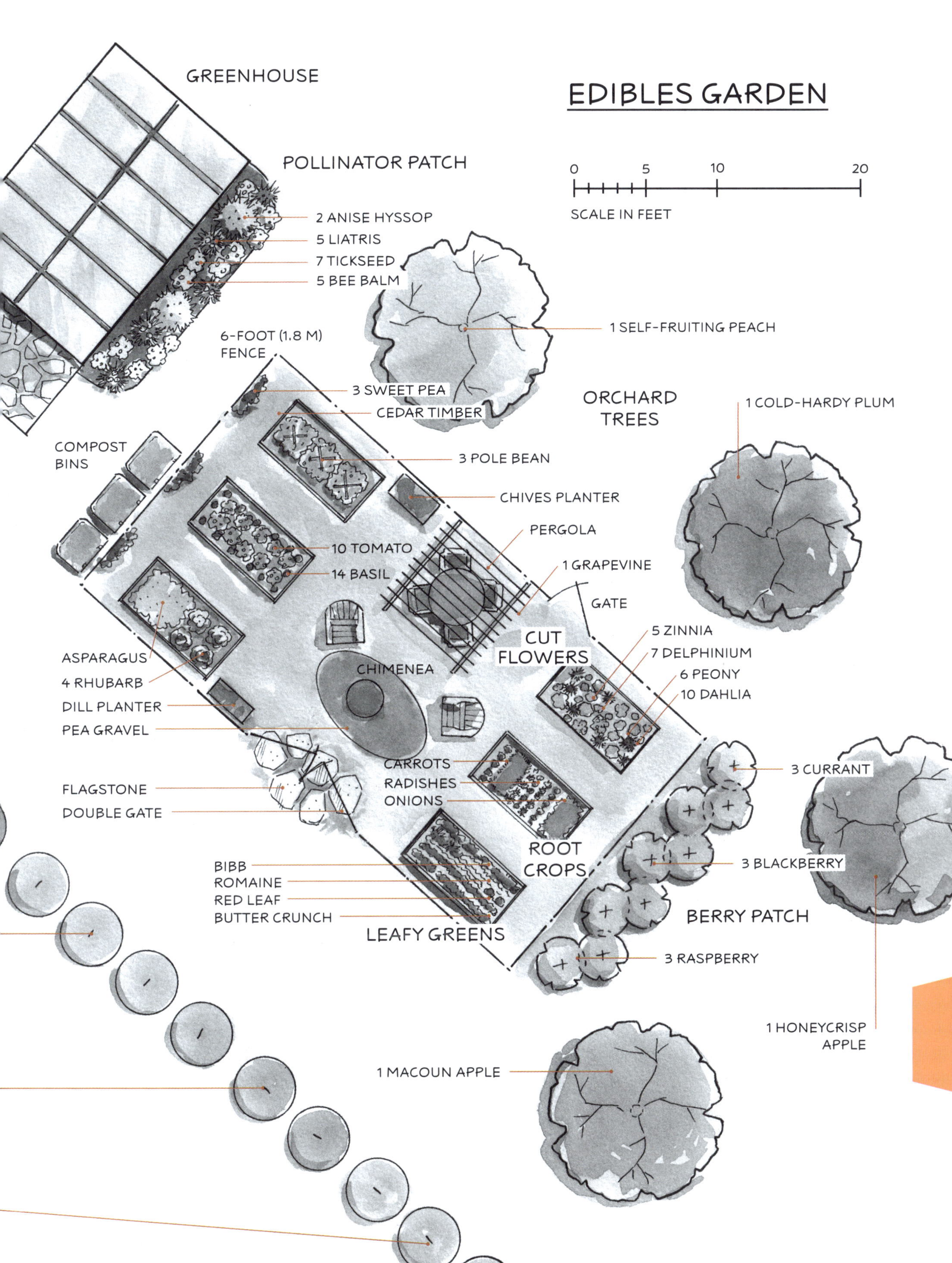

EDIBLES GARDEN
0
5
10
20
SCALE IN FEET
GREENHOUSE
POLLINATOR PATCH
2 ANISE HYSSOP
5 LIATRIS
7 TICKSEED
5 BEE BALM
1 SELF-FRUITING PEACH
6-FOOT (1.8 M)
FENCE
3 SWEET PEA
CEDAR TIMBER
ORCHARD
TREES
1 COLD-HARDY PLUM
COMPOST
BINS
3 POLE BEAN
CHIVES PLANTER
PERGOLA
10 TOMATO
14 BASIL
1 GRAPEVINE
GATE
CUT
FLOWERS
5 ZINNIA
7 DELPHINIUM
6 PEONY
10 DAHLIA
ASPARAGUS
4 RHUBARB
DILL PLANTER
PEA GRAVEL
CHIMENEA
CARROTS
RADISHES
ONIONS
3 CURRANT
FLAGSTONE
DOUBLE GATE
ROOT
CROPS
3 BLACKBERRY
BIBB
ROMAINE
RED LEAF
BUTTER CRUNCH
LEAFY GREENS
BERRY PATCH
3 RASPBERRY
1 HONEYCRISP
APPLE
1 MACOUN APPLE

Herb Garden

LOCATION: Central Georgia
HARDINESS ZONE: 8a
SUN EXPOSURE: Full Sun
SOIL: Clay Loam

This formal herb garden is a perfect discrete garden room set within the larger context of a Southern estate garden. Balance through symmetry and strong rectilinear geometry are the hallmarks of this garden set within stone walls. Two main axis lines are indicated by intersecting pea gravel paths set within metal edging, and a large central fountain focal feature. Single cut-stone steps at each of the three entryways mark a clear transition when passing into this garden. Flanking pillars indicate the main entry, and an iron gate signals a secondary side exit. Square stepping-stones allow visitors to enter the four-quadrant herb beds to get closer to the collection of fragrant plants. Two curved benches line the inner circle, and a stone bench flanked by two flower urns lies at the end of an axis line and wall. Two more flower urns flank the secondary entrance and four others are positioned atop the wall at the corners, contributing to the formal geometry of the design. Within the walls are orderly arrangements of herbs positioned within each of the four quadrants on either side of the stepping-stones, each square bed highlighted by a rose topiary. Outside the walls, carefully positioned trees and shrubs tie the walled garden to the surrounding landscape.

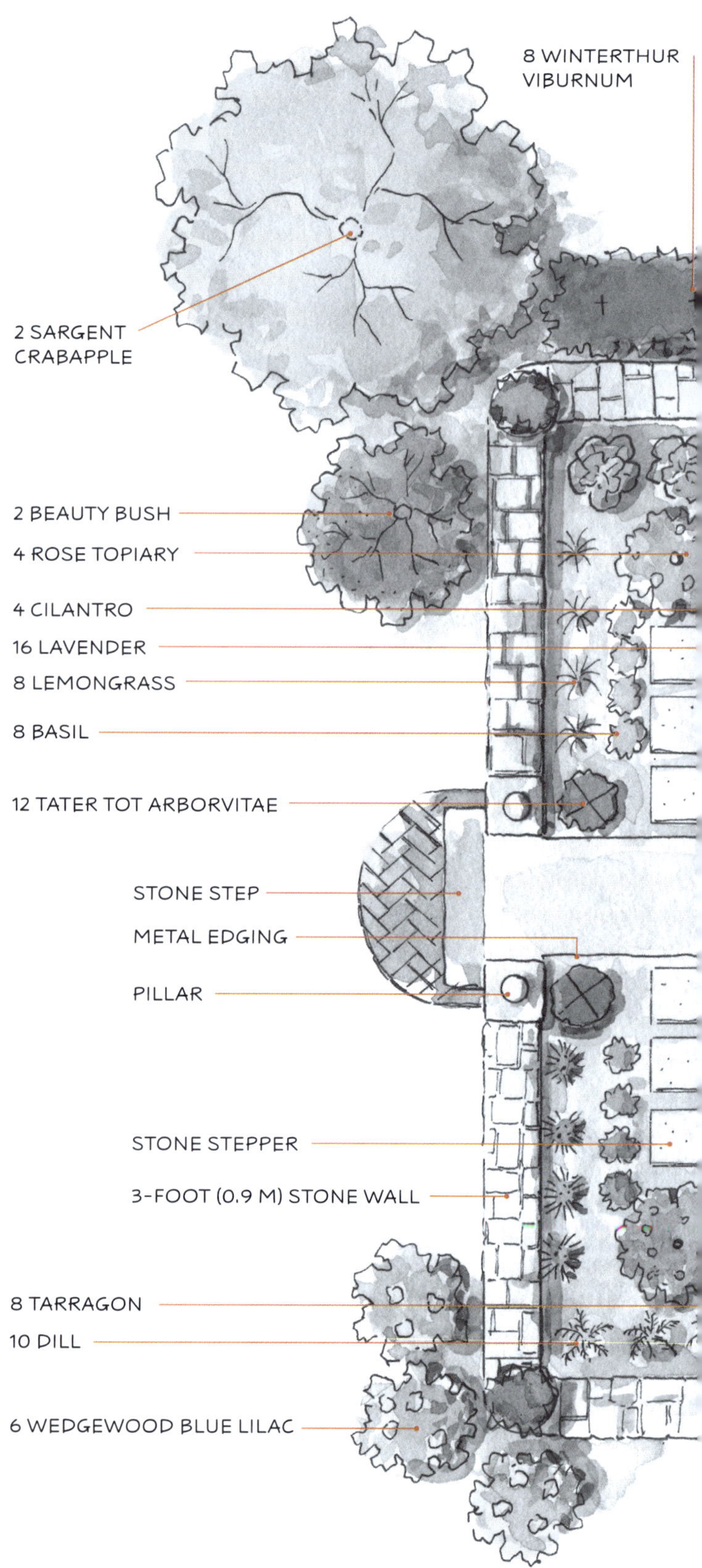

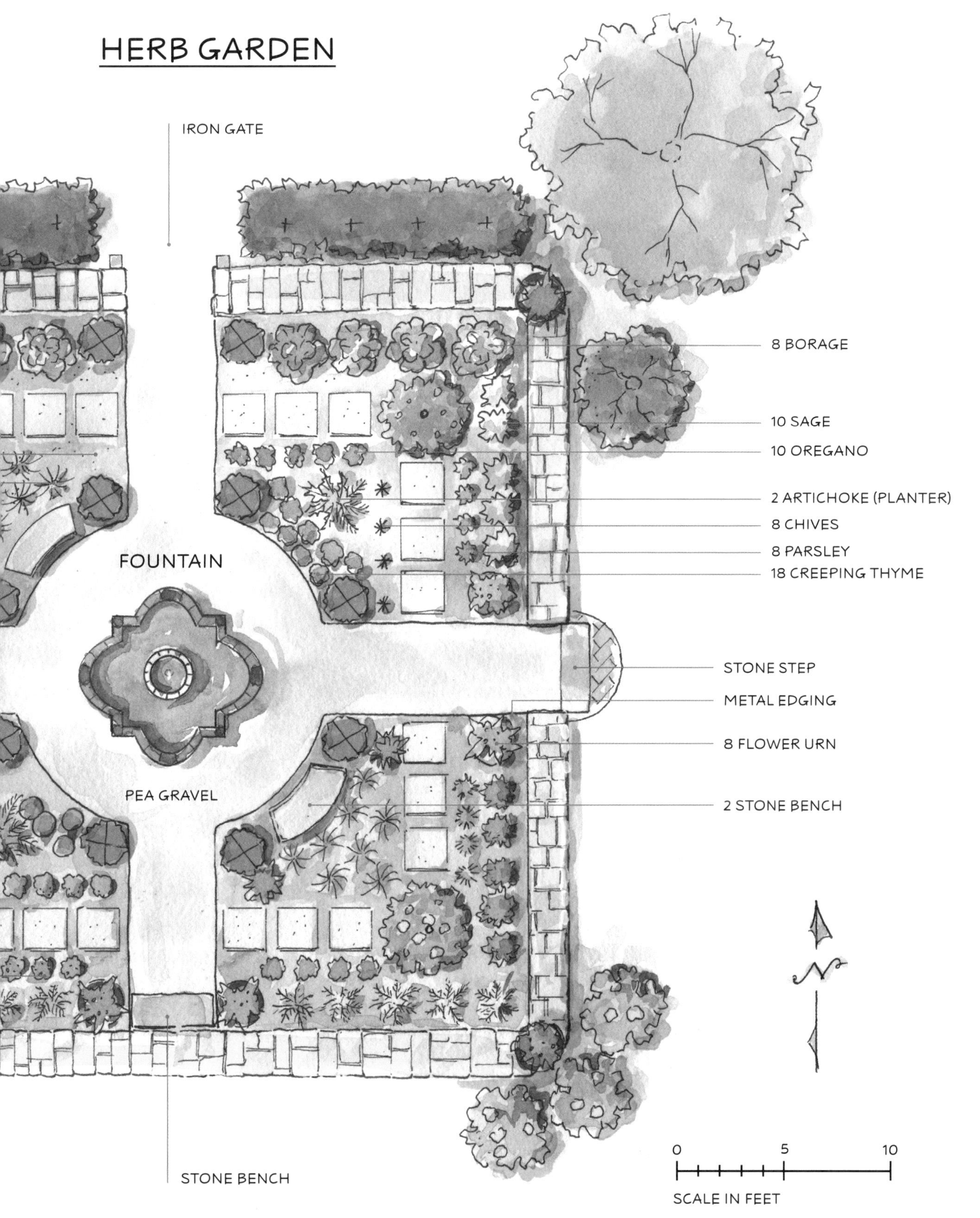
HERB GARDEN
IRON GATE
8 BORAGE
10 SAGE
10 OREGANO
2 ARTICHOKE (PLANTER)
8 CHIVES
8 PARSLEY
18 CREEPING THYME
FOUNTAIN
STONE STEP
METAL EDGING
8 FLOWER URN
PEA GRAVEL
2 STONE BENCH
N
0
5
10
SCALE IN FEET
STONE BENCH

CHAPTER 10

After the Design

Lessons on *how to evaluate a design*, *determine budgeting*, *begin implementation*, and *approaches to maintenance*.

Evaluating a Garden Design

As we work on a new design plan, we should have a sense of whether the process is going well as multiple versions distill our ideas into the best design possible. While it helps to step away from a design for a day or two and return with a fresh set of eyes, sooner or later we must put down the pen or pencil, roll up the drawing, and say we're done. We can, however, help our designs by learning how to evaluate other gardens already created or still on the drawing board. Here are a few questions to ask when evaluating a design.

IS IT PLEASING?

It's as simple as asking, "Do we like it?" If a design strikes us as pleasing because of an interesting landform pattern, an eye-catching terrace geometry, or a jungle of unique plants, sometimes that's all it takes. A successful design can be read and recognized on the design sheet or, better yet, when the garden is experienced in person. Go with your gut and let your aesthetic instincts kick in to indicate something special is here.

DOES IT WORK?

Does the design solve the problems we identified during the site survey and scope of design phase? Are they solved in the best way possible? Does the front entry walk guide guests to the right door? Are the slopes outside the house aimed away from the foundations? Will the plants on the plant list thrive in this region? If the answers to questions like these are all a resounding "yes," then the garden design works.

DOES IT MAKE SENSE?

A little more subtle than the "Does It Work?" question, this evaluation applies to what it feels like to experience the garden. This may not become completely clear until the garden takes shape in the real world, but even on a plan we can tell if paths take us places or if the garden rooms belong. It's a double check that something isn't off, or odd, about the design, like an overengineered wall, or a habitat area that's too small.

IS IT MEMORABLE?

This may be the most important question asked when evaluating a design. A memorable garden

◂ Turning your design into a reality requires forethought, planning, and some good old hard work.

is a great garden. Whether it is a novel approach to the geometry of the layout, a new way to use structures, or an unconventional application of plants, something about the garden must be so compelling as to stick in our mind and be remembered long after we've seen or experienced it.

WILL IT MATURE WELL?

On a practical level, we must ask whether the garden as planned will mature well. This falls heavily upon the plant layer because that is the most dynamic aspect of any garden design. If the trees and other key specimen plants are selected and spaced so they are able to grow into their full glory as the garden evolves over time, with or without maintenance, then we can say the garden will mature well.

Budgeting

At the beginning of the design process, we didn't want budget concerns to get in the way of our potential ideas for the garden, but once it is time to turn plans into reality, budget concerns enter the picture. Prices for labor, hardscape materials, and plants vary from city to city and state to state so it's not practical to suggest exactly what any given garden will cost to make. Plant prices vary greatly depending upon their size and variety, as well as seasonal availability. Even labor charges are seasonal. Tree work is cheaper in winter, and stonework in summer. Any time contractors aren't busy and need the work is the best time to hire them. These are the categories of work to consider when budgeting the costs of implementing a design.

- **LAND CLEARING** Tree and brush removal, major transplants, and tree protection
- **GRADING AND DRAINAGE** Preparing the land for hardscape elements, grading for surface water runoff, possibly supplemented with underground drainage
- **HARDSCAPING** Contract work with masons for stonework, carpenters for pergolas and arbors, and fencing contractors
- **TREE PLANTING** Landscape crew for large ball-and-burlap specimen trees
- **BED PREPARATION** Landscape crew for large areas, and delivery of compost or garden soil by the cubic yard for soil improvements
- **SHRUB AND PERENNIAL PLANTING** Landscape crew for large plantings of one hundred plants or more; can be performed by the gardener if the beds are prepped and plants are limited to 1-, 3-, and 5-gallon pot specimens; includes mulching the new plantings
- **LAWN OR GROUNDCOVER** For large areas especially, seed is cheaper than sod and easier to install; requires seed, fertilizer, and covering straw
- **BULBS AND ANNUALS** Seasonal, and best done by the gardener unless it's thousands of bulbs
- **ACCESSORIES AND DÉCOR** Go slow—find and buy these over the years; includes outdoor furniture, containers for plants, and garden art
- **IRRIGATION** Contract work and expensive, plus yearly repairs and a service contract

- **LANDSCAPE LIGHTING** Typically one-and-done with a licensed contractor for best results
- **MAINTENANCE** Ongoing contract work, or performed by owner/gardener with level of care dependent upon the size and type of garden

Implementation

The actual implementation of a garden design is an entirely new challenge, and even the best designs can be botched if they aren't made as planned. That said, plan for adjustments along the way when turning a garden design into reality. Expect some aspects of the design to change, especially within the plant layer, though this is occasionally true of some landform and structure elements. Often, hidden and unexpected challenges arise during construction so it behooves the designer to stay involved during the implementation phase to ensure everything stays on track, and the work stays true to the goals and objectives of the design.

ORDER OF OPERATION

The order of operation for implementing a garden design follows the same order as the design process: Start with landform, then structures, and finally plants. The landform work can be minimal or significant. Either way, start with landform as it will affect the rest of the design implementation and, once the structures and plants are in place, it may become impossible to use heavy equipment to make any extensive landform changes. Cut and fill comes first to level slopes or provide other usable space, followed by a rough-surface grading to control surface runoff or complete aesthetic contouring. This work also includes bringing in extra fill required to raise the grade as needed.

After any major landform adjustments are complete, the structural hardscape is next. It is always best to install walls, patios, and walks early on because they play such an important role in the garden's layout and because retaining walls work hand in hand with landform adjustments. At this stage, the garden is still a construction site so protecting existing plants is more important than adding new ones. Large stones for walls or patios require machinery that can compact soil, not to mention all the bootsteps of the masons hard at work. With the stonework in place, it may also be the right time to install other significant structures, like pergolas, fences, or fountains, while unfettered access throughout the garden is available.

After landform and structures come the plants. Start with large trees, which also might require equipment to get in place, then work out the understory shrubs and ground-layer plants. Finish with any new or renovated lawn areas and plan to return in autumn with bulbs.

SITE PREPARATION

Even before landforming, some plant editing may be required. If the site survey and analysis identified any problem plants that, for whatever reason, need to be removed, it's best to do this first. This could include taking out some unsafe trees or eliminating invasive brush, but it could also include rescuing good plants and preparing them to be transplanted elsewhere within the design. Timing is key when it comes to site preparations. Early spring or late winter in temperate climates, and early winter in warm winter regions is when plants are dormant. That's the best time to dig and transplant them. If they are very large specimens, root prune a year before so they are ready to be moved the following spring. Smaller plants don't need the prep work but should still be moved when dormant.

If there is no new hardscape involved in the design, we can jump right to planting bed preparation. Bed prep entails drawing out all the bed lines on the ground, with either marking paint, rope, or garden hose. With the lines defined, remove the lawn, weeds, or whatever is covering the soil all throughout the bed. This is also the time to turn the soil, adding fresh compost or other amendments to prepare the ground for new plants. Finish by smoothing the soil and fine-grading the beds. If there is hardscape work planned, wait until it is complete before doing the bed prep.

HARDSCAPING

Building hardscape structures starts with retaining walls required for landform adjustments, such as changing a slope to create level ground within the new garden plan. From there, we move on to structures on established landform or level areas, like patios and pools. Walkways and decorative walls that connect and define new garden rooms come next, along with wooden structures, like decks, pergolas, and small sheds. It's important to work from the back of the property to the front, or wherever there is ample access, to get the needed materials in place and make installation easy and efficient. Wait to install any fencing that might cut off access to the gardens for future work, like planting large trees that may need machinery to set them in place. The last major hardscape step should be any changes or improvements to the driveway because work vehicles and other construction equipment will take a toll on new pavement or concrete.

PLANTINGS

After the planting beds have been prepared, place the trees first. These are the large, ball-and-burlap, canopy, screening, and ornamental trees. Some may be planted in the beds; others might go directly in lawn areas. Make sure they are exactly where they should be before planting because it's never a good idea to move a new tree after it goes into the ground.

Once the large trees are planted, bring in the shrubs and perennial ground-layer plants. These are often in containers and can be manipulated easily and shifted into place. Follow the planting plan but be prepared to make on-the-spot adjustments to improve the design. This is often necessary if the specified plants on the planting plan aren't available and substitutions were made. Put them all in place and review their arrangement. Walk from spot to spot to observe how they look together and shift them as needed until it feels just right. Then and only then begin planting.

If drip irrigation is going to be installed in the beds, wait until after all the plants are in the ground, then lay out the irrigation. Once the drip lines are installed, apply the mulch to hide the drip lines. Mulching after planting conserves soil moisture, inhibits weed growth, and provides that finished look to the garden. If bulbs are part of the planting plan, set aside the funds to order them in fall and plant them then.

Design with Maintenance in Mind

Savvy garden designers think about the future maintenance needs of a garden during the design process. By working through long-term care requirements, we can ensure the continued success of our gardens through the years and possibly find ways to save money on maintenance.

WOODY VS. HERBACEOUS

Herbaceous plants typically require more maintenance than woody shrubs. A well-conceived perennial flower garden will have many different species of plants, all of which require regular visits to keep them happy and healthy, unlike shrubs which may require yearly pruning but not much else once established. Herbaceous plants are more dynamic and may need lifting, dividing, or transplanting to keep them in bounds. They can also be short-lived, or may simply die out for no obvious reason, necessitating new plants to replace them. Herbaceous perennials not part of a wild planting and left to their own devices may also require staking, pruning, feeding, deadheading, and deadleafing to keep them looking fresh. All edibles require a high level of continual care to produce the crops we hope for, making edible gardens, with woody or herbaceous plants, the most maintenance intensive.

MASSES VS. MATRIX PLANTINGS

Planting in masses requires more maintenance than a matrix scheme simply because large groups of the same species require attention at the same time, such as deadheading after their flowers fade, or rejuvenation pruning to stimulate fresh new growth. This happens at different times of year for each species, which means repeated visits to the same planting bed throughout the year. With matrix planting, part of the aesthetic is a messy look, so we can cut back and clean up all the plants in a bed during a single visit, once or twice a year, depending on the plants. This becomes even simpler if we work with native plant communities and design the plantings to be self-sustaining so they need very little, if any, maintenance at all.

NATURAL VS. MANUFACTURED MATERIALS

In almost every instance, natural materials, like stone, wood, and fired clay, look and fit better in a garden. Plastic and plants don't go together, however, there are many manufactured products that work well. Composite decking and fence materials often look a lot like the real thing but require a fraction of the upkeep. Sooner or later, wood will rot. Not so with composites. Stamped concrete patios and walks are less expensive and easier to care for than natural stone hardscape, and there are new technologies that make them look like natural stone. The trick is to use these manufactured materials where they work well but don't detract from the design aesthetics. For example, a PVC property line fence located far from the house will look like the real thing from a distance, while hand-hewn timbers for a terrace pergola increase the level of fit and finish to an installation.

MASTER PLAN

GARDEN DESIGN CONCEPTS

Treat the completed final design drawing as a guide, not an immutable plan, as you implement the design ideas that will transform your unremarkable property into a memorable landscape garden.

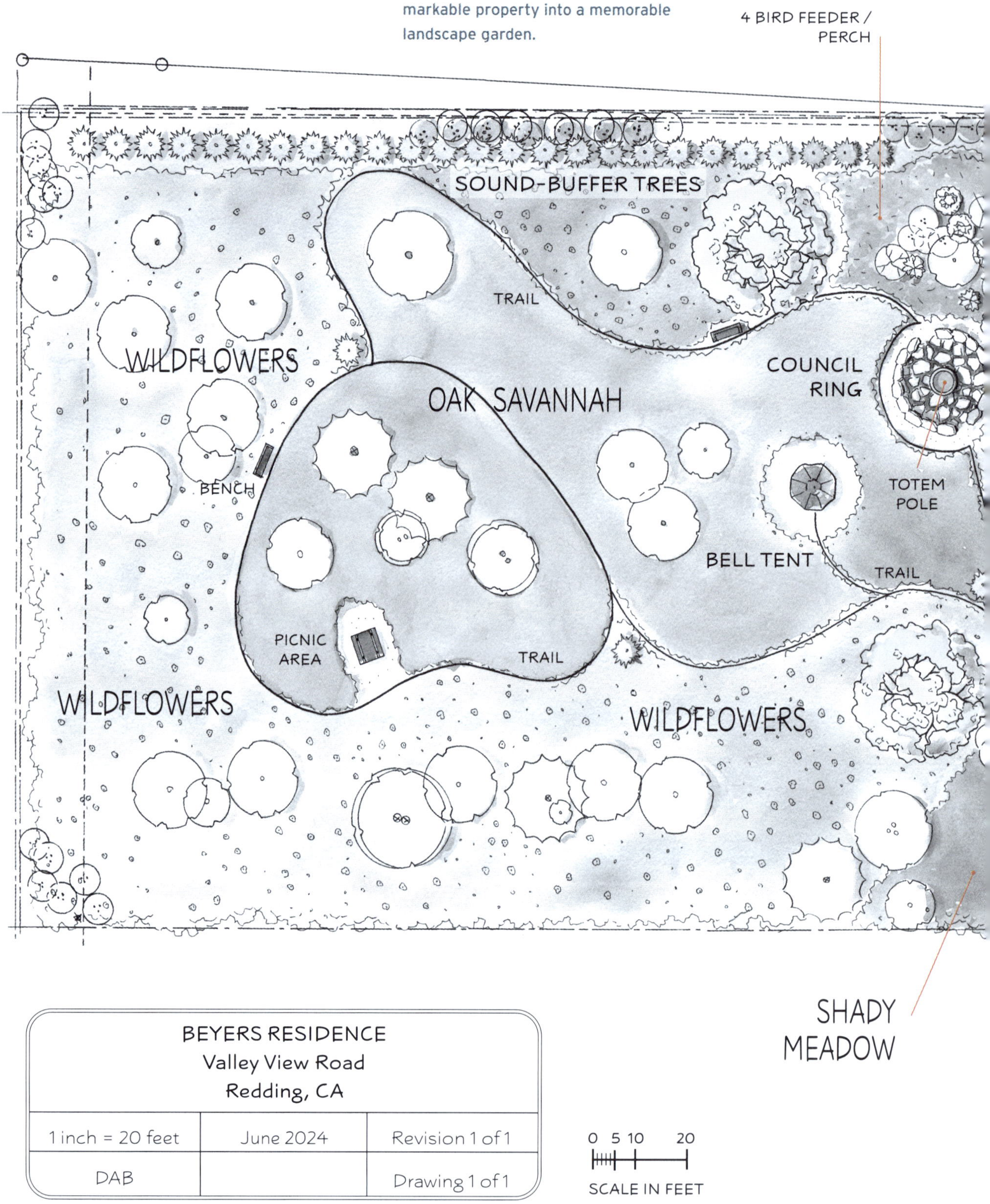

4 BIRD FEEDER / PERCH

SOUND-BUFFER TREES

TRAIL

WILDFLOWERS

OAK SAVANNAH

COUNCIL RING

BENCH

TOTEM POLE

BELL TENT

TRAIL

PICNIC AREA

TRAIL

WILDFLOWERS

WILDFLOWERS

SHADY MEADOW

BEYERS RESIDENCE Valley View Road Redding, CA		
1 inch = 20 feet	June 2024	Revision 1 of 1
DAB		Drawing 1 of 1

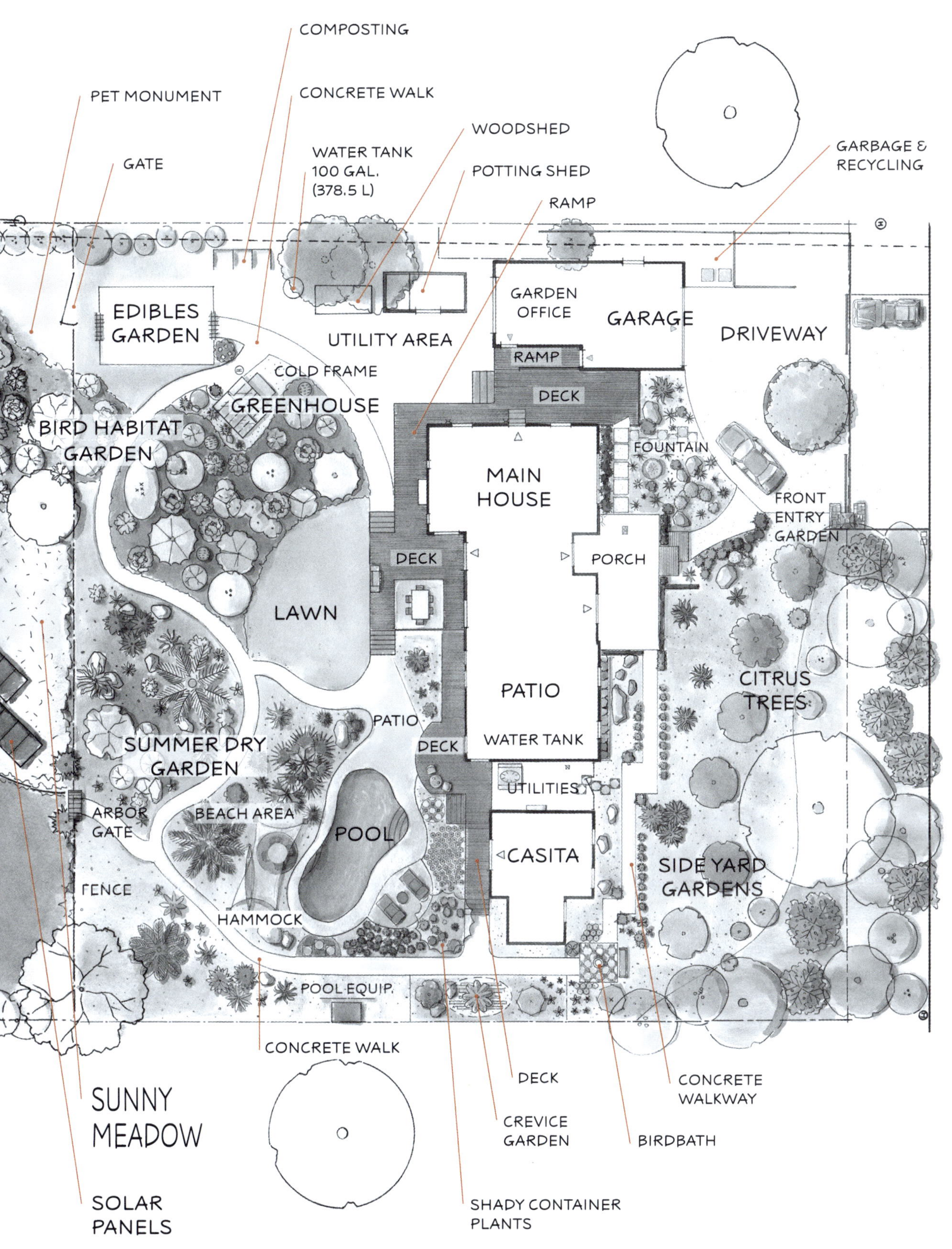

COMPOSTING
PET MONUMENT
CONCRETE WALK
WOODSHED
WATER TANK
100 GAL.
(378.5 L)
GATE
POTTING SHED
GARBAGE &
RECYCLING
RAMP
EDIBLES
GARDEN
UTILITY AREA
GARDEN
OFFICE
GARAGE
DRIVEWAY
RAMP
COLD FRAME
DECK
GREENHOUSE
BIRD HABITAT
GARDEN
FOUNTAIN
MAIN
HOUSE
FRONT
ENTRY
GARDEN
DECK
PORCH
LAWN
CITRUS
TREES
PATIO
PATIO
SUMMER DRY
GARDEN
DECK
WATER TANK
UTILITIES
ARBOR
GATE
BEACH AREA
POOL
CASITA
SIDE YARD
GARDENS
FENCE
HAMMOCK
POOL EQUIP.
CONCRETE WALK
DECK
CONCRETE
WALKWAY
SUNNY
MEADOW
CREVICE
GARDEN
BIRDBATH
SOLAR
PANELS
SHADY CONTAINER
PLANTS

WORKING WITH CURVILINEAR BED LINES

The shape and layout of beds and hardscaping should be formed so mowing any adjacent lawn areas is easy and efficient. Avoid tight angles that end in points. Terminate bed lines at obtuse or right angles, making it easier for a lawn mower to maneuver.

LAWN TYPES: TRADITIONAL, ALTERNATIVE, ARTIFICIAL

Everyone loves a little patch of lawn to walk barefoot upon, or as a place for the kids to play, and though most true garden making means finding ways to have less lawn, we often want a patch of grass here or there. So the decision must be made between a traditional turfgrass lawn or one of the many alternatives available. Traditional turfgrass requires a lot of maintenance, especially if we want it to look like a golf course fairway or sports field, and the larger the area the more work and expense it requires. So, either keep the lawn small, or grow an alternative lawn with one of several species of plants that act like turf but aren't. These alternatives don't allow for the same amount of foot traffic as a traditional lawn, but they fulfill the look and feel of a lawn without all the upkeep. Clover, sedge, and buffalograss are popular alternatives. Basically, any herbaceous plant that grows low and spreads will work, but these three can take foot traffic now and then. In arid regions, many gardens opt for artificial lawns. They provide the open garden floor of a real lawn but with almost no maintenance, and good ones look and feel almost real.

Multiyear Implementation

The implementation of a new garden, especially a full property master plan, takes time, effort, and money, making it useful to spread the work over several years. By proceeding in the right order, it is possible to implement most of a large plan in four or five years, allowing the gardens to develop gradually and settle into a mature form. What follows is a helpful year-by-year approach to a multiyear implementation.

YEAR ONE: Transplants, Grading, Major Hardscape, Large Specimen Trees, and Cover Crops

At the start of year one, all transplants are completed, and any major land clearing or grading starts first thing in spring. This includes any surface or buried drainage infrastructure like dry wells or French drains. Once the landform is set, major hardscapes, especially masonry work like walls, terraces, and walkways, begin. This is good summer work. Come fall, once all the grading and hardscape equipment is offsite and the stonework materials cleaned up, canopy trees and large specimen shrubs are safe to plant. Broadcast seed for cover crops or turfgrasses or native annuals on any disturbed ground to keep weeds down and prevent soil erosion.

YEAR TWO: Bed Building, Understory Shrubs, Ground Plants for Curb Appeal, and Smaller Hardscapes

Start year two with bed building to prepare for planting the understory shrubs and perennial ground-layer plants. Loosening the soil and bringing in fresh amendments like compost make planting easier and help ensure successful plant establishment. Layout and cut in all new beds, then plant and mulch. Focus on the front yard for improved curb appeal, but don't block access to the sides or back of the property. After spring planting season, install smaller hardscape features like trellises, fencing, or fountains.

YEAR THREE: Finish Backyard Plantings, Tweak Ground Plants

Come year three, we turn our attention to completing the plantings in the backyard, focusing on understory shrubs, perennial ground-layer plants, or lawn areas, filling in and around the garden beds and new hardscape. It's also time to tweak the herbaceous perennial plants from the previous year's planting. Lift and move any that aren't thriving or add new ones where others have been lost. In autumn, plant spring-blooming bulbs and perform corrective pruning to established trees and shrubs from the year-one planting.

YEAR FOUR: Finish Side Yards and Final Structures

With the front and backyards nearly complete, turn to the side yards and finish those gardens with new beds and plants to complement any hardscaping installed in year two. Now is the time to think about adding a layer of annuals or tender perennials to the planting schemes and completing the final structures, like property line fences or garbage and recycling bin stations.

YEAR FIVE: Adjustments, Special Features, Maintenance, and More Bulbs

Every season from here on should focus on spring planting adjustments to the ground-layer perennials and the potential for a new structure element or specimen plants to improve the design. Maintenance will begin to play a significant role in the yearly garden task list as the plantings become fully established, and keep adding bulbs each fall to fill out those plantings.

Afterword

After the publication of my first gardening book, *The New Gardener's Handbook*, I received a lot of reader feedback asking for equally accessible lessons on how to design and create gardens. This book is my answer to those requests and is meant to serve as a companion text to the earlier work. My goal for both books is to make it easier for new gardeners and garden designers to get started and grow confident in their knowledge and skills. Gardening is about making, whereas garden design is about imagining. Together they unite our efforts and actions in transforming our outdoor spaces into memorable places.

Always remember, every garden is a work in progress and the garden represented in a design drawing almost never becomes the garden on the ground. The metaphor I use is that a design plan is not a completed novel, written, edited, and published. The design is a guide, akin to the script of a movie or stage play. The basic story structure is there, along with the characters (plants and materials), settings (outdoor spaces), and dialog (garden functions), but it is up to us, the actors (garden designers and gardeners), to perform the play and manifest the garden. I hope this book succeeds in teaching how to see garden design as an action plan for a rewarding life in gardens.

Appendix: Recommended Plant Lists

Shade Trees

This list includes the most reliable species commonly available for purchase, though there are countless other species, cultivars, and varieties to choose from each genus represented. Species available at local garden centers and plant nurseries should be suited to the local climate, but always verify hardiness zone.

- Alder (*Alnus* spp. and cvs.)
- American hophornbeam (*Ostrya virginiana*)
- American sycamore (*Platanus occidentalis*)
- Amur cork (*Phellodendron amurense*)
- Bur oak (*Quercus macrocarpa*)
- Copper beech (*Fagus sylvatica* 'Purpurea')
- Elm (*Ulmus americana* 'Princeton')
- English walnut (*Juglans regia*)
- Golden catalpa (*Catalpa bignonioides* 'Aurea')
- Golden weeping willow (*Salix alba* 'Niobe')
- Hackberry (*Celtis occidentalis*)
- Honey locust (*Gleditsia triacanthos* f. *inermis*)
- Kentucky coffee tree (*Gymnocladus dioicus*)
- Maidenhair tree (*Ginkgo biloba*)
- Red horse chestnut (*Aesculus* × *carnea* 'Briotii')
- Shagbark hickory (*Carya ovata*)
- Small-leaved linden (*Tilia cordata*)
- Southern live oak (*Quercus virginiana*)
- Southern magnolia (*Magnolia grandiflora*)
- Sugar maple (*Acer saccharum*)
- Tulip tree (*Liriodendron tulipifera*)
- Tupelo (*Nyssa sylvatica*)
- Winter king hawthorn (*Crataegus viridis* 'Winter King')

Ornamental Trees

This list includes the most reliable species commonly available for purchase, though there are countless other species, cultivars, and varieties to choose from each genus represented. Species available at local garden centers and plant nurseries should be suited to the local climate, but always verify hardiness zone.

- Amur chokecherry (*Prunus maackii*)
- California palm (*Washingtonia filifera*)
- Chinese pistache (*Pistacia chinensis*)
- Date palm (*Phoenix dactylifera*)
- Flowering dogwood (*Cornus florida*)
- Franklin tree (*Franklinia alatamaha*)
- Fruitless olive (*Olea europaea* 'Wilsonii')
- Jacaranda (*Jacaranda mimosifolia*)
- Japanese stewartia (*Stewartia pseudocamellia*)
- Mountain ash (*Sorbus americana*)
- Ornamental pear (*Pyrus calleryana* 'Chanticleer')
- Palo verde (*Parkinsonia aculeata*)
- Purple-leaf redbud (*Cercis canadensis* 'Forest Pansy')
- Quaking aspen (*Populus tremuloides*)
- Redbay (*Persea borbonia*)
- Rutgers dogwood (*Cornus kousa* × *Cornus florida*)
- Sargent crabapple (*Malus sargentii*)
- Saucer magnolia (*Magnolia* × *soulangeana*)
- Seven-son flower (*Heptacodium miconioides*)
- Shadblow (*Amelanchier canadensis*)
- Silverbell (*Halesia carolina* spp. and cvs.)
- Silver birch (*Betula pendula*)
- Snowbell (*Styrax japonicus*)
- Sourwood (*Oxydendrum arboreum*)
- Weeping cherry (*Prunus subhirtella* 'Autumnalis')
- Weeping katsura (*Cercidiphyllum japonicum* 'Pendulum')
- Western redbud (*Cercis occidentalis*)
- White fringe tree (*Chionanthus virginicus* cvs.)
- Zelkova (*Zelkova serrata*)

Patio Trees

This list includes the most reliable species commonly available for purchase, though there are countless other species, cultivars, and varieties to choose from each genus represented. Species available at local garden centers and plant nurseries should be suited to the local climate, but always verify hardiness zone.

- American hazelnut (*Corylus americana*)
- Bladdernut (*Staphylea trifolia*)
- Bristlecone pine (*Pinus aristata*)
- Columnar crabapple (*Malus* 'Red Barron')
- Dwarf hinoki cypress (*Chamaecyparis obtusa* 'Nana Gracilis')
- Dwarf weeping dogwood (*Cornus kousa* 'Lustgarten Weeping')
- Florida anise tree (*Illicium floridanum*)
- Goldenchain tree (*Laburnum × watereri*)
- Japanese maple (*Acer japonicum*)
- Parasol pink snowbell (*Styrax japonicus* 'Marley's Pink')
- Purple-leaf elderberry (*Sambucus nigra* 'Black Beauty')
- Snow Fountains weeping cherry (*Prunus ×* 'Snofozam')
- Star magnolia (*Magnolia stellata* 'Royal Star')
- Weeping snowbell (*Styrax japonicus* 'Carillon')
- Witch hazel (*Hamamelis × intermedia* 'Jelena')

Screening Trees

This list includes the most reliable species commonly available for purchase, though there are countless other species, cultivars, and varieties to choose from each genus represented. Species available at local garden centers and plant nurseries should be suited to the local climate, but always verify hardiness zone.

EVERGREENS

- American holly (*Ilex opaca*)
- Blue point juniper (*Juniperus chinensis* 'Blue Point')
- Canadian hemlock (*Tsuga canadensis*)
- Japanese cedar (*Cryptomeria japonica* 'Yoshino')
- Leyland cypress (*Cupressocyparis leylandii*)
- Norway spruce (*Picea abies*)
- Umbrella pine (*Sciadopitys verticillata*)
- Western arborvitae (*Thuja plicata*)
- White fir (*Abies concolor*)

DECIDUOUS

- Austree willow (*Salix × matsudana × alba*)
- Columnar English oak (*Quercus robur* 'Fastigiata')
- Hornbeam (*Carpinus betulus* 'Frans Fontaine')
- Lombardy poplar (*Populus nigra* 'Italica')

Flowering Deciduous Shrubs

This list includes the most reliable species commonly available for purchase, though there are countless other species, cultivars, and varieties to choose from each genus represented. Species available at local garden centers and plant nurseries should be suited to the local climate, but always verify hardiness zone.

LARGE

- American snowbell (*Styrax americanus*)
- Beauty bush (*Kolkwitzia amabilis*)
- California lilac (*Ceanothus arboreus*)
- Common lilac (*Syringa vulgaris*)
- Forsythia (*Forsythia × intermedia* 'Lynwood Gold')
- Northern bayberry (*Myrica pensylvanica*)
- Purple-leaf ninebark (*Physocarpus opulifolius* 'Diabolo')
- Pussy willow (*Salix discolor*)
- Redvein enkianthus (*Enkianthus campanulatus*)
- Rose of Sharon (*Hibiscus syriacus* 'Blue Satin')
- Saskatoon serviceberry (*Amelanchier alnifolia*)
- Siebold viburnum (*Viburnum sieboldii*)
- Winterberry (*Ilex verticillata*)

MEDIUM AND SMALL

- Abelia (*Abelia × grandiflora*)
- Alpine currant (*Ribes alpinum*)
- Beach plum (*Prunus maritima*)
- Black chokeberry (*Aronia melanocarpa*)
- Blue mist shrub (*Caryopteris × clandonensis*)
- Bridal wreath (*Spiraea × vanhouttei*)
- Carolina allspice (*Calycanthus floridus*)
- Diervilla (*Diervilla × splendens*)
- Flame azalea (*Rhododendron calendulaceum*)
- Fragrant viburnum (*Viburnum carlesii*)
- Japanese rose (*Kerria japonica*)
- Northern spicebush (*Lindera benzoin*)
- Oakleaf hydrangea (*Hydrangea quercifolia*)
- Pink cinquefoil (*Dasiphora fruticosa* 'Pink Beauty')
- Purple-leaf sand cherry (*Prunus × cistena*)
- Red osier dogwood (*Cornus sericea*)
- Rugosa rose (*Rosa rugosa*)
- Strawberry bush (*Euonymus americanus*)
- Summersweet (*Clethra alnifolia*)
- Sweet mock orange (*Philadelphus coronarius*)
- Sweetspire (*Itea virginica*)
- Weigela (*Weigela* 'Florida Variegata')
- Witch alder (*Fothergilla gardenii*)

Evergreen Shrubs

This list includes the most reliable species commonly available for purchase, though there are countless other species, cultivars, and varieties to choose from each genus represented. Species available at local garden centers and plant nurseries should be suited to the local climate, but always verify hardiness zone.

DECORATIVE CONIFERS

- Bristlecone pine (*Pinus longaeva*)
- Dwarf black spruce (*Picea mariana* 'Nana')
- Dwarf Japanese cedar (*Cryptomeria japonica* 'Rein's Dense Jade')
- Globe cypress (*Chamaecyparis lawsoniana*)
- Golden dwarf hinoki (*Chamaecyparis obtusa* 'Verdoni')
- Grey owl juniper (*Juniperus virginiana* 'Grey Owl')
- Montgomery blue spruce (*Picea pungens* 'Montgomery')
- Mugo pine (*Pinus mugo*)
- Silver Korean fir (*Abies koreana* 'Horstmann's Silberlocke')
- Spreading plum yew (*Cephalotaxus harringtonia* 'Prostrata')
- Weeping blue atlas cedar (*Cedrus atlantica* 'Glauca Pendula')
- Weeping hemlock (*Tsuga canadensis* 'Pendula')

FLOWERING BROADLEAF EVERGREENS

This list includes the most reliable species commonly available for purchase, though there are countless other species, cultivars, and varieties to choose from each genus represented. Species available at local garden centers and plant nurseries should be suited to the local climate, but always verify hardiness zone.

- Andromeda (*Pieris japonica* 'Dorothy Wycoff')
- Camellia (*Camellia japonica*)
- Dog hobble (*Leucothoe fontanesiana* 'Rainbow')
- Fringe flower (*Loropetalum chinense rubrum*)
- Gardenia (*Gardenia jasminoides*)
- Grape holly (*Mahonia aquifolium*)
- Manzanita (*Arctostaphylos crustacea*)
- Mountain laurel (*Kalmia latifolia*)
- Oleander (*Nerium oleander*)
- Red tip (*Photinia × fraseri*)
- Rosebay rhododendron (*Rhododendron maximum*)
- Skimmia (*Skimmia japonica*)
- Spotted laurel (*Aucuba japonica*)
- Sweet tea olive (*Osmanthus fragrans*)

Hedging Shrubs

This list includes the most reliable species commonly available for purchase, though there are countless other species, cultivars, and varieties to choose from each genus represented. Species available at local garden centers and plant nurseries should be suited to the local climate, but always verify hardiness zone.

- Amur maple (*Acer ginnala*)
- Hick's yew (*Taxus* × *media* 'Hicksii')
- Holly (*Ilex* 'Nellie R. Stevens')
- Hornbeam (*Carpinus betulus*)
- Inkberry (*Ilex glabra*)
- Japanese boxwood (*Buxus microphylla*)
- Skip laurel (*Prunus laurocerasus* 'Schipkaensis')

Climbing Vines

This list includes the most reliable species commonly available for purchase, though there are countless other species, cultivars, and varieties to choose from each genus represented. Species available at local garden centers and plant nurseries should be suited to the local climate, but always verify hardiness zone.

- Autumn clematis (*Clematis terniflora*)
- Boston ivy (*Parthenocissus tricuspidata*)
- Chocolate vine (*Akebia quinata*)
- Climbing hydrangea (*Hydrangea anomala* var. *petiolaris*)
- Climbing rose (*Rosa* 'Strawberry Hill')
- Common honeysuckle (*Lonicera periclymenum*)
- Grape vine (*Vitis vinifera*)
- Japanese hydrangea vine (*Schizophragma hydrangeoides*)
- Kiwi (*Actinidia arguta*)
- Passionflower (*Passiflora incarnata*)
- Star jasmine (*Trachelospermum jasminoides*)
- Trumpet vine (*Campsis radicans*)
- Wisteria (*Wisteria sinensis*)

Groundcover Shrubs

This list includes the most reliable species commonly available for purchase, though there are countless other species, cultivars, and varieties to choose from each genus represented. Species available at local garden centers and plant nurseries should be suited to the local climate, but always verify hardiness zone.

- Bearberry (*Arctostaphylos uva-ursi*)
- Carpet rose (*Rosa* 'Flower Carpet')
- Creeping juniper (*Juniperus horizontalis* 'Blue Chip')
- Creeping rosemary (*Rosmarinus officinalis* var. *repens*)
- Dwarf slender deutzia (*Deutzia gracilis* 'Nikko')
- Gro-Low sumac (*Rhus aromatica* 'Gro-Low')
- Rockspray (*Cotoneaster horizontalis*)
- Sweet box (*Sarcococca ruscifolia*)
- Tide Hill boxwood (*Buxus sinica* var. *insularis* 'Tide Hill')

Sun-Loving Perennials

This list includes the most reliable species commonly available for purchase, though there are countless other species, cultivars, and varieties to choose from each genus represented. Species available at local garden centers and plant nurseries should be suited to the local climate, but always verify hardiness zone.

- Anise hyssop (*Agastache foeniculum*)
- Bearded iris (*Iris germanica*)
- Beard tongue (*Penstemon digitalis* 'Dark Towers')
- Bee balm (*Monarda fistulosa*)
- Bee blossom (*Gaura lindheimeri* 'Siskiyou Pink')
- Black-eyed Susan (*Rudbeckia fulgida* 'Goldsturm')
- Blanket flower (*Gaillardia aristata* 'Arizona Red Shades')
- Blue star (*Amsonia hubrichtii*)
- Calamint (*Calamintha nepeta*)
- California poppy (*Papaver orientale*)
- Century plant (*Agave americana*)
- Cheddar pink (*Dianthus gratianopolitanus*)
- Chrysanthemum (*Dendranthema* × *grandiflorum*)
- Creeping thyme (*Thymus serpyllum*)
- Cushion spurge (*Euphorbia polychroma*)
- Daylily (*Hemerocallis* 'Rosy Returns')
- False sunflower (*Heliopsis helianthoides*)
- Feather reed grass (*Calamagrostis* × *acutiflora* 'Karl Foerster')
- Flag iris (*Iris pseudacorus*)
- Garden phlox (*Phlox paniculata* 'David')
- Goldenrod (*Solidago altissima*)
- Gray santolina (*Santolina chamaecyparissus*)

- Great blue lobelia (*Lobelia siphilitica*)
- Hardy sage (*Salvia nemorosa* 'Caradonna')
- Ice plant (*Delosperma cooperi*)
- Joe-Pye weed (*Eupatorium maculatum*)
- Large-flower tickseed (*Coreopsis grandiflora*)
- Little bluestem Grass (*Schizachyrium scoparium*)
- Meadowsweet (*Filipendula rubra* 'Venusta')
- Native milkweed (*Asclepias incarnata*)
- New England aster (*Aster novae-angliae* 'Purple Dome')
- Ornamental onion (*Allium millenium*)
- Peony (*Paeonia lactiflora*)
- Prairie dropseed (*Sporobolus heterolepis*)
- Prickly pear (*Opuntia engelmannii*)
- Purple coneflower (*Echinacea purpurea*)
- Russian sage (*Salvia yangii*)
- Sea thrift (*Armeria maritima*)
- Sneezeweed (*Helenium autumnale*)
- Snow-in-summer (*Cerastium tomentosum*)
- Spanish dagger (*Yucca gloriosa* 'Variegata')
- Speedwell (*Veronica spicata*)
- Stonecrop (*Sedum* 'Matrona')
- Switch grass (*Panicum virgatum*)
- Yarrow (*Achillea millefolium*)

Sun or Shade Perennials

This list includes the most reliable species commonly available for purchase, though there are countless other species, cultivars, and varieties to choose from each genus represented. Species available at local garden centers and plant nurseries should be suited to the local climate, but always verify hardiness zone.

- Astilbe (*Astilbe chinensis* 'Visions')
- Candelabra aloe (*Aloe arborescens*)
- Baby's breath (*Gypsophila repens*)
- Balloon flower (*Platycodon grandiflorus*)
- Bellflower (*Campanula glomerata*)
- Bigroot geranium (*Geranium macrorrhizum*)
- Catmint (*Nepeta faassenii*)
- Columbine (*Aquilegia canadensis*)
- Coral bells (*Heuchera americana* 'Peppermint Spice')
- Creeping mazus (*Mazus reptans*)
- Creeping phlox (*Phlox subulata*)
- Culver's root (*Veronicastrum virginicum*)
- False indigo (*Baptisia australis*)
- Fountain grass (*Pennisetum alopecuroides*)
- Foxglove (*Digitalis* × *mertonensis*)
- Germander (*Teucrium chamaedrys*)
- Hayscented fern (*Dennstaedtia punctilobula*)

- Ironweed (*Vernonia noveboracensis*)
- Lady's mantle (*Alchemilla mollis*)
- Lamb's ear (*Stachys byzantina*)
- Lily turf (*Liriope spicata*)
- Ostrich fern (*Matteuccia struthiopteris*)
- Penn sedge (*Carex pensylvanica*)
- Pink muhly grass (*Muhlenbergia capillaris*)
- Red hot pokers (*Kniphofia uvaria*)
- Rodger's flower (*Rodgersia aesculifolia*)
- Spiderwort (*Tradescantia virginiana*)
- Swamp rose mallow (*Hibiscus moscheutos*)
- Woodland phlox (*Phlox divaricata*)

Shade-Loving Perennials

This list includes the most reliable species commonly available for purchase, though there are countless other species, cultivars, and varieties to choose from each genus represented. Species available at local garden centers and plant nurseries should be suited to the local climate, but always verify hardiness zone.

- Barrenwort (*Epimedium* × *rubrum*)
- Bleeding heart (*Lamprocapnos spectabilis*)
- Bugbane (*Actaea racemosa*)
- Cinnamon fern (*Osmunda cinnamomea*)
- Foamflower (*Tiarella cordifolia*)
- Forest grass (*Hakonechloa macra* 'Beni Kaze')
- Goat's beard (*Aruncus dioicus*)
- Golden spikenard (*Aralia cordata* 'Sun King')
- Hosta (*Hosta* 'Guacamole')
- Jacob's ladder (*Polemonium reptans*)
- Lenten rose (*Helleborus orientalis*)
- Leopard plant (*Ligularia dentata* 'Othello')
- Lungwort (*Pulmonaria angustifolia*)
- Mayapple (*Podophyllum peltatum*)
- Meadow rue (*Thalictrum rochebruneanum*)
- Mexican feather grass (*Nassella tenuissima*)
- Siberian bugloss (*Brunnera macrophylla* 'Jack Frost')
- Solomon's seal (*Polygonatum odoratum*)
- Sweet woodruff (*Galium odoratum*)
- Toad lily (*Tricyrtis hirta*)
- Trout lily (*Erythronium americanum*)
- Turtlehead (*Chelone obliqua*)
- Virginia bluebells (*Mertensia virginica*)
- Wake robin (*Trillium grandiflorum*)
- Windflower (*Anemone robustissima*)
- Wood fern (*Dryopteris intermedia*)

Annuals

This list includes the most reliable species commonly available for purchase, though there are countless other species, cultivars, and varieties to choose from each genus represented.

- African marigold (*Tagetes erecta*)
- Candytuft (*Iberis umbellata*)
- Cockscomb (*Celosia plumosa*)
- Coleus (*Coleus scutellarioides*)
- Cosmos (*Cosmos bipinnatus*)
- Fan flower (*Scaevola aemula*)
- Floss flower (*Ageratum houstonianum*)
- Garden geranium (*Pelargonium × hortorum*)
- Impatiens (*Impatiens walleriana*)
- Lantana (*Lantana camara*)
- Lobelia (*Lobelia erinus*)
- Love-in-a-mist (*Nigella damascena*)
- Mealycup sage (*Salvia farinacea*)
- Million bells (*Calibrachoa × hybrida*)
- Nasturtium (*Tropaeolum majus*)
- Pansy (*Viola × wittrockiana*)
- Petunia (*Petunia × atkinsiana*)
- Pot marigold (*Calendula officinalis*)
- Scarlet sage (*Salvia splendens*)
- Snapdragon (*Antirrhinum majus*)
- Spider flower (*Cleome hassleriana*)
- Summer snapdragon (*Angelonia angustifolia*)
- Sunflower (*Helianthus annuus*)
- SunPatiens (*Impatiens × hybrida*)
- Wax begonia (*Begonia cucullata*)
- Wishbone flower (*Torenia fournieri*)
- Zinnia (*Zinnia elegans*)

Flowering Bulbs

This list includes the most reliable species commonly available for purchase, though there are countless other species, cultivars, and varieties to choose from each genus represented. Species available at local garden centers and plant nurseries should be suited to the local climate, but always verify hardiness zone.

- Asiatic lily (*Lilium auratum*)
- Autumn crocus (*Colchicum autumnale*)
- Checker lily (*Fritillaria affinis*)
- Daffodil (*Narcissus pseudonarcissus*)
- Dutch iris (*Iris × hollandica*)
- Garden hyacinth (*Hyacinthus orientalis*)
- Garden tulip (*Tulipa gesneriana*)
- Glory of the snow (*Chionodoxa luciliae*)
- Grape hyacinth (*Muscari armeniacum*)
- Madonna lily (*Lilium candidum*)
- Ornamental onion (*Allium giganteum*)
- Siberian squill (*Scilla siberica*)
- Snowdrops (*Galanthus nivalis*)
- Spring crocus (*Crocus tommasinianus*)
- Summer snowflake (*Leucojum aestivum*)

Tender Perennials

This list includes the most reliable species commonly available for purchase, though there are countless other species, cultivars, and varieties to choose from each genus represented.

- Buttercup (*Ranunculus × hybrida*)
- Caladium (*Caladium bicolor*)
- Calla lily (*Zantedeschia aethiopica*)
- Canna lily (*Canna indica*)
- Dahlia (*Dahlia pinnata*)
- Elephant's ear (*Colocasia esculenta*)
- Ginger lily (*Hedychium coronarium*)
- Gladiolus (*Gladiolus palustris*)
- Hibiscus (*Hibiscus rosa-sinensis*)
- Mandevilla (*Mandevilla sanderi*)
- Tuberous begonia (*Begonia × tuberhybrida*)

Vegetables

This list includes the most reliable species commonly available for purchase, though there are countless other species, cultivars, and varieties to choose from each genus represented.

- Arugula
- Beans
- Beets
- Bok choy
- Broccoli
- Brussels sprouts
- Cabbage
- Carrots
- Chard
- Corn
- Cucumber
- Eggplant
- Endive
- Kale
- Leek
- Lettuce
- Mustard greens
- Oats
- Onions
- Peas
- Peppers
- Potatoes
- Pumpkin
- Radishes
- Rye
- Summer squash
- Tomato
- Turnips
- Watercress
- Wheat
- Yams
- Zucchini

Culinary Herbs

This list includes the most reliable species commonly available for purchase, though there are countless other species, cultivars, and varieties to choose from each genus represented.

- Basil
- Chives
- Cilantro
- Dill
- Fennel
- Lemongrass
- Marjoram
- Mint
- Oregano
- Parsley
- Rosemary
- Sage
- Tarragon
- Thyme

Berry Shrubs

This list includes the most reliable species commonly available for purchase, though there are countless other species, cultivars, and varieties to choose from each genus represented. Species available at local garden centers and plant nurseries should be suited to the local climate, but always verify hardiness zone.

- Blackberry
- Blueberry
- Boysenberry
- Currant
- Elderberry
- Goji berry
- Honeyberry
- Lingonberry
- Loganberry
- Raspberry

Orchard Trees

This list includes the most reliable species commonly available for purchase, though there are countless other species, cultivars, and varieties to choose from each genus represented. Species available at local garden centers and plant nurseries should be suited to the local climate, but always verify hardiness zone.

- Apple
- Avocado
- Cherry
- Fig
- Grapefruit
- Lemon
- Lime
- Nectarine
- Olive
- Orange
- Pawpaw
- Peach
- Pear
- Persimmon
- Plum
- Pomegranate

Cool-Season Edibles

Refer to a vegetable planning and transplanting guide for detailed growing information for each crop.

BEST IN SPRING

- Beets
- Cabbage
- Carrots
- Lettuce
- Onion
- Peas
- Radishes
- Spinach
- Swiss chard

BEST IN FALL

- Broccoli
- Brussels sprouts
- Cauliflower
- Celery
- Kale
- Leek
- Parsnips
- Turnips

Warm-Season Edibles

Refer to a vegetable planning and transplanting guide for detailed growing information for each crop.

- Beans
- Corn
- Cucumbers
- Eggplant
- Melons
- Peppers
- Pumpkin
- Summer squash
- Sweet potato
- Tomato
- Watermelon
- Winter squash
- Zucchini

Photo and Illustration Credits

All illustrations by Elara Tanguy

All photos are by the author, except for the following:

Chicago Botanic Garden, Evening Island, 194
U.S. National Arboretum, 157

Dreamstime

Ivandzyuba, 250

iStock

BasieB, 189 (left)
Binnerstam, 153
DanaDowling, 133
Fotolinchen, 162
Glasslanguage, 139 (top center)
Gloszilla, 202 (right)
HannamariaH, 106
iv-serg, 18
Janaka Maharage Dharmasena, 202 (left)
Ken Wiedemann, 229
MagicDreamer, 139 (top left)
Mdoculus, 190 (right)
Nancykennedy, 134
PurpleImages, 146
SeanPavonePhoto, 12
Sebastien Mercier, 190 (left)
Solidago, cover (top right)
Welcomia, 128

Shutterstock

365 Focus Photography, 90
Bonnie Watton, 138 (middle left)
Cindy Carlsson, 167
Cristina Ionescu, 139 (middle right)
Gardens by Design, 189 (right)
HeiSpa, 139 (bottom center)
Kristine Radkovska, 139 (middle center)
Lamyai, 36
Md. Nadir Hasan, 139 (middle left)
Pixel-Shot, 64

Wikimedia

Public Domain

Jmeeter, 138 (bottom left)

CC 2.0 Generic

James St. John, 138 (top left)

CC 2.5 Generic

Marc Ryckaert (MJJR), 138 (middle right)

CC 3.0 Unported

Kroton, 139 (top right)

CC SA 4.0 International

Agnieszka Kwiecień, Nova, 139 (bottom left)
David J. Stang, 136 (bottom right), 139 (bottom right)
Libraryisme, 138 (top right)

Model design by Zoali Alavarez and Green Day Co., 89

Index

G

H

I

J

K

Q

R

S

T

U

V

W

X

Y

Z

Daryl Beyers is the author of *The New Gardener's Handbook* (Timber Press, 2020) and is Gardening Certificate Program Coordinator at the New York Botanical Garden, where he helps shape the continuing education department's gardening curriculum and teaches the capstone "Fundamentals of Garden Design" course. With over three decades of professional landscaping experience, specializing in residential garden design and development, he has created and cared for hundreds of gardens throughout the United States. He authored two special issues on garden design for *Fine Gardening* magazine, was a contributing garden editor for *Martha Stewart Living*, and his articles on gardening and garden design appear regularly in *Horticulture* and other national publications. Daryl continues to provide design expertise for client gardens while maintaining an active public-speaking schedule and honing his gardening and design skills at his home in Shasta County, California.